State College

at

Framingham

10-68-948217

CONGREGATIONAL COMMONWEALTH
Connecticut, 1636–1662

CONGREGATIONAL

COMMONWEALTH

Connecticut, 1636-1662

BY

MARY JEANNE ANDERSON JONES

WESLEYAN UNIVERSITY PRESS

Middletown, Connecticut

Library of Congress Catalog Card Number: 68-27543

Manufactured in the United States of America

FIRST EDITION

TO RICHARD

Contents

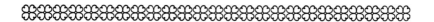

Illustrations

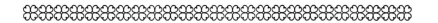

Preface

FROM 1636 until 1662 an anomalous colony existed in the New World. Originally it was composed of several hundred "Inhabitants and Residents of Windsor, Harteford and Wethersfield . . . now cohabiting and dwelling in and vppon the River of Conectecotte and the Lands thereunto adioyneing." By the close of the period several thousand Congregationalists had made their homes in the fifteen towns of Connecticut. The inhabitants and residents of the towns of Connecticut were Puritan men and women who had wrenched themselves and their families from their ancestral settings in England to sail westward as part of the Great Migration. They settled temporarily in Massachusetts Bay, but soon uprooted themselves once again in search of the promised land. Their wanderings finally came to a halt in the Connecticut River Valley. There they erected a unique commonwealth which professed allegiance neither to the King of England, nor to the Lord Protector, nor to the Colony of Massachusetts Bay, nor to the directors of a joint-stock company. The Commonwealth of Connecticut existed independently under its own constitution—the Fundamental Orders of Connecticut.

Traditionally, Connecticut has been classified with the charter colonies in history textbooks, but actually it was a commonwealth from the time of its settlement until it achieved corporate status in 1662. Prior to its incorporation under the Great Seal, England exercised no authority over this Congregational commonwealth. Connecticut's churches and state were autonomous. Each church had its own covenant and the state its own written instrument of government, the first adopted anywhere in the New World.

The Commonwealth's precise boundaries remained undefined under the Fundamental Orders. Before 1644 the Congregationalists built their towns on the western bank of the Connecticut River and along the shore of Long Island Sound on land claimed by the Warwick Patentees. In 1644 they purchased the Warwick Patent and for the remainder of the period asserted their alleged rights to the territory on both sides of the river by authority of the Patent, but no survey was made to establish Connecticut's exact bounds. Throughout the period of the Commonwealth, New Haven and its satellite communities remained a separate entity, outside the jurisdiction of Connecticut.

The first Europeans arrived in the Connecticut Valley in 1633, but 1636 is here considered the year of the Commonwealth's birth. In that year formal government was first instituted with the Massachusetts Bay Commission. In that year also, the Particular Court held its first session and Thomas Hooker led a major party to the plantation that soon became Hartford. From the beginning the Commonwealth bore an Algonquian name. The Dutch traders knew the river as the *Versche Riviere*, the "Fresh River," but the six or seven thousand resident Algonquian Indians called the area *Quanet-ta-cut*, meaning "on the long tidal river." The Indian nomenclature prevailed.

Only because of the unsettled conditions in England during these years was Connecticut permitted to develop without interference from its mother country. While the men and women in the Connecticut Valley were performing their wilderness work with courage and perseverance, turning dense forests into fields, building new towns, and establishing their churches and governments in accordance with their divine mission in spite of the Dutch, Indians, and wild wolves, Charles I was occupied at home with a constitutional crisis and the Civil War. After his defeat at the Battle of Naseby in 1645 and his execution on the block in 1649, his successor, Oliver Cromwell, was equally unable to divert his attention from an insurrection in Ireland, from a war with the Dutch, or from his efforts to mold a stable government in England. Until the Restoration the King and Lord Protector had little interest in the Commonwealth of Connecticut, inconspicuous in area, population, and mercantile value. The Congregationalists in Connecticut did not have to fight for their independence. They were independent by default. Unmolested, they built their New Jerusalem in the wilderness.

The Fundamental Orders, which served as the constitution for Connecticut from 1639 until 1662, first attracted the writer to this early period of Connecticut's history and are the focal point of the study. To determine what the vigorous little community on the Connecticut River was rebelling against, its heritage from England and Massachusetts Bay had to be examined. To understand early Connecticut's political philosophy, the government of its Congregational churches had to be considered. To judge the practicality of the constitution following its enactment, the legislative, executive, and judicial systems it fostered had to be investigated and the myth of Connecticut's being a democracy in the modern connotation dispelled. Finally, to evaluate the constitution, it was necessary to consider the fact that in 1662 it was supplanted by a royal patent granted at the request of the Commonwealth of Connecticut itself.

The purpose of this book is not to provide a social, economic, or general history of Connecticut from its founding until it became a charter colony. These aspects of the Commonwealth have been scrutinized ably by such eminent historians as Benjamin Trumbull, Charles M. Andrews, and Albert E. Van Dusen. Instead, the purpose is to present the Fundamental Orders of Connecticut in their Puritan environment, to analyze the origin of the constitution, to study the system of government it sanctioned, and to evaluate it as a phenomenon of seventeenth-century Puritanism. Every effort has been made to assure accuracy, a difficult task at times because of the archaic spellings and abbreviations prevalent in seventeenth-century court records, letters, and books. Citations to original works, nevertheless, are generous and opinion has not been substituted for fact. My hope is that this study of early Connecticut may enable the citizens of twentieth-century Connecticut, who have so recently adopted a fourth constitution for the state, to become cognizant of their heritage and to better understand this product of their forefathers' enmities, experience, and ingenuity.

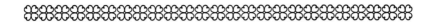

Acknowledgments

THIS study of Connecticut under the Fundamental Orders has evolved over a period of ten years. During that time numerous people have encouraged my interest in the Commonwealth and its constitution. The first was Professor Thomas Perkins Abernethy of the University of Virginia, the leading authority on southern history, who introduced me to colonial America. I am grateful also to Professor David Alan Williams of the University of Virginia for the hours he spent advising me while I was a graduate student. And I should particularly like to thank my father, Buist M. Anderson, Esq., my mother, Dorothy C. Anderson, and my husband, Dr. Richard F. Jones, III, for their critical advice.

The major part of the research was performed in Hartford at The Connecticut Historical Society, the Hartford Seminary Foundation, Trinity College, and the Connecticut State Library. Two years later, after our move to Charlottesville, the majority of the published works were still available to me in the University of Virginia's Alderman Library, particularly in the McGregor Room. I should like to thank the many librarians, especially Miss Katherine Beville, for their patience in helping me locate the sources. Some of the works on Congregationalism understandably were not among the collections of the University of Virginia, far removed from Connecticut and Puritanism. Without Miss Helena C. Koiner and the Interlibrary Loan the completion of this study would have been impossible.

M.J.A.J.

Ziegelhausen über Heidelberg
West Germany
February 1, 1968

CONGREGATIONAL COMMONWEALTH
Connecticut, 1636–1662

I

Prelude to Connecticut

THE Commonwealth of Connecticut became a formally constituted independent state with the adoption of the Fundamental Orders in January 1638/39.[1] But the story of this Congregational commonwealth does not begin then, nor even in 1633, when the first white men invaded the virgin forests and undisturbed wilderness of the Connecticut River Valley. The beginnings of the Commonwealth of Connecticut lie deep in the 1620's with events that were transpiring three thousand miles away. Contrary to popular thought, it was not the lure of the wilderness that tempted adventurous souls to settle Connecticut. It was the political and religious tyranny imposed by King Charles I and Archbishop William Laud that drove the Englishmen from their homes to Connecticut, in spite of the wilds.

The extent of the crisis in England was so great that twenty thousand men, women, and children fled across the Atlantic Ocean between 1629 and 1640.[2] Thousands of these Puritan exiles sought refuge first in the Massachusetts Bay Colony, but hundreds of them had yet to find their promised land and soon pressed westward into Connecticut. During the eleven years of the Great Migration, one after another dissident Puritan forsook his ancestral home and undertook the grueling two-, three- or even four-month voyage, where the specter of sickness and death hovered nearby at all times and only a frontier settlement awaited him. All for one reason: Puritanism was being defeated. Writers from the seventeenth century until modern times are virtually unanimous in agreeing that the primary cause of the exodus to New England was the unrest within the Church of England.

The crisis within the Established Church had smoldered from the days of Henry VIII until 1625, when Charles I and William Laud came to power. Then it exploded. On one side the King and Bishop of London were determined to throw out the staying measures effected by the Elizabethan Compromise, preferring to imitate the absolutism in church and state attained by their contemporary, Louis XIII, in France. Their attempt to impose the divine right of kings on the English nation occurred at precisely the moment when the Puritan preachers at the other pole realized the power of the pulpit and the popular press. Literacy had increased in England directly in proportion to the extent the King James Version of the Bible had spread. By 1629 it had been in public circulation for eighteen years, more than long enough to teach one generation of children to read and write. Taking advantage of the more literate public and the more numerous printing presses, the Puritan intellectuals preached their controversial doctrines from pulpits not dependent on bishops' approval, or, like John Milton, fought heated battles for their cause in the war of pamphlets. Using simple language and humble images, instead of the classical tongues and erudite references, the "Spiritual Brotherhood" proclaimed the duty of the individual to strive continually for his own salvation.

Outspoken in their pulpits and pamphlets, the Puritans within the Anglican Church demanded a continuation of the Reformation. The ideal they sought was the primitive apostolic church described in the New Testament. They preached that salvation could be attained directly through the Word of God without the intercession of any mortal, regardless of his position in the Church. Salvation could be achieved only through individual faith and divine grace, not through works. Despising the ignorant and inebriated pluralists who held so many of England's benefices, they urged the Church to replace its unqualified incumbents with an intelligent, university-educated ministry.

These Puritans railed against the innovations and corruptions they found within the Church. In the Bible they found no ecclesiastical vestments, no caps and surplices, no recognition of saints' days, no use of the sign of the cross in baptism nor of the ring in the marriage ceremony, and no bowing of the head at the mention of Jesus' name. They found the ritual, the standing during the credo and kneeling during prayers, the communion service and the Book of Common Prayer to be without biblical precedent, as were the ecclesiastical courts, which they both hated and feared. Their pleas for reform appealed to the middle classes and occasionally to the gentry; but in trying to convince the authorities, they ran into one obstacle after another. In England the Puritan demands for the abolition of these detested practices met with discouraging frustration.

First in 1628 as Bishop of London and then after 1633 as Archbishop of Canterbury and Chancellor of London, Laud, unlike his predecessors, was able to dominate the Church of England by combining the power of his own offices with that of the Court of Star Chamber and the High Commission to crush the Puritan opposition. The hated Oath of Supremacy became obligatory for Anglican and Puritan alike, and the Act of Unformity applied to all Englishmen. Laud's intentions were honorable: to strengthen the Church by reforming and unifying it; but the Puritans only saw him leading the Church of England directly into the camp of the Pope. The Queen openly professed Catholicism, and Pope Urban VIII had even offered the cardinal's insignia to the Archbishop of Canterbury.[3] Laws against the Papists went unheeded. Arminian theories on election and predestination prevailed.

Furthermore, to silence the Puritan protest Charles I and Bishop Laud issued in 1628 a declaration that the King was the Supreme Governor of the Church and that the Thirty-Nine Articles represented the true doctrine, not to be debated. In 1629 Laud persuaded the King to restrict the activities of Puritan lecturers and chaplains hired by wealthy gentlemen. In 1633 the King ordered the dissolution of the feoffees, a committee of twelve Puritans who had been purchasing impropriations since 1626 and using the income to fill lectureships with men sympathetic to their own beliefs.[4] In the same year he reissued the Declaration of Sports, to the horror of the Puritans, and in 1636 the bishops began visitations in their dioceses, silencing or suspending nonconformists.[5]

In the spiritual courts the nonconformists risked fines and imprisonments, ear-croppings and nose-slittings without the right to a trial by jury, to a writ of habeas corpus, or to being informed of their alleged offense. This concentrated persecution of the dissenters by Archbishop Laud and Charles I did not quell the protest, but curtailed its force by depriving its spokesmen of their livings and their pulpits and forcing its leaders, like Thomas Hooker and John Cotton, to flee from England.

Up to this point the majority of the Puritans had conformed at least outwardly, but now the only hope for reform seemed to be in the New World. Expressing the general disillusionment, Hooker lamented immediately before his departure from England that "England hath seene her best dayes, and now evill dayes are befalling us: God is packing up his Gospell, because no body will buy his wares, nor come to his price." [6] John Cotton added in 1634 that he and his "brother Hooker" had emigrated, feeling that

> God having shut a door against both of us from ministering to him and his people in our wonted congregations, and calling us, by a remnant of our people, and by others of this country, to minister to them here [in New England], and opening a door to us this way, who are we that we should strive against God, and refuse to follow the concurrence of his ordinance and providence together, calling us forth to minister here? If we may and ought to follow God's calling three hundred miles, why not three thousand.[7]

As the ecclesiastical despotism increased and the Puritan chances for success diminished, the emigration movement gained momentum. During the summer of 1633 ten or twelve ships sailed from England to New England. The next year seventeen ships followed their lead, and then came thirty-two in 1635, eleven in 1637, and twenty in 1638.[8] These Puritans had lost all hope of reforming the Anglican Church by remaining in England. They felt that they had been called anew to serve God in the wildernesses of America, unmolested by King or Archbishop. The strength of their conviction that *sustinet qui transtulit* (He who has transplanted, sustains), which has been proclaimed through the centuries on Connecticut's seal, and the absolute certainty that they represented the true church and the Anglicans a false one forced these dedicated crusaders to forfeit their positions and leave their homes and families to tackle the untamed forests of

New England in order to continue the Reformation. Samuel Eliot
Morison called Puritanism the *leit-motif* of the colonization of
New England.[9]

The critical situation within the Anglican Church during the
first third of the seventeenth century was the primary cause of the
Great Migration, but it was not the sole factor in the removal.
The period of the Great Migration coincided exactly with the
personal rule of Charles I. The years immediately preceding the
migration had been dominated by the struggle for predominance
in the government between the King, supported by his prelates
and favorites, and the Parliament of the Puritans and gentry.
Prior to 1629 Charles I had exacted forced loans without Parliament's sanction and had violated the Petition of Right repeatedly.
He imposed ship money, established monopolies, and revived
obsolete forest laws to support the extravagant whims of his
luxury-loving courtiers. He imprisoned the Puritans Pym and
Eliot, and wooed the Catholic monarchs in France and Spain. But
the Puritan middle classes were not defeated until he dissolved
his third Parliament in four years, rather than grant its demands
for reforms. From early 1628/29 until 1640 the King governed
England absolutely, without the aid, or rather the interference,
of Parliament. The dissolution of Parliament in 1629 brought ulti-
mate despair to the Puritans and gentry. For eleven years they had
no political voice.

Between March 2, 1628/29, when Charles dissolved his third
Parliament, and November 3, 1640, when the Long Parliament
convened, colonization flourished in the New World. Puritans of
the caliber of the Earl of Warwick, Viscount Saye and Sele, and
Lord Brooke, who otherwise would have been leaders in Parliament, turned their energies to the Providence Company's activities at Saybrook and in the Caribbean.[10] Others who were local
leaders like John Winthrop and Roger Ludlow joined the Massachusetts Bay Company, immigrated to New England, and directed their talents to serving Massachusetts and Connecticut
rather than England. While of less importance in forcing the
Puritans to leave Britain than the attempt to establish uniformity
within the Church, this constitutional conflict must not be over-
looked as a second force driving the gentry across the ocean.

A third element in the exodus from England was the economic instability of the country. From 1629 until the fall of 1632 England was in the midst of a depression. England was still in the throes of the transformation from a medieval, feudal economy to a modern, capitalistic economy. The incessant demands for English woolens only aggravated the situation by stimulating the enclosure movement. Thousands of yeomen and tenant farmers were driven from their lands to the overcrowded cities, where they became not only landless but also jobless. To compound the problems of the weavers in particular, a sudden influx of Flemish competitors glutted the country. Norfolk, Suffolk, and Essex were dealt the greatest blows. By April 17, 1629, the economic pressures had reached such proportions that the Justices of the Peace of Essex reported to the Privy Council that two hundred persons had petitioned them on behalf of the weavers of Braintree and Bocking, complaining of the lack of jobs for the clothiers and warning that thirty thousand men would join the ranks of the unemployed momentarily.[11] In spite of the opinion that the 1629–1632 depression principally affected the poorer classes who did not migrate to New England,[12] it must not be forgotten that Hooker's Company came from Chelmsford and Braintree.

Considering the religious, constitutional, and economic unrest in England, it is not surprising that many Englishmen should seek a Utopia in the New World. Thomas More's *Utopia* had been in print since 1516, but Bacon's *Novus Atlantis* had just appeared in 1627 to generate a faith in the possibility of a new and better world elsewhere. The Puritans were a thinking people, capable of visualizing an ideal society in contrast to the realities of the times. William Hubbard was probably the first to catch this element in the Great Migration. He wrote in 1680 that the "Utopian fancy of any projector, may easily in imagination frame a flourishing plantation, in such a country as was New England; but to the actual accomplishing thereof there is required a good number of resolved people, qualified with industry, experience, prudence, and estate, to carry on such a design to perfection."[13] Among the Connecticut Congregationalists there were "a good number" of people capable of creating a commonwealth to correspond with their ideals.

These nonseparating Puritans who left England with the Great Migration never advocated withdrawal from the Church of England, but with God's aid they intended to complete the Reformation of the Church in America. Unhampered by hostile civil and ecclesiastical authorities, they thought that there they could accomplish their "errand into the wilderness" by gathering their churches according to the example provided in the New Testament. In them they would be united by a covenant and could at last live according to the Word of God. As John Winthrop emphasized in his *Model of Christian Charity*, written while he sailed for Massachusetts aboard the *Arbella* in 1630, the New England churches would then serve as an example for the reform of the Church of England.

Closely associated with the ideal churches would be an ideal Bible commonwealth originating in a political convenant and serving to maintain peace and order in the godly community so that the Puritans might worship unhindered by human innovations and impositions.[14] Its rulers would be militant members of the Congregational churches, who could take office only after they had sworn to uphold Puritanism and to punish sinners not abiding by the Word of God. They would not force upon an unwilling people erroneous Anglican doctrines and ceremonies; instead, they would enforce uniformity according to Congregational doctrine and discipline. The exact form of this government was not evolved prior to the migration; the details were worked out in Massachusetts and Connecticut as the necessity arose to satisfy the demands of a religious people alone in the wilderness.

How many mighty forces contributed in driving the thousands of Englishmen across the ocean is debatable. Some adventurers came in response to the challenge of subduing the New England frontier. Others followed the lead of their friends, relatives, or minister who had already made the crossing. Lion Gardiner, the engineer who constructed Saybrook Fort, migrated because Hugh Peter and John Davenport, whom he had known in Rotterdam, had already embarked for the New World.[15] Roger Clap, a resident of Dorchester in Massachusetts Bay, admitted, "I never so much as heard of New-England until I heard of many godly persons that were going there, and that Mr. Warham was to go also." [16] Even the Reverend Thomas Hooker undoubtedly considered migrating to New England because many of his followers from Essex had already sailed and because his sister lay buried there. [17]

Englishmen thus eager to emigrate were becoming aware of the Massachusetts Bay area of New England long before they knew the Connecticut Valley existed. Governor William Bradford's *A Relation or Iournall of the beginning and proceedings of the English Plantation setled at Plimouth in New England, by certaine English Aduenturers both Merchants and others* (generally known as *Mourt's Relation*) was published in 1622, and Edward Winslow's *Good Newes from New England* followed in 1624. In 1630 the Reverend Francis Higginson's *New-Englands Plantation* appeared, describing the beautiful open fields, the abundance of wine and corn, fish and fowl in a land where few were ever sick and the Indians were friendly. What Puritan could resist the appeal of a country where

> that which is our greatest comfort, and meanes of defence aboue all other, is, that we haue here the true Religion and holy Ordinances of Almightie God taught amongst vs: Thankes be to God, wee haue here plenty of Preaching, and diligent Catechizing, with strickt and carefull exercise, and good and commendable orders to bring our People into a Christian conuersation with whom wee haue to doe withall. And thus we doubt not but God will be with vs, and *if God be with us, who can be against us?* [18]

In 1634 William Wood's *New-England's Prospect* appeared in a similar vein.

Who were these Puritans fleeing from England in the early part of the seventeenth century in tiny, uncomfortable, crowded ships? They were a relatively homogeneous group. Ethnically, they were Anglo-Saxons from East Anglia, the London area, or the western counties of Devon, Somerset, and Dorset. In faith they were still nonseparating Puritans. The Puritan Revolution had not yet reached the more radical stage of the Cromwellian Commonwealth and the later supremacy of the Levellers when they departed from England. They were not fanatics—not as radical as the Pilgrims who had recently settled Plymouth. Instead, they were devout, dedicated Englishmen striving toward a truer religion in the promised land.

Socially and economically the Puritans belonged to England's middle classes. Few of the nobility and few of the desperately poor in the jails and slums, poorhouses and asylums, migrated to New England. The country squires, experienced as justices of the peace in the shires, as leaders in the courts-leet and occasionally as members of the House of Commons, provided the leadership for the movement. John Haynes, Edward Hopkins, George Wyllys, Henry Wolcott, and Roger Ludlow were members of the English gentry and continued to be referred to as "Mr." or "Esq." in the Connecticut commonwealth and town records. They belonged to the same class that produced Pym, Hampden, and Oliver Cromwell. The ecclesiastical leaders of the exodus were Puritan ministers like Thomas Hooker, Samuel Stone, John Warham, Ephraim Huit, and Henry Smith, who had been preachers of note in England. The majority of them were alumni of Emmanuel College, Cambridge, where Puritanism ran rampant. The other nine-tenths of the emigrants were artisans, yeomen, and husbandmen. New England was not yet the melting pot for peoples of divers national and class origins that it became in the nineteenth century.

In their dress and habits the Puritans were not radical. They wore bright colors and silver buttons on their waistcoats and dresses, as long as they were obtainable. But they also dressed in leather and homespun on working days. These were far more appropriate to their stations than would have been the lace and silks adorned with expensive jewelry found at Court. Only the ministers wore black habitually. Children played with dolls and toys, though simple ones, of course. The Puritans frowned on secular music and art, but not on beauty in itself. Wine and beer formed an important element in their daily diet, but inebriation they abhorred. Their morals were reasonable, contrary to popular conception, and not Victorian. Love in the home was a vital part of the marriage.

These men and women, leaders and followers, brought to the Connecticut River the traditional belief in the principle of *cujus est regio, illius est religio*, soon to be propounded on the Continent at the Peace of Westphalia in 1648. It recognized the principle of the close relationship between church and state, the state determining whether the official religion should be Catholicism or Protestantism. Neither civil nor ecclesiastical diversity was permissible thereafter. They also brought with them England's time-honored belief in the merits of a stratified society, not an ideal democracy in which all men possessed equal political, social, and religious privileges.

The Puritans who left England for Massachusetts Bay and later for Connecticut transplanted themselves and their families to a land which belonged to the Crown of England by right of discovery. In 1494 John Cabot, who was an Englishman by birth but by heredity the scion of a Venetian family, had claimed Newfoundland and the Island of St. Johns for Henry VII. Cabot's son Sebastian reinforced the discovery in 1497 with explorations as far south as Florida. In 1606, over a century later, James I granted the territory between the forty-fifth and fortieth degrees of north latitude as far west as the Pacific to the Plymouth merchants in the Virginia Company. In 1620 this corporation was reorganized by letters patent and emerged as the "Council established at Plymouth, in the County of Devon, for the planting, ruling, ordering, and governing of New England in America," that is, the Council for New England. The King was in dire need of a buffer against the French in Quebec.

All subsequent charters for New England until the demise of the Council in 1635 were based on this charter to the Council for New England. The Council's first important grant was awarded to John Peirce for the Plymouth Plantation. A second involving Puritan interests was the Dorchester Company's charter of 1623, which approved the fishing settlement at Cape Anne. This jurisdiction was then reconveyed to "the Governor and Deputy of the New England Company for a Plantation in Massachusetts Bay" by a subsequent charter dated March 19, 1627/28, but it transferred the title to the land only. To obtain governmental rights a royal patent was requisite. Ironically, during the same week that Charles I dismissed his final Parliament, he transformed the New England Company into the "Governor and Company of the Massachusetts Bay in Newe England." The letters patent dated March 4, 1628/29, granted corporate status to the Massachusetts Bay Company and endowed it with comprehensive political, legislative, and judicial powers, as well as the right to acquire and transfer land in New England, in return for one-fifth of all gold or silver ore found.[19] The King lived to regret his action.

Many of the Puritans who eventually migrated to Connecticut crossed the Atlantic Ocean with the Winthrop Fleet in 1630 and settled first in the Bay Colony under the auspices of the Massachusetts Bay Company. The Connecticut towns of Windsor, Wethersfield, and Hartford are direct offshoots of the Bay Colony's towns of Dorchester, Watertown, and Newtown, respectively. The Dorchester Church was the only New England church gathered on English soil before the migration across the Atlantic. The founding fathers of Dorchester in Massachusetts Bay and Windsor in Connecticut had united into a church while in Plymouth, England, prior to their embarkation under the guidance of the Reverend John White, Rector of Holy Trinity Church in Dorchester. White did not himself make the journey to the New World; instead, on a day of fasting and prayer in March 1630 the congregation chose John Warham, formerly a well-known minister in Exeter, as their pastor and John Maverick as teacher. The lay leaders, Roger Ludlow and Edward Rossiter, were also assistants in the Massachusetts Bay Company. Unlike the majority of the settlers in the Bay Colony, the Dorchester people had lived in the western counties of England. About one hundred and forty of them sailed together from Plymouth on the four-hundred-ton *Mary and John* soon after their church was gathered. Theirs was the first of the seventeen ships of the Winthrop Fleet to land in Massachusetts, arriving in Nantasket at the end of May in 1630, only to be abruptly abandoned by the captain. They were forced to find a second ship to carry them and their belongings first to Watertown and then to "Mattapan," which they promptly renamed "Dorchester" in honor of their home in England. The people of Dorchester remained together in Massachusetts and later in Windsor in greater harmony than did the settlers in either Hartford or Wethersfield.

Watertown was also settled in 1630 by members of the Winthrop Fleet. Its original planters were followers of Sir Richard Saltonstall and George Phillips in Essex, but they had not united into a church in England. Instead, on August 27, 1630, in Massa-

chusetts Bay the Church of Watertown was gathered and Phillips
was chosen and ordained pastor.[20] He remained in this capacity
for approximately fourteen years, not removing to the Connecticut
Valley to participate in the settlement of Wethersfield. Wethersfield alone of the three river towns was settled by individuals
rather than by a migrating church or town; its institutions originated in Connecticut and consequently suffered the greatest discord.

The third town in Massachusetts Bay involved in the founding
of Connecticut was Newtown (now Cambridge, Massachusetts).[21]
In December 1630 the site had been selected with the intention of
founding the capital of the colony there and fortifying it heavily
against the Indians. The first settlements took place the following
spring, and in 1632 the Braintree Company arrived. In England
these people had long been thorns in the side of the Anglican
Church. Complaining about them during January 1631/32, the
Vicar of Braintree grumbled that it

> is no easy matter to reduce a numerous congregation into order that has
> been disorderly these 50 years, and for the last seven years has been en-
> couraged in that way by all the refractory ministers of the country by
> private meetings and leaving schismatical books among them. These per-
> sons have laboured to make his person and ministry contemptible and
> odious, because he would not hold correspondence with them.[22]

Later that year William Goodwin led the Braintree Company to
Massachusetts Bay. The Vicar must have breathed an audible sigh
of relief when the Company waved its final farewell.

Under the date of August 14, 1632, Governor Winthrop noted
that the "Braintree company, (which had begun to sit down at
Mount Wollaston,) by order of court, removed to Newtown.
These were Mr. Hooker's company." [23] This was Governor Winthrop's first mention of Thomas Hooker or his followers from
Chelmsford, Colchester, and Braintree, England. The Church of
Newtown was gathered before Hooker's arrival, but undoubtedly
with the understanding that he would join it in the Bay as its
pastor. The Center Church in Hartford, as the Newtown Church
is known 236 years later, considers 1632 as the year of its founding, although at that date it had neither pastor nor teacher. For

about a year the Elders William Goodwin and Andrew Warner officiated in the church.

Not until September 4, 1633, did the *Griffin* finally arrive, bringing Hooker and Samuel Stone with about two hundred other passengers to Newtown. Hooker's sojourn in Newtown marked a temporary halt in the wanderings of this nonseparating Puritan minister, whom Cotton Mather eulogized in his biography, styling him *"The Light of the Western Churches* . . . the Renowned Pastor of *Hartford*-Church, and Pillar of *Connecticut*-Colony, in *New-England."* [24] His career typified the harried life of a prominent nonconformist during the reigns of James I and Charles I. It is worth pausing over, for no man exerted a greater influence over the infant Commonwealth of Connecticut than did Thomas Hooker.

Born about 1586 in the tiny hamlet of Marfield in Leicestershire to a yeoman father and mother, he was educated at a small school at Market Bosworth, about twenty-five miles from his home. He matriculated at Queen's College, Cambridge, but soon transferred to Emmanuel College. He received his A.B. in 1608 and his M.A. in 1611, but continued at Emmanuel College until 1618 as a Dixie Fellow. Emmanuel College was then seething with Puritanism. Among his contemporaries there were William Ames, Peter Bulkeley, John Cotton, Francis Higginson, John Wilson, and Nathaniel Ward. It was while at Cambridge that he experienced an agonizing regeneration.

Soon afterward he was appointed rector of St. George's Church in Esher, Surrey, a position he could hold without the bishop's approval because it was endowed by Francis Drake, a nephew of the Elizabethan sea dog and circumnavigator. From there repute of his forceful, stimulating sermons spread. From about 1626 until 1629 he served as lecturer at St. Mary's in Chelmsford, where his congregation included such personages as the Earl of Warwick. But his fame was becoming too great. People from all parts of Essex flocked to his sermons. Inevitably he attracted the notice of Laud, then Bishop of London, and became a target of the Establishment.

On May 20, 1629, Samuel Collins, Vicar of Braintree, reported to Dr. Duck, Laud's Chancellor, that he had spoken with Thomas

Hooker, who had requested that the Bishop of London not arraign him before the High Commission, but allow him to leave the diocese quietly. Collins added that he had been advised by reliable authorities that this would be the safest means of silencing the non-conformist without repercussions. He urged caution because the economic hardships in the area had created an incendiary situation among the "tumultuous vulgar" which might be ignited by any proceedings against Hooker. Collins also reported Hooker's intention to settle with his followers elsewhere in Essex, as maintenance had been promised him should he be suspended by the High Commission. His great popularity was certain to endure and his influence spread to other pulpits.[25] Laud's spy feared the power of this Puritan divine.

Two weeks later Collins reported to Dr. Duck that Mr. Hooker was headed first for Leicestershire and then for London, where he intended to appear before the Bishop of London. Collins advocated letting Hooker leave the diocese unobtrusively. Already his presence had caused too great a stir. "All men," he warned, "are taken up with expecting what will be the conclusion of Mr. Hooker's business. Cambridge disputes it *pro et con*. It drowns the noise of the great question of tonnage and poundage." [26]

Still the complaints continued. In November 1629 Dr. John Browning, Rector of Rawreth, Essex, begged help from Laud. He reported that Hooker continued to preach and implored the Bishop's assistance at least in protecting the obedient members of the Church of England from Hooker's lectures and the addiction of his following, if silencing the nonconformist were not feasible. Like Collins he added that caution must be employed in suppressing his lectures, because of the inevitable reaction of his followers.[27] But on November 10, 1629, forty-nine conformist clergymen in Essex wrote to Bishop Laud, taking the opposite position by defending Hooker and vouching that he "be for doctrine, orthodox, for life and conversation, honest, and for disposition, peaceable, no ways turbulent or factious," to no avail.[28] This letter was hastily followed by one from forty-one clergymen begging for the stringent enforcement of all the statutes against nonconformism.

Laud's party prevailed. Thomas Hooker was forced to relinquish his lectureship at St. Mary's. Four miles away in Little Bad-

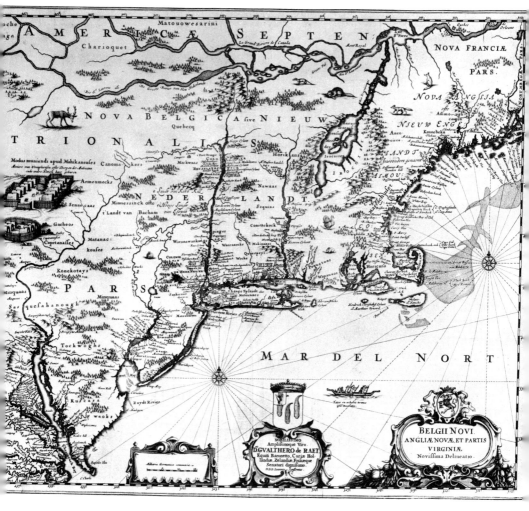

The Jansson, or Janssonius, Prototype, depicted 1647–1651, issued
c. 1660. *Courtesy of The New-York Historical Society, New York City.*

dow he ostensibly took on the new and more pacific role of a schoolmaster, assisted by John Eliot, but surreptitiously he continued to hold monthly meetings until in 1630 the spiritual court sitting at Chelmsford silenced him and bound him over to appear before the High Commission. Instead of obeying the Anglicans at the risk of having his ears cropped or his nose slit, Hooker jumped bail, forfeited the £50 which a Puritan farmer named Nash had given for surety, and fled to Holland, where he preached his views for three years. One wonders if Laud had listened to the warnings of Collins and Browning and intentionally looked the other way. In the Netherlands, Hooker lectured first in Amsterdam, but found his views incompatible with those of the Presbyterian John Paget. In Delft he served as an assistant to the Reverend Hugh Peter, but soon moved on to join William Ames in Rotterdam, where he wrote the preface for Ames's *A Fresh Suit against Human Ceremonies in God's Worship.*

Not yet satisfied, he decided to accept the invitation of the Church of Newtown in Massachusetts Bay. But first he had to return to England to settle his affairs. Cotton Mather, illustrating well the fact that even Puritans were capable of both wit and deceit, has preserved this tale of his narrow but humorous escape from the Bishop. Hooker, he wrote

was quickly scented by the Pursevants; who at length got so far up with him, as to knock at the Door of that very Chamber, where he was now discoursing with Mr. *Stone;* who was now become his designed Companion and Assistent for the *New English* Enterprize. Mr. *Stone* was at that Instant smoking of *Tobacco;* for which Mr. *Hooker* had been reproving him, as being then used by few Persons of Sobriety; being also of a sudden and pleasant Wit, he stept unto the Door, with his Pipe in his mouth, and such an Air of Speech and Look, as gave him some Credit with the Officer. The Officer demanded, *Whether Mr.* Hooker *were not there?* Mr. *Stone* replied with a braving fort of Confidence, *What* Hooker? *Do you mean* Hooker *that liv'd once at* Chelmsford! The Officer answered, *Yes,* He! Mr. *Stone* immediately, with a Diversion like that which once helped *Athanasius,* made this true Answer, *If it be he you look for, I saw him about an Hour ago, at such an House in the Town; you had best hasten thither after him.* The Officer took this for a sufficient Account, and went his way; but Mr. *Hooker,* upon this Intimation, concealed himself more carefully and securely, till he went on Board, at the *Downs*, in the Year 1633. the Ship which brought him, and Mr. *Cotton*, and Mr. *Stone* to *New-England*.[29]

Thus arrived in New England Thomas Hooker, whose imprint on the churches and state of Connecticut was so bold.[30]

As Cotton Mather quipped, the people of Massachusetts Bay now had "*Cotton* for their *Cloathing, Hooker* for their *Fishing,* and *Stone* for their *Building*." [31] During September, Hooker and Stone were admitted to the Church at Boston, and on October 11 there was held a "fast at Newtown, where Mr. Hooker was chosen pastor, and Mr. Stone teacher, in such a manner as before at Boston." [32] Unfortunately, Governor Winthrop did not go into greater detail concerning this final step in the organization of the Church of Newtown, which was soon to be transplanted from Massachusetts Bay to Connecticut.

Some of the future inhabitants of the Commonwealth of Connecticut were thus in Massachusetts Bay during the formative years of that colony, the time when both its religious and political institutions evolved. These were difficult years, but they contributed to the experience of those going to Connecticut, enabling them to establish their comparable institutions more facilely. While they were in the Bay, the form of the New England Congregational churches emerged as an amalgamation of Puritan ideals and Plymouth's experience. A working civil government developed from the original trading-company structure to operate in close harmony with the churches. Towns prospered, homes and fortifications soon appeared against the hilly sky line, and the fields yielded their first produce.

All was not perfection in this Puritan world, however. Within only a few months of Hooker's arrival, rumblings of discontent began to be heard, particularly among the settlers of Dorchester, Watertown, and Newtown. Economic grievances instead of religious unrest predominated in the determination to migrate a second time. In the official explanation of the removal expressed in the petition to Charles II for the Charter in 1661, the General Court of Connecticut explained that its people had left the Bay "in hope of better accomodacõns." [33] Newtown was hemmed in by

Charlestown, Watertown, Boston, and Roxbury. The first planters had made a tactical error in locating the towns so close together. What land Newtown possessed was arid and sandy. On May 15, 1634, its inhabitants complained to the General Court "of straitness for want of land, especially meadow, and desired leave of the court to look out either for enlargement or removal." The Court granted the request.[34] Today the problem seems incomprehensible because the population was then only a fraction of what it is now, but much of the land was still wilderness, uncleared and untillable. Cleared land became more precious as the Bay's population swelled with the influx of wealthy Puritans, who relied on large herds of cattle to provide their livelihood and were dependent on adequate meadows and pastures.[35]

Soon Watertown and Dorchester reiterated the complaint of land hunger. Watertown's physical situation presented a special difficulty: the town itself was divided by many rivulets "which hath caused her inhabitants to scatter in such manner, that their Sabbath-Assemblies prove very thin if the season favour not," a distressing situation for the religiously minded leaders.[36] In contrast to their own land shortage they began receiving reports of the rich alluvial soil and open meadows situated on a navigable river in a valley where the Indian population had been depleted by a smallpox epidemic.

In addition to the land problems a second factor, the opposition to the political regime in Massachusetts, was instrumental in the removal. As early as February 17, 1631/32, the pastor and elder of Watertown had publicly challenged the right of the colonial government to levy taxes without the consent of the people, but they were forced to humbly retract their statements.[37] Many inhabitants also criticized the limitation of the franchise to church members, but the practice in Connecticut was to be little different. Others objected to the virtual veto power which the assistants (comparable to our modern senators) had over the deputies (the representatives) in the General Court and to the fact that on March 3, 1635/36, the General Court ordered that a standing council with life tenure be chosen from the assistants.[38] This action was soon modified, but stirred up considerable contention and was not duplicated in the Fundamental Orders of Connecticut.

Perhaps the overt discontent over the shortage of land was only
a disguise for covert dissatisfaction, for deep-seated personal rivalries existed. Competition between Hooker and Cotton was first
mentioned by William Hubbard about 1680. "Two such eminent
stars," he observed, "such as were Mr. Cotton and Mr. Hooker,
both of the first magnitude, though of differing influence, could
not well continue in one and the same orb." [39] Thomas Hooker's
church had extended an invitation to John Cotton to serve as his
assistant in the Bay, but he declined, and Stone was chosen instead.
Hooker had achieved greater fame in England, but in the Bay
Colony, Cotton was the more prominent pastor.

Historians from Benjamin Trumbull to Perry Miller have
agreed with Hubbard, in spite of the fact that the conciliatory John
Winthrop, writing home to Sir Simonds D'Ewes, a Suffolk lawyer,
antiquary, and Member of Parliament, absolutely denied it, re-
iterating his conviction that "Mr Hooker is like to goe thither [to
Connecticut] next yeare, not for any difference between Mr Cotton
& him (soe reporte) for they doe hould a most sweet & brotherly
comunion together (thoughe their judgm^{ts} doe somewhat differ
about the lawfullnesse of the Crosse in the ensigne) but that the
people & cattle are so increased as the place will not suffice
them." [40] The report that reached Archbishop Laud in October
1637 emphasized the theological conflict between them over questions of whether justification were achieved by faith or by works,
the state of the soul requisite for the attainment of grace, and the
degree of faith required before sanctification. [41] They had taken
opposing sides during the Antinomian Controversy and differed
greatly on how strict the admission requirements to the churches
should be.

In civil matters Hooker was more liberal than Cotton, but the
difference was in degree only. As Albert E. Van Dusen has emphasized, Hooker was still a theocrat. [42] He was more inclined to
listen to the views of his congregation and more optimistic on the
fate of man in general. And he opposed the negative voice of the
assistants, particularly when they vetoed the removal of Newtown
in 1634. But his belief that civil government should be limited to
the regenerate of the Congregational churches, rather than being
open on a parochial basis to all freeholders, was little different

from Cotton's. Each had a large body of prominent supporters, but while many of Hooker's followers—William Pynchon, Roger Ludlow, Edward Rossiter, and John Haynes, for instance—had been early and important members of the Massachusetts Bay Company and among the first arrivals, Cotton's adherents had greater seniority and held more of the reins of power. These Puritan divines were not immune to human jealousy. Massachusetts Bay was not large enough for two such strong-willed spokesmen of the true religion.

The precarious position of the Colony of Massachusetts was a final factor in the removal. The Bay Colony was being threatened by both internal and external forces at the time when the removal to Connecticut was under consideration. Its cohesion was first shaken by Roger Williams, who leveled attacks on its basic purposes until the General Court on September 3, 1635, sentenced him to banishment on the grounds that he "hath broached & dyvulged dyvers newe & dangerous opinions, against the aucthoritie of magistrates, as also writt lres of dafamacõn, both of the magistrates & churches here, & that before any conviccõn, and yet mainetaineth the same without retraccõn." [43] At the trial Thomas Hooker was chosen to debate the issue with him, just as centuries before the Apostles had debated with nonbelievers.

At the same time the Antinomians, led by Anne Hutchinson, her brother-in-law, the Reverend John Wheelwright, and Governor Henry Vane, expounded religious doctrines in the colony tantamount to heresy from 1634 until 1637, when their opinions were declared erroneous and they were excommunicated and banished. They preached that salvation depended on the covenant of grace, which God and the individual believer concluded without the intercession of a pastor or priest. Their controversial stand virtually divided Massachusetts into two camps at a time when solidarity was essential for its preservation. In May 1636 the influence of the Antinomians reached its peak. Henry Vane won the gubernatorial election, and Hooker was scorned as a minister under a covenant of works. It hardly appears to be coincidental that this was the point when he led the trek to Connecticut.

Simultaneously, rumors ran rampant in Massachusetts Bay that the arrival of a governor-general was imminent. Archbishop Laud

was becoming more cognizant of the scope of the Great Migration
as reports besieged him that prominent Puritans like Lord Saye
and Sele contemplated escaping to New England and when enemies of the Bay Colony like Sir Ferdinando Gorges began spreading malicious reports about it. On February 21, 1633/34, the King
in Council issued an order that all ships in the Thames River remain there until further notice. Later in 1634 Laud succeeded in
having Charles I appoint a commission, the Lords Commissioners
for Plantations in General, whose specific duties included the
power to revoke letters patent, to pass laws for the colonies, to
enforce religious uniformity, to appoint justices and magistrates for
them, to remove governors, and to hear complaints.[44] In 1635 the
Court of Kings Bench, instigated by Gorges, issued a writ of quo
warranto against the governor, deputy governor, and assistants of
the Massachusetts Bay Company, ordering the return of their
charter. The colonists ignored the writ and fortified Castle Island
instead, appointing Roger Ludlow its superintendent. Nevertheless,
the Connecticut Valley offered a site for a Bible commonwealth
farther inland and one more step removed from the sight of the
unsympathetic officials of the King and Archbishop.

The Connecticut Valley was in the early seventeenth century
nine-tenths covered with primeval hardwood forests, thick under-
neath with matted vines. There were also the softwoods: pines,
cedars, and fruit trees. Never had the birds and wild animals been
disturbed by the white man. The only cleared lands were the
swamps and small meadows which the Indians burned over period-
ically to trap game or to plant their corn, pumpkins, and tobacco.
Estimates of the number of Indians of the Algonquian Confederation resident in the valley in the 1630's run as high as twenty
thousand, but the actual figure was probably closer to six or seven
thousand.[45]

The Indians were primitive savages, no farther advanced than
the Stone Age. Not until the Europeans brought them steel and
iron knives, hoes, and guns did they have weapons other than
their bows, arrows, and wooden spears. The relatively peaceful
River Indians were being squeezed between the warlike Mohawks
on the west and the fierce Pequots on the east when the Puritans
arrived in New England. Natawanute and his Mantianucks of

Windsor, Sequassen and the Suckiaugs at Hartford, and Sowheag and his Pyquaugs at Wethersfield welcomed the English to their valley. Here were extra forces to fight their Indian enemies, as well as buyers for their furs.

Land shortages, personal rivalries, disquiet within the Bay Colony, and the threatened interference from abroad all played their part in promoting the removal to this valley. But in spite of all these provocations, the first Europeans to migrate to Connecticut were not men from Massachusetts Bay. They were Dutch traders attracted there by the prospect of a profitable beaver trade with the Indians, rather than by the possibility of a permanent settlement. The Dutch based their right to the Connecticut Valley both on discovery and on Indian purchase. In 1614 Adrian Block had explored the river he named the "Fresh River" and had established the Dutch claim by his actual visit. This right was conveyed by the States-General of Holland to the Dutch West India Company in 1621.[46] To reinforce the claim, on June 8, 1633, the Dutch Governor Jacob van Curter purchased from the Pequot sachem, Nepuquash, a twenty- to thirty-acre parcel of land on the south side of the Park River where it flowed into the Connecticut River and hastily erected a fort defended by two cannons. Today this property retains the name Dutch Point, in memory of its original white settlers. Fort Good Hope, or the House of Good Hope, as it was also known, was completed before permanent settlements were made by the English, thus reinforcing the Dutch rights by prior occupation.

The most valid English title to the Connecticut River was a charter, the Warwick Patent, granted by the Council for New England to Puritan interests.[47] Many doubts concerning the actual existence of this patent have been expressed, but throughout this period the Connecticut men accepted its authenticity even though they never saw the original document. In 1630 the Council for New England had granted the tract of land which included the Connecticut River to its president, Robert Rich, the second Earl of Warwick. Its action possibly was confirmed by a royal patent from Charles I. On March 19, 1631/32, the Earl presumably transferred his interest in the territory to several Puritan nobles and gentlemen of the Providence Company, who intended to establish a refuge to which they could flee if the political and religious situation in England should become critical. During the 1630's the defeat of Puritanism always seemed at hand, and these gentlemen could well afford a little foresight. The most prominent of the grantees were Lord Saye and Sele, Lord Brooke (Baron Brooke of Warwick Castle), Lord Rich (the Earl's eldest son and heir), Sir Nathaniel Rich (a close relation), Sir Richard Saltonstall, John Pym, and John Hampden. The family ties are obvious. So is the Puritan flavor.

In the Patent the Earl of Warwick conveyed "all that part of New-England, in America, which lies and extends itself from a river there called Narraganset river, the space of forty leagues upon a straight line near the sea shore towards the southwest, west and by south, or west, as the coast lieth towards Virginia, . . . to the south sea." In addition to this vague parcel of land the Earl granted the gentlemen "all jurisdictions, rights, and royalties, liberties, freedoms, immunities, powers, privileges, franchises, preeminencies, and commodities whatsoever, which the said Robert, Earl of Warwick, now hath or had," reserving for the King and his heirs the customary one-fifth of all gold and silver found.[48] The Patent represented the transfer of the title to the land, rather than the authorization of a corporation with governmental powers.

Asserting their rights under the Warwick Patent, nevertheless, the lords and gentlemen commissioned John Winthrop, Jr., as their agent in New England. He sailed on the *Abigail* and in October 1635 landed in Massachusetts Bay to inquire about the Patentees' territory and to secure their title. His instructions were to erect a fort at the mouth of the Connecticut River with the £2,000 allotted him and to begin the initial divisions of the land surrounding it.

In November, Winthrop hurriedly sent a thirty-ton ship loaded with twenty men and their provisions, two pieces of cannon, and enough ammunition to thwart a Dutch attempt to occupy the strategic position at Kievit's Hoek at the river's mouth. His mission was successful; the Dutch were warded off, and the fort was soon constructed by Lion Gardiner. The next year the Lords sent an inquiry to make certain that their rights and titles as nobility would be recognized should they flee to Saybrook, but the events in England never occasioned their removal. Shortly thereafter Puritanism gained the upper hand, and the nonconformists remained in England. Only George Fenwick represented their interests at Saybrook when Winthrop's commission expired in 1636. No governor again served over their entire jurisdiction.[49]

Before the Warwick Patentees built their fort at Saybrook, other Englishmen had begun settlements up the river. In 1631 Chief Wahginnacutt of the Podunk Indians had tried to convince Plymouth that it and Massachusetts Bay should combine their resources in a profitable trading venture in the Connecticut Valley. Plymouth was unable to persuade the Bay of the merits of the scheme and so in 1632 sent Edward Winslow to select a site on the river. It was determined to trade there alone.

Later in the summer of 1633, the year that Laud became Archbishop of Canterbury, the bold but reprobate John Oldham, a freeman of Massachusetts Bay, and three men had followed Indian paths to Pyquaug (Wethersfield) to investigate the area. Oldham returned to the Bay with reports of a potentially profitable trade with the Indians of the valley. Perhaps his visit is the event the General Court relied on about 1658, when it decided that Wethersfield was Connecticut's "most Auncient Towne" and awarded it the right to determine the time and place for the annual perambulations of the towns' boundaries.[50] Who should know better than the magistrates and deputies sitting as the General Court of Connecticut in the 1650's, which of the Connecticut towns was the most ancient? Their decision could only mean either that Oldham was in Wethersfield at least temporarily before the Dutch settled at Fort Good Hope at Hartford and Lieutenant Holmes and his party from Plymouth erected their trading house at Windsor or that the General Court did not consider trading houses as permanent settlements.

In the fall of 1633 adventurers from Plymouth entered the valley, lured there by the beaver, hemp, and black lead. In October 1633 William Holmes and his party sailed past the Dutch at Fort Good Hope, purchased land from the River Indians, erected a frame house at Mattaneaug (Windsor) near the mouth of the Farmington River, and surrounded it with a palisade. Plymouth was anxious to repay its debt to the merchants who had financed

its pilgrimage to the New World. Seventy Dutchmen marched
north hastily to drive out the intruders, but quickly retreated
without firing a shot when they realized the strength of Plymouth's fortifications. The Dutch shortly thereafter attempted to
start another trading center above Holmes's but were soon discouraged. The Indian population had succumbed to the white
man's smallpox.

Trade was not the only reason Englishmen eyed the valley;
many in the Bay were growing restless for the reasons already
mentioned and were determined to settle there. In the spring of
1634 the Newtowners petitioned the General Court for permission to leave. On May 14, 1634, the Court granted their request
to search for other lands provided they look only within the
jurisdiction of Massachusetts. They then sent explorers to investigate the Merrimack River, but the report brought no satisfactory
news. Thereupon they sent six of their men on the *Blessing* "to
discover Connecticut River, intending to remove their town
thither." [51] The September 1634 sessions of the General Court
held on the third and twenty-fifth dealt with the question of the
removal of Newtown to Connecticut. During the debate, which
lasted several days, the Newtowners complained that their land
was inadequate for grazing their cattle, supporting their minister,
and accommodating new inhabitants. They explained the attrac-
tion of the Connecticut Valley and the "strong bent of their
spirits to remove thither." [52]

The vote in the General Court nearly caused a constitutional
crisis. The deputies voted fifteen to ten in favor of Newtown's
departure. They were supported by Governor Thomas Dudley
and two assistants, but the deputy governor, Roger Ludlow, and
a majority of the assistants opposed it on the grounds that the
Bay Colony would be more vulnerable with its population depleted. Ludlow and others also objected to the removal as a
breach of covenant. A deadlock ensued. To settle the issue they
agreed to a day of humiliation, after which the Court reassembled.
John Cotton preached a sermon attacking the removal and convinced a majority of its evils. The people of Newtown therefore
agreed to augment their lands with meadow and river bank donated by Watertown and Boston. And "so the fear of their re-

moval to Connecticut was removed" [53]—at least temporarily. However, during the fall of 1634 John Oldham and eight or nine companions again left Watertown without permission of the General Court and remained during the winter at Pyquaug, the site of the future town of Wethersfield. There these adventurers lived in log huts. Probably they sowed the first crop of winter wheat in the valley, marking the beginnings of agricultural life in Connecticut.

By May 1635 Watertown and Dorchester were openly complaining of insufficient land. Therefore, on May 6 the General Court granted the inhabitants of Watertown permission to remove to a place of their choosing, "pvided they continue still vnd[r] this goumt." [54] Thereupon a band of settlers under the leadership of John Oldham journeyed to the Connecticut River Valley, increasing the number of white inhabitants in Watertown (Wethersfield) to twenty-five or thirty. [55]

On June 3 permission to remove was also granted the town of Dorchester, but in it a different note was sounded. The record states, "There is like leave graunted to the inhabitants of Dorchest[r], for their removeall, as Waterton hath graunted to them." But immediately following this is: "Also, there are three peeces graunted to the plantacõns that shall remove to Conecticott, to ffortifie themselues withall." [56] By June it had become evident that many important persons in these towns would resettle in Connecticut, whether or not they had permission from the General Court.

The determination to migrate from Massachusetts Bay was unrestrainable. During the summer of 1635 the removal began. Suddenly, Plymouth, Dorchester, and the Warwick Patentees began quarreling over the meadowland surrounding the Plymouth trading house at Mattaneaug (Windsor). The newcomers from Dorchester, led by Roger Ludlow, ignored the rights of the Plymouth traders by usurping their lands and instructing their surveyor, Matthew Grant, to lay out home lots on the high land west of the river, known as the "Lord's Waste." Ill will existed between Plymouth and Massachusetts Bay for years as a result of this abusive treatment. Edward Winslow gave vent to Plymouth's fury in a letter to John Winthrop, the younger, writing

that these "oppressors deserue no favor, their pride would be
taken down. Tis pitty religion should be a cloake for such
spirits." [57] This antagonism was only partially mitigated in May
1637, when the Dorchester proprietors purchased the Plymouth
rights, except for the trading house, 43¾ acres of meadow, 40
acres of high land adjacent to the Hartford line, and certain lands
not yet divided, for £37 10s.[58] The determined Dorchester settlers
also forced Francis Stiles and his two brothers and eighteen indentured servants, whom Sir Richard Saltonstall had sent in behalf of the Warwick Patentees, to vacate the site or rest content
with peripheral lands. Sir Richard stormed, but after 1635 the
Dorchester Puritans were triumphant in Windsor. Half the population of Dorchester in the Bay migrated to Connecticut, led by
its most influential citizens, Edward Rossiter and Roger Ludlow,
and the Reverend John Warham.

So many pioneers reached Connecticut by September 1635
that the General Court of the Bay decided it had to participate
in the removal and assert its influence over the development of
the embryonic towns, as it could not prevent their growth. In the
September 3 session several steps were taken to establish its authority over the new settlements: the General Court authorized
the loan of defensive equipment to the plantations on the river,
and it swore in William Westwood as constable for the Connecticut plantations until others should be chosen to replace him. It
gave the settlements in Connecticut liberty to choose their own
constables in the future, and it empowered the assistants of the
Bay to swear in the constables upon the request of the withdrawers.
The constable had been responsible for keeping the King's peace
in England. In Connecticut he was the sole military officer until
the militia was raised. The first constable, William Westwood,
served as a temporary link between Massachusetts Bay and Connecticut.[59]

By October, Hooker had decided to leave the Bay, giving
impetus to the movement. On the fifteenth of the month a preliminary migration of permanent settlers took place. About sixty
men, women, and children followed an Indian trail, arriving
safely with their cows, horses, and swine only "after a tedious and
difficult journey." [60] Some went to the northernmost settlement

near the Plymouth trading house. Others from Newtown, led by their church's teacher, Samuel Stone, its ruling elder, William Goodwin, and the constable, proceeded southward to Suckiaug, where Hartford now stands. The brave Puritans at Suckiaug built their temporary shelters of turf and branches on a ridge above the meadow and surrounded their new homes with a palisade. They were designated the "Northsiders" in the early Hartford records. Winter descended suddenly and cruelly that year all along the Connecticut River, catching the Puritan newcomers unprepared. Many were forced to trudge back to the Bay to escape the icy blasts little abated by their flimsy dwellings or fled to Saybrook, where the *Rebecca* was frozen into the river, but was soon freed by a warm rain. Others cheated famine and death by surviving on acorns and roots.

In spite of these winter hardships, final preparations for removal were being made back in Newtown, Dorchester, and Watertown. The *Register Book of the Lands and Houses in the "New Towne"* reveals the situation in one of the towns. The first complete liquidation of landholdings occurred on August 28, 1635, when John Steele "sould and past over all that right title and Intrest wch he hath in all his parcells of land lyeinge and beeing in Newtown." [61] The majority of the lands were transferred between April 1 and May 30, 1636. Fortunately for Newtown, the Reverend Thomas Shepard arrived from England with his people in October 1635. In February 1635/36 they gathered their church and eagerly purchased the property from Hooker's followers. Not all the property held in the Bay could be liquidated before the departure. For instance, when his will was probated in March 1640/41, William Spenser's estate included land in Concord valued at £120. [62] But this was the exception; the majority of the lands changed hands before the removal.

On March 3, 1635/36, the General Court of the Bay took another crucial step in the removal. Grudgingly, it bestowed its tacit approval by providing a provisional government for the new plantations. [63] Historians have never been able to explain this action, as no one at that time was certain within whose jurisdiction the Connecticut Valley lay. As late as February 24, 1635/36, Governor Winthrop recorded the fact that Edward Winslow of Plymouth had come to Dorchester to discuss their quarrel over the land in Connecticut, it "being doubtful whether that place were within our patent or not." [64]

The territory at the mouth of the river belonged to the War-wick Patentees, but their agent, John Winthrop, Jr., had been delegated no authority by the Patentees to establish an independent government up the river. The eighteenth-century Massachusetts historian Thomas Hutchinson, suggested that perhaps the action was in accordance with the then generally accepted principle that once a man had taken an oath of fidelity to a commonwealth, he was bound to it even though he should no longer reside in it. [65] This interpretation rationalized the extension of the authority of the Massachusetts Bay General Court over the persons of the settlers, even though the Court possessed no rights over the land they occupied. The action was obviously an expedient measure taken by the General Court and by John Winthrop, Jr., repre-senting the Patentees, to provide a semblance of legality for the new plantations.

Undoubtedly there were secret meetings attended by the John Winthrops, elder and younger, Thomas Hooker, Roger Ludlow, Samuel Stone, and others concerned with the exodus during the winter of 1635–1636 to determine the best means of providing legal sanction for the new Puritan communities inevitably destined to be planted on the bank of the Connecticut River. The final compromise agreed on recognized the general authority of John Winthrop, the younger, as agent of the Patentees over the river territory, even though the gentlemen had not bestowed their blessings, but the provisional government emanated from the General Court of the Bay. Thereby both parties participated in the action. [66]

The General Court of Massachusetts Bay and the agent of the Warwick Patentees created a commission to govern Connecti-cut. The Court and the Patentees' agent drew up the new govern-ment and provided the authority for its existence, but they re-tained no rights other than the stipulation that

it shalbe lawfull for this Court to recall the said psents if they see cause, and if soe be there may be a mutuall and setled goum^t condiscended vnto by & with the good likeing & consent of the saide noble psonages, or their agent, the inhabitants, & this comōnwealthe; provided, also, that this may not be any preiudice to the interst of those noble psonages in the sᵈ ryver & confines thereof within their seuall lymitts.⁶⁷

It was an unusual commission created to govern Connecticut for the twelve months from March 1636 through March 1637. It is probable that Roger Ludlow drew up this document as well as the Fundamental Orders and the Code of 1650. All the commissioners appointed intended to migrate; there was no absentee rule over the river towns. Two were chosen for each of the four communities, including Agawam (Springfield). Roger Ludlow, who two years previously had so violently opposed the settlement of Connecticut, and William Phelps intended to live in the Connecticut town of Dorchester (Windsor); John Steele and William Westwood, in Newtown (Hartford); William Swain and Andrew Ward, in Watertown (Wethersfield); and Henry Smith and William Pynchon, in Agawam (Springfield). It is worth noting that of these men Ludlow, Pynchon, Smith, and Phelps sat as magistrates on the last General "Corte" ⁶⁸ recorded before the adoption of the Fundamental Orders and that Steele and Ward sat on it as "committees." Ludlow became Connecticut's first deputy governor, and Phelps was elected a magistrate and Steele a deputy in the first court of elections held under the new constitution.

These eight commissioners were appointed to serve as a resident court with full authority to hear and determine judicial cases, to examine witnesses in disputes between individuals, to judge misdemeanors, and to sentence the guilty to corporal punishment, imprisonment, or fine. There is no evidence that appeals from their decisions were returned to the Bay. The Commission was authorized to serve as a temporary legislative body and in that capacity pass the requisite orders to regulate trade, planting, building, the distribution of land, and military discipline and, if necessary, wage war for the public good of the incipient plantations.⁶⁹ The General Court further decreed that the eight commissioners, "or the greatʳ p̄te of them, shall haue power, vnder the greatʳ p̄te of their ha[nds], att a day or dayes by them appoyncted, vpon convenient not[ice], to convent the said inhabitants of the said townes to any convenient place that they shall thinke meete, in a legall & open manner, by way of Court, to pceede in execute[ing] the power & aucthoritie aforesaide." [70]

Thus the General Court of the Bay Colony provided comprehensive legislative, judicial, and administrative powers for the first governing body in the Connecticut Valley. From this moment it was the Commonwealth that was of primary importance. Under the Massachusetts Bay Commission, Windsor, Hartford, and Wethersfield were not recognized as autonomous city-states like ancient Athens or Sparta, or medieval Florence and Venice, nor were they later in the Fundamental Orders. The Commission was designed to provide a formal government for the whole settlement on the Connecticut River, not for the individual towns.

The question frequently arises as to whether the General Court intended that Connecticut should remain within its control or whether it should be allowed to develop independently after the expiration of the Commission. On June 2, 1641, the Bay's Court merely stated that "the said comission was not granted upon any intent either to dismise the psons frō us, or to determine any thing about the limits of iurisdictions, the interest of the lands & oʳ owne limits being as then unknowne; therefore it was granted onely for one yeare." [71]

Technically, Connecticut was the child of the Bay Colony and the Warwick Patentees for the year. Actually, Connecticut was an independent commonwealth from its beginning because of the difficulties of transportation and communication. The new settlements never acknowledged John Winthrop, Jr., as their governor in spite of his commission from the Warwick Patentees, and he never asserted his rights by attending the meetings of the Commission. The name of Roger Ludlow appeared first on the roll, indicating that he, rather than the governor's son, presided at the eight sessions held between April 26, 1636, and March 28, 1637.

About three months subsequent to the creation of the Massachusetts Bay Commission, Hooker's parishioners uprooted themselves from their temporary homes in the Bay and removed to Connecticut. In his journal for May 31, 1636, Governor Winthrop jotted down the often quoted note that "Mr. Hooker, pastor of the church of Newtown, and the most of his congregation, went to Connecticut. His wife was carried in a horse litter; and they drove one hundred and sixty cattle, and fed of their milk by the way." [72] These hundred Newtowners forwarded their heavy goods by boat and then proceeded themselves on foot westward along an Indian trail until they reached the Connecticut River near the spot where Springfield now stands. They followed the river south for a few miles, crossing it from a point opposite the Plymouth trading house. Finally, after the two-week journey through swamps, over mountains, and through virgin forests, Master Hooker led the body of his church south to Suckiaug, already occupied by the Dutch at Fort Good Hope and by the advance party of his church. He and the leaders of the Newtown Church settled north of the Little, or Park, River with the Stone and Goodwin parties, who had preceded them in the removal from the Bay, while the majority of his followers crossed the Little River to make their homes on its southern side.

The migration of the Dorchester Puritans was also as a church. Twenty-four full communion members, a majority of the church, voted to leave the Bay.[73] Because the greater part of the church approved the exodus, Pastor Warham and Teacher Maverick agreed to the move. Maverick died in March before the removal, but in September 1636 Warham arrived in the valley to join his church. Later a second church was gathered in the mother town of Dorchester to serve the minority of the members who had remained in the Bay.

Of the three towns, only Watertown did not migrate as a church. Sir Richard Saltonstall, the Reverend Mr. Phillips, and the majority of the church decided to stay in Massachusetts Bay. Six members—Andrew Ward, John Sherman, John Stickland, Robert Coo, Robert Reynold, and Jonas Weede, a minority of the church—were dismissed with the specific understanding that they form a new church on the Connecticut River, but they brought no minister with them.

Few men of great wealth cared to face the frontier settlements of Connecticut, and those venturous souls who challenged the wilderness managed to bring with them only the minimum number of servants. But there were great names in the Connecticut Valley early in the seventeenth century: Edward Hopkins had been a wealthy Turkey merchant in London, but migrated to the New World in the company of John Davenport and Theophilus Eaton; John Haynes retained vast estates in Hertfordshire and Essex which provided him with an annual income of over £5,000; George Wyllys, of County Warwick, arrived in Connecticut in 1638, after his steward and men had purchased a homesite and built his home. In Hartford were intelligent, devoted men like John Talcott, John Webster, Thomas Welles, and William Whiting. In Windsor there were Henry Wolcott, William Phelps, Captain John Mason, and Matthew Grant, while Wethersfield boasted of William Swain, Thurston Rayner, Henry Smith, and Andrew Ward. These men poured their fortunes and their energies into the Commonwealth of Connecticut in a determined effort to found an ideal Congregational community.

By the end of 1636 about eight hundred Englishmen had migrated to the Connecticut Valley and founded three plantations on the western bank of the river.[74] It had been a long and arduous journey to the New World for everyone in Connecticut. Primarily because of their opposition to the Church of England and Archbishop Laud's efforts to enforce strict uniformity, but also because of the political and economic unrest, they had relinquished their ancestral homes. At first they had come to the Bay under the auspices of the Massachusetts Bay Company with no intentions of migrating further into the wilderness. In the Bay they hoped to establish a Bible Commonwealth to serve the demands of their Congregational churches. But for many, particularly in the towns of Dorchester, Watertown, and Newtown, their wanderings were not over. Within only a few years they grew so dissatisfied with their land and lot that they preferred to face the hardships of the frontier once again, to fight Indians, to clear stubborn fields, to build new homes, and to create a government which would harmonize with their ideals.

Here was an early instance of westward migration in America. The Commonwealth of Connecticut, while retaining contact with Massachusetts Bay in matters concerning both ecclesiastical and civil affairs, became a completely independent state even before the Fundamental Orders were enacted. It was not settled under the Great Seal of England. There were no humble petitions to the King or Parliament. No royal servants resided on the Connecticut River, nor did any assistants or deputies speak for them in the Bay's General Court. Once created, the Massachusetts Bay Commission acted as the governing body of an autonomous state. The Puritans in Connecticut never swore allegiance to the King, the Warwick Patentees, or the Massachusetts Bay Company.

Cotton Mather was in error when he beckoned, "Reader, come with me now to behold some Worthy, and Learned, and Genteel Persons going to be *Buried Alive* on the Banks of *Connecticut*, having been first *Slain* by the Ecclesiastical Impositions and Persecutions of *Europe*."[75] These men, women, and children did not go to the banks of the Connecticut River to be buried alive; instead, they withdrew from odious religious, political, and economic institutions in England and the Bay, only to return to the world in a few short years, having created a unique civil and ecclesiastical state.

II

The Way of the Churches of Connecticut

IsolATED from Europe by the tumultuous events occurring there and by the Atlantic Ocean, Connecticut's Congregationalists [1] did not vegetate. Instead, free at last to establish their own religious and civil institutions without meddlesome, unsympathetic interference, they attacked their wilderness work with vigor. Their foremost concern was their churches. In Hartford, Windsor, and Wethersfield they gathered their churches before they adopted the Fundamental Orders and gave their plantations formal political organization. They then borrowed heavily from their church polity and incorporated it into the civil government of the Commonwealth. The Fundamental Orders were the written solution provided by this Congregational people, determined that the primary purpose of their political institutions should be the preservation of their churches. Congregationalism was the way of the churches of Connecticut and the Fundamental Orders the result.

The Connecticut Congregationalists differed from other Englishmen, not economically or socially, but only in the fervor of their conviction that the reform in the Church should be continued without delay. It led to their staunch determination to worship in purity and simplicity even if they had to travel three thousand miles to escape from sin and corruption. Once in the New World, the men and women who had made the pilgrimage strove to behave like saints. A burning desire to lead godly, righteous lives pervaded the thoughts of laymen and clergy alike. The later infractions of the civil and moral codes rarely involved the

Congregationalists who had come to Connecticut initially. Trouble in Connecticut, inevitable in any community, in most instances involved the servants, indentured and otherwise, the newcomers, and often the younger generation.

The first generation of Connecticut Congregationalists took their religion seriously. Many were the fast days and many the hours spent in prayer and self-examination. Happy events like the passing of an epidemic in October 1661 were celebrated with days of public thanksgiving, while sad events like "the sudden death of o^r late Governor [Haynes], & the like mortallity of o^r neibours in the Bay, & some eminent removalls of others, & spreading opinions in the Collonies, the condityon of o^r natiue Countrey, the alienations of the Colonies in regard of the Combinations" in March 1653/54 were marked by days of humiliation. So convinced were they that they were a chosen people that the General Court on October 10, 1639, ordered that Deputy Governor Roger Ludlow, Captain John Mason, and the Reverend Samuel Stone, together with Elder William Goodwin of the Hartford Church, Clement Chaplin, and George Hubberd, record the "passages of Gods p^{r}vidence wch haue beene remarkable since o^r first undertaking these plantačons" and that they continue to note down the signs proving that God smiled on the Commonwealth.[2]

Cotton Mather's description of Edward Hopkins' day illustrates well the depth of devotion of a typical inhabitant of Connecticut. Mather wrote of Hopkins:

> It was his manner to *Rise early*, even before Day, to enjoy the Devotions of his *Closet:* after which he spent a considerable time in Reading, and Opening, and Applying the *Word* of God unto his *Family*, and then *Praying* with them: And he had one particular way to cause Attention in the People of his Family, which was to ask any Person that seemed Careless in the midst of his Discourse, *What was it that I Read or Spoke last?* Whereby he Habituated them unto such an Attention, that they were still usually able to give a ready Account. But as for his *Prayers*, they were not only *frequent*, but so *fervent* also, that he frequently fell a *Bleeding* at the Nose through the *Agony* of Spirit with which he labour'd in them. And, especially when imploring such *Spiritual Blessings*, as, *That God would grant in the End of our Lives, the End of our Hopes, even the Salvation of our Souls*, he would be so Transported, that the Observing

and Judicious Hearers would say sometimes upon it, *Surely this Man can't be long out of Heaven*. Moreover, in his Neighbourhood he not only set himself to Encourage and Countenance real *Godliness*, but also would himself kindly visit the *Meetings* that the Religious Neighbours privately kept for the Exercises of it; and where the least Occasion for *Contention* was offered, he would, with a prudent and speedy Endeavour, Extinguish it. But the *Poor* he so considered, that besides the *Daily Reliefs* which with his own Hands he dispenced unto them, he would put considerable Sums of Money into the Hands of his Friends, to be by them employed as they saw *Opportunity to do good unto all, especially the Household of Faith*.[3]

Hopkins was a wealthy man with more time than the average settler to devote to worship, but his attitude and fervency were not unusual. Nor has the vitality of Congregationalism been exaggerated because historians like Cotton Mather and Benjamin Trumbull were themselves churchmen. Congregationalism in the seventeenth century was a militant movement.

Under the Fundamental Orders there was no religious liberty. Connecticut was not founded as a haven for all religions. It was founded specifically for the Congregational community alone, to provide it with a place to worship God as it chose. In England the nonseparating Puritans had asked for toleration, but Laud had refused to listen to their pleas. In turn the Congregationalists were equally intolerant of dissenters. Originally, non-Puritans had migrated to Massachusetts Bay and then to Connecticut only as servants. Later, in 1656, when the first threat to the Connecticut churches arrived on the New England shores in the form of a group of Quaker women seeking proselytes, the General Court acted quickly to forbid any Quakers, Ranters, Adamites, or "such like notorious heritiques" to remain in any town more than fourteen days. The Court imposed a fine of £5 a week and ordered the townsmen to notify a magistrate or assistant of the contaminating presence. He should be quarantined in prison until he could be banished. It also ordered that no masters of ships permit heretics to land in Connecticut, but at the same time added the reasonable qualification that if the master should happen to permit such a person to disembark, he would be held responsible for carrying him away when the ship sailed. The fine this time was set at £20.[4]

In August 1657 the original order was re-enacted, but with more stringent penalties prescribed. Anyone in Connecticut found entertaining or speaking with a heretic was liable to a fine of £5. In October of the same year a fine of 10 shillings was imposed on anyone, except the teaching elders, possessing Quaker books or manuscripts. The danger had abated a year later, when the Court relented a bit and left the punishment of the Quakers to the discretion of the magistrates or assistants, but armed them with the authority to fine, banish, or inflict corporal punishment on any heretic or anyone responsible for bringing him into the Commonwealth. So great was the fear of Quakerism or any rival religion to the Congregational churches that the General Court acted with haste and severity.[5]

Intolerance was the most powerful weapon the Congregationalists possessed to protect their churches. In these churches Connecticut's Puritans of the seventeenth century accepted Calvinist theology as modified by the Church of England. It was the elaborate rites and ceremonies, the liturgy and discipline, and particularly the polity that they revolted against. Their solution to the evils within the Anglican Church was the elimination of all but the purest and simplest forms of worship, their emphasis on the independence and equality of each particular church, and the restriction of membership to the regenerate.

The unique church organization which evolved in New England resembled that espoused in England by both Independents and Separatists, but was not identical to either form. Rather than duplicate a contemporary church, the Puritans in New England modeled their churches on the primitive ones in the New Testament, particularly as described by Luke in the Book of Acts. The determination of the Connecticut Congregationalists to turn to the Bible as their authority rested on their conviction that the precedent for each element of their church government should be found there rather than being left to the discretion of men, churches, or states.[6] "For," as Thomas Hooker added, "the Ordinances of Christ and rules of the Gospel serve, not only for the *constitution* of a Church, but for the *preservation* of it." [7] Polity rather than doctrine was the major point of divergence between the New England Puritan churches and the reformed churches of England and the Continent.

In the 1640's, when Presbyterianism was on the offensive in England and Congregationalism on the defensive, several explanations of the New England way were written to bolster its position. Fortunately for posterity, the best of these, Thomas Hooker's *A Survey of the Summe of Church-Discipline* and the Cambridge Platform of 1648, have survived to explain in detail the polity of Connecticut's churches. Hooker completed his manuscript in 1645 in reply to Samuel Rutherford's *Due Right of Presbyteries* and attacks on the New England churches by other Presbyterian pamphleteers. A meeting of the ministers of Hartford, Windsor, Wethersfield, New Haven, Guilford, Milford, Stratford, Fairfield, and some of the Bay towns approved his treatise, but together with many of the writings of John Davenport, it was lost at sea in January 1646/47 in the last ship which New Haven sent abroad in its futile attempt to become a major trading colony. Only after much persuasion was Hooker enticed to rewrite it. Published posthumously, *A Survey of the Summe of Church-Discipline* presents an excellent exposition of Congregationalism by the man who was more responsible for molding its polity than any other. Numerous explanations were written in answer to English questions, but Hooker's is the most pertinent for a study of the churches of Connecticut.[8]

Also valuable in explaining the polity and doctrine of the churches of Connecticut is the Cambridge Platform of 1648, drafted by Richard Mather of the Dorchester, Massachusetts, Church. The Cambridge (Massachusetts) Synod of 1646-1648 adopted the Platform as a statement of New England's Congregational principles, to assert Congregational solidarity against the threatening Presbyterianism then gaining supremacy in England. The Synod refused to incorporate into the Platform the discipline previously agreed on by the Westminster Assembly in England because it espoused Presbyterian polity, but it did include the Westminster Confession in the preface of the Platform to prove the orthodoxy of Congregational theology to the world. This the Synod could afford to do, as Oliver Cromwell and the Independents had by then gained control of the English government. By 1651 the churches of Connecticut had approved the Cambridge Platform as a written expression of their beliefs. Just as the Fundamental Orders served as the civil constitution for the Commonwealth, the Cambridge Platform became the written constitution for the churches of Connecticut. To this and to Hooker's *Survey* the student of Connecticut as a commonwealth must turn in order to understand the philosophy behind the civil institutions described in the Fundamental Orders.

In the Cambridge Platform and in their sermons and written works, Hooker and the Congregationalists of Connecticut readily acknowledged their debt to the older generation of nonseparating Puritans which included William Bradshaw, William Ames, Henry Parker, Paul Baynes, Richard Sibbes, John Forbes, and Henry Jacob in the early years of the seventeenth century.[9] Like them, the Connecticut Congregationalists, while they remained in England, had been nonseparating nonconformists, willing to accept Anglican doctrine and to continue to worship within the Church even though they opposed the hierarchy, the rites and ceremonies, and their rigid enforcement by Archbishop Laud and the High Commission. From their pulpits they had loudly proclaimed the need to reform the Church, but they advocated the Church's playing the leading role in its own purge.

They were more reluctant to acknowledge any resemblance to the early sixteenth-century radical reformers, although the Congregationalists borrowed many of their precepts. They denied any heritage from the Anabaptists on the Continent, who also rebelled against the parish as the basis of church membership, or from Thomas Cartwright, who equally disapproved of a ministry appointed by the Crown or lay patrons. They admitted no ties with the controversial Robert Browne, who had organized the first Independent church at Norwich and like the Congregationalists expounded a theory of each church's originating in a covenant between the saints and God, followed by one between the saints themselves. Their position was precarious enough without being branded with a Brownist or Anabaptist stigma.

The Congregationalists in Connecticut also refused to admit any connection with the London-Amsterdam Separatist Church, where the officers were chosen by the brethren and ordained by fasting, prayers, and the laying on of hands in the fashion of the primitive church. But by the time Hooker wrote his *Survey* the churches of Connecticut were no longer churches of nonseparating Puritans, worshiping within the Anglican Church. In Connecticut they became in fact Separatist churches, although they were unwilling to acknowledge the transformation. They had adopted enough of the ideology of the earlier and more radical reformers so that their polity closely resembled that of the Separatist church of the Pilgrims in Plymouth.

There are two schools of thought on the cause of the close resemblance in church government between the Separatist church of Leyden and Plymouth and the officially nonseparating Congregational churches of New England. Champlin Burrage and Perry Miller felt that the reconciliation occurred in Europe. They argued that about 1610 Henry Jacob, Robert Parker, Paul Baynes, and William Ames, who were nonseparating Puritans living in Holland, convinced the Separatist John Robinson that salvation might be found by remaining within the Established Church.[10] Burrage and Miller emphasized the essential similarity between the nonseparating Puritans and the Separatists even in Europe; they felt that the Pilgrim Separatists had become less radical before migrating to America. In doctrine Separatists and nonseparating Puritans alike were Calvinists determined to use the apostolic church as a guide for the polity and ritual in their own churches. They agreed that the officers should be called by the congregation, that the membership should be restricted to the saints, and that only the regenerate should be permitted to receive the sacraments. Both the Puritan John Cotton and the Separatist John Robinson had been students of Robert Parker, and both had finally decided to uproot themselves and their families to escape to America or Holland, where they could establish their churches in peace.

The other theory is that Separatism entered into Congregational polity after the migration to New England. It resulted from the contact of the Massachusetts Bay churches with the Plymouth Church in the New World. The *avant-garde* of nonseparating Puritans sent across the Atlantic by the Massachusetts Bay

Company under the leadership of John Endecott settled at Naumkeag (Salem) in 1629. Attacked by scurvy soon after their arrival, they sought the aid of Dr. Samuel Fuller, of Plymouth, who had previously been a deacon in John Robinson's church in Leyden. While Dr. Fuller was in Salem, he convincingly explained the expediency of Separatist polity. The result was that while the scurvy was being cured, the prejudices against the Plymouth Pilgrims, who had been scorned as radicals in Europe, were overcome. In gratitude for the medical aid and spiritual awakening John Endecott wrote to Plymouth's Governor Bradford:

> I acknowledge my selfe much bound to you for your kind love and care in sending M^r. Fuller among us, and rejoyce much y^t I am by him satisfied touching your judgments of ye outward forme of Gods worshipe. It is, as farr as I can yet gather, no other then is warrented by ye evidence of truth, and ye same which I have proffessed and maintained ever since ye Lord in mercie revealed him selfe unto me; being farr from ye commone reporte that hath been spread of you touching that perticuler.[11]

This was one of the few occasions when a nonseparating Puritan acknowledged any connection with the Separatists.

The churches of Connecticut, like the Commonwealth under the Fundamental Orders, never publicly announced their separation from either the Church of England or the Crown. While in Amsterdam, Thomas Hooker, in reply to searching questions put to him by the Reverend John Paget, had reiterated his conviction that "To *Separate from the Faithful Assemblies and Churches in* England, *as no Churches, is an Error in Judgment, and Sin in Practice, held and maintained by the Brownists.*"[12] Two generations later Cotton Mather, John Cotton's grandson, described these original settlers as "*Truer Sons* to the Church of *England,* than that part of the *Church,* which, then by their misemploying their heavy *Church-keys,* banished them into this Plantation."[13] Yet in practice the Congregationalists, once in Connecticut, severed all outward ties with the Church of England.

Their actual separation from the government of the Anglican Church was equal to that of the avowed Separatists; they never recognized the authority of the Bishop of London, as did the colonies in the South. In the wilderness, where the Congregational churches of Connecticut became the established churches instead of a minority group, they were wiser than to proclaim their secession. They were physically separated by the Atlantic Ocean and free to purge human corruption from their churches and to model their polity on previously expounded ideals without broadcasting their intentions.

As William E. Barton said, "A Congregational church is not necessarily a church of Congregationalists; it is a church of Christians, Congregationally governed." [14] In matters of faith, as attested by the adoption of the Westminster Confession in 1648, the three original Connecticut churches of Windsor, Hartford, and Wethersfield and the later ones gathered in other parts of the Commonwealth were little different from the Church of England; in matters of polity, however, there was virtually no resemblance. It was these innovations in polity which were in turn transferred to the state government through the medium of the Fundamental Orders.

In their polity the Congregationalists recognized the existence of a catholic church, a universal church, but it was not an organic church like the Church of Rome. It was composed of mortal saints, "the whole company of those that are elected, redeemed, & in time effectually called from the state of sin & death vnto a state of Grace, & salvation in Iesus Christ." [15] It was both invisible and visible, "Invisible, in respect of their relation wherin they stand to Christ, as a body unto the head, being united unto him, by the spirit of God, & faith in their hearts: Visible, in respect of the profession of their faith, in their persons, & in their particuler Churches." [16] Thus there were recognized both a universal invisible church comprised of all the saints, which had no human officers and no political organization, and the particular visible churches like those of Hartford, Windsor, and Wethersfield, which, as Samuel Stone wrote, were each considered descendants of the Church at Jerusalem. [17]

Congregational polity emphasized the absolute autonomy of each particular visible church, instead of the subjection of the local church to the rule of a diocesan, provincial, or national church, as in both Anglican and Presbyterian England. Throughout the *Survey*, Hooker stressed this local independence. "*We deny*," he wrote emphatically, *"that Christ hath given power of Iurisdiction to one particular congregation over another,"* and asserted that each "Congregation compleatly constituted of all Officers, hath sufficient power in her self, to exercise the power of the keyes, and all Church discipline, in all the censures thereof." [18] The Church of Hartford, for example, could call and ordain its own officers, admit members, censure and excommunicate offenders, receive the sacraments, and regulate its services. Each church was equal to all others. It retained its identity even though it changed its location, provided a majority of its members remained together. The Dorchester Church moved as a body from England to Massachusetts Bay and finally to Connecticut, and the Newtown Church migrated from the Bay to the river, but a majority of the Watertown Church voted to remain in the Bay, and so a new church had to be gathered in Connecticut.

During the period of the Fundamental Orders there was only one church in each town. The town became the local unit of worship, just as the parish had been in England. With the approval of the General Court each new church was formed by the visible saints living in close proximity to one another in the manner described by Thomas Lechford of Massachusetts Bay. Lechford wrote that a "convenient, or competent number of Christians, allowed by the generall Court to plant together, at a day prefixed, come together, in publique manner, in some fit place, and there confesse their sins and professe their faith, one unto another, and being satisfied of one anothers faith & repentance, they solemlny [*sic*] enter into a Covenant with God, and one an other." [19] The General Court made the regulations regarding the formation of new churches more explicit in March 1657/58, when it ordered that no churches could be gathered without the consent of both the Court and the neighboring churches.[20] This order was required at the time because of the schisms taking place in the Hartford and Wethersfield churches and the determination of the minority factions to withdraw from the parent churches and form new ones more to their liking.

Covenants united each Congregational church. The covenant appeared in three forms in Connecticut. The first was the covenant of grace, which was the original agreement between God and the individual saint. It was contracted at God's discretion, not man's, for the Congregationalists believed that only God knew which souls had been retrieved from the sinful world through faith and His mercy and had accepted His calling.[21] The covenant bound the saint to the authority of God alone, not to any archbishops, kings, or classes and their law. Its sequel was the covenant of the particular church, which united the saints living within the locale into the visible church body. The Fundamental Orders, the civil covenant, represented the third covenant. Its object was to bind man to man in a civil relationship, as the other two had been contracts designed to unite God and saint, and saint and saint.

The church covenant—the second type—concerns us here. It was a voluntary agreement by the prospective members of a particular church to unite. The mutual "covenanting and confoederating of the Saints in the fellowship of the faith according to the order of the Gospel," Hooker wrote, "is that which gives constitution and being to a visible Church." [22] He preferred that the covenant between the regenerate be explicit, rather than implicit,[23] which also explains why the constitution of Connecticut soon appeared in written form among the records of the General Court.

The original Covenant of the First Church of Hartford has not endured the centuries, but we have the second *in toto*. In it the covenanters agreed:

> Since it hath pleased God, in His infinite mercy, to manifest Himself willing to take unworthy sinners near unto Himself, even into covenant relation to and interest in Him, to become a God to them and avouch them to be his people, and accordingly to command and encourage them to give up themselves and their children also unto Him.
>
> We do therefore this day, in the presence of God, His holy angels, and this assembly, avouch the Lord Jehovah, the true and living God, even God the Father, the Son and the Holy Ghost, to be our God and give up ourselves and ours also unto Him, to be his subject and servants, promising through grace and strength in Christ (without whom we can do nothing,) to walk in professed subjection to Him as our only Lord and Lawgiver, yielding universal obedience to his blessed will, according to what discoveries He hath made or hereafter shall make, of the same to us; in special, that we will seek Him in all His holy ordinances according to the rules of the Gospel, submitting to His government in this particular Church, and walking together therein, with all brotherly love

and mutual watchfulness, to the building up of one another in faith and love unto His praise in all which we promise to perform, the Lord helping us through His grace in Jesus Christ.[24]

This covenant is thought to be a longer version of the 1632 agreement. Each church had its individual covenant in which its members, in "owning the covenant," swore to give up themselves unto the Lord, to observe His ordinances, to abide by the Gospel, and to unite politically into one church.[25] The occasion was then solemnized by fasting and prayers. Thereafter no one could withdraw without the permission of his brethren. The covenant was perpetuated through succeeding generations by admitting the children of the saints to the church by the rite of infant baptism.

Originally the churches of Connecticut did not have a confession of faith other than that of the Anglican Church. In October 1647, however, the Windsor Church adopted its Creed-Covenant, the first confession of faith in Connecticut.[26] It was composed as part of the same movement that was forcing Thomas Hooker and the Cambridge Synod to set down the principles of Congregationalism in writing.

Each Connecticut church united by its covenant was a mixed government. In the Cambridge Platform it was explained, "In respect of *Christ*, the head & King of the church, & the Soveraigne power residing in him, & exercised by him, it is a *Monarchy:* in respect of the body, or *Brotherhood* of the church, & powr from Christ graunted unto them, it resembles a *Democracy*, In respect of the *Presbyetry* & powr comited to them, it is an *Aristocracy.*" [27] In Connecticut during its Commonwealth period Christ ruled as King of the churches and the earthly power resided with the officers of the church, as interpreters of the Bible. The churches, like the state, were monarchical and aristocratic, rather than democratic. The brethren, like the freemen of the Commonwealth were a select group, but their influence was limited. Outside the church remained many residents of the Connecticut towns, compelled to attend the religious services, to pay taxes for the support of the church and its pastor, and to abide by its law, but not welcomed as members and not permitted to vote or to partake of the sacraments.

Christ was the King of the church; He represented its monarchical element. Instead of an earthly pope or king, He was

recognized as the head of each Congregational church because of
the commission He had received from God.[28] Similarly, He was
recognized as the head of the Commonwealth of Connecticut in
the Fundamental Orders. All authority was derived from Him.
This Thomas Hooker emphasized in a sermon delivered on May
1, 1639, which unfortunately has been preserved only in note
form. Hooker proclaimed Christ's role in the Congregational
church, saying:

> doctrine   the lord sits as a sovereign controller of the works of all
> creatures in the very height of their rage confusion and tumult
> 1   wherein this sovereignty of God consists
> 1   there is no power in the creatures but the hand of the lord gives it
> 2ly   unless the lord give commission though they have power they can-
> not put it forth
> 3   it is in Gods power how and when he will stop the creature
> 4ly   the lord by his almighty power doth over work the creature to the
> accomplishment of his own pleasure
> 1st reason   from the absolute privilege royal of the lord he is the 1st and
> last
> 2 reason   reason is taken from the infinite distance that is between the
> power of God and the weakness of the creature.[29]

It was Christ who called each church together, provided it with
ordinances and laws, appointed ministers to explain and enforce
them, and defended it from its enemies.[30]

As Christ reigned as the church's monarch, so the brethren
were its democracy. They were the people of the church, the
electorate, comparable to the freemen and admitted inhabitants
in the civil government. To be one of the saints was a great privilege, but this was the weakest part of the church. Congregational
polity rejected the idea of a true democracy; man was still the
fallen creature.

The membership in the churches during the period of the
Fundamental Orders included only a minority of the town's population. The first church of Windsor had twenty-four members and
that of Wethersfield only seven. No one was admitted to a Congregational church in Connecticut merely because he was a Christian
residing in the particular area; the town and church were not
synonymous, as the parish and church had been in England, but

existed as separate entities.[31] In theory only visible saints, such "as haue not only attained the knowledge of the principles of Religion, & are free from gros & open scandals, but also do together with the profession of their faith & Repentance, walk in blameles obedience to the word, so as that in charitable discretion they may be accounted Saints by calling," could qualify for membership.[32] Both in the Cambridge Platform and in Hooker's *Survey*, however, it was readily admitted that errors were committed and hypocrites inadvertently voted into the church. The consensus is that Hooker's leniency in welcoming members was responsible for more hypocrites being in the Hartford Church, but this was balanced by there being fewer saints left outside the church.[33]

A person became a full communion member only after he had received the seal of baptism and had been voted into the church by the brethren. Baptism throughout most of the period of the Fundamental Orders was administered only to the infant children of saints or to adults who could give convincing proof of their faith and determination to follow Christ. Baptism was considered a preliminary step in being admitted to the covenant of the church. The issue of eligibility for baptism and the resultant Halfway Covenant became a matter of controversy, seriously debated and not settled by the end of the period.

The second step in the admission to the church was the confession of faith. Usually the saint had experienced a traumatic conversion shortly before. It might have followed his reading a thought-provoking book or pamphlet or hearing a particularly moving sermon. The saint, once called and redeemed, realized the necessity of leading a holy, righteous life within the church. Therefore, he would express his desire to unite with the brethren to the ruling elder, who would investigate his qualifications and present his findings to the body of the church. The members would then consider the candidate privately or summon him to appear before them to confess his faith and convince them of his worthiness and his repentance for his sins. Perhaps he would also relate the events which occurred during his conversion. Often the profession of faith was given before the elders alone, if the individual were afraid to make it before the whole church. After proclaiming his faith in Jesus Christ, he agreed to unite in the covenant and abide by the Word of God. After this the church voted on his admission.[34]

These were the only prerequisites for membership in the Connecticut churches. Women were admitted, as well as men, although they were not allowed to speak in church unless they were presenting vital testimony in their own defense or in proof of their repentance after being censured. Probably this was in reaction to the Hutchinson incident in Massachusetts Bay, when Mistress Anne created such commotion with her teachings; it was identical to the policy advocated by John Cotton in *The Keyes Of the Kingdom of Heaven.* No property qualifications were required, and servants were admitted, provided they could prove their regeneracy.[35] However, their social inferiority was recognized by their being assigned inconspicuous pews within the church. Occasionally persons also entered the church on the strength of a letter of recommendation from another Congregational church to which they had previously belonged. For example, Elizabeth Allen, Samuel Stone's second wife, was admitted on the basis of letters written by the Boston Church to the Hartford Church.[36]

The feeling was strong that the size of the membership should be limited to the number of people who could conveniently travel to the church, fit comfortably inside a single meetinghouse, and be known by the pastor and the teacher. The first meetinghouse in Hartford is thought to have been a crude wooden building only 36 feet long and 23 feet wide. It was soon given to Hooker to use as a barn and replaced before 1640 by one large enough to accommodate all the inhabitants of Hartford. The first church stood at the corner of Central Row and Prospect Street, and its successor occupied a lot just to the west of it. The site was carefully selected so that the townfolk could reach it easily even in the most inclement weather. As the towns grew, inevitably the petitions for winter privileges, the right to be excused from the meetings, increased. Because of the initial shortage of buildings, the meetinghouse, even in Congregational Connecticut, had to double as an armory, capitol, and courthouse, as well as serve as a house of worship.

Once becoming a member of a church, a man or woman had the right to receive the sacraments himself, to have his children baptized, to vote for officers and new members, and in theory to dismiss or excommunicate offenders. Each was bound by the law of God and subject to public censure by the entire congregation, or even excommunication. The Congregationalists believed that the struggle against the temptations of the devil never ended, even after sainthood had been achieved. Even the most devout of the brethren required continual prayers, contemplation, Bible reading, and attendance at church to insure their salvation. The saint's colleagues helped prevent his relapse into sin by keeping an eye on his behavior, known as "holy watching." But the emphasis, particularly while Thomas Hooker served as minister to the Hartford Church, was on the forgiveness and understanding of God and the church, rather than on the hell-fire and damnation preached by later New Englanders.

The members of each church, joined on Sundays and lecture days and on days of fasting and of thanksgiving by the rest of the populace, heard the sermon delivered by the pastor or teacher. In the meetings there was no organ or harpsichord accompaniment to the hymns. The Puritans frowned on music within the church as a profanation. Instead, the congregation, unaccompanied, chanted discordantly the psalms from the Bay Psalm Book (or *The Whole Book of Psalmes Faithfully Translated into English Metre*, as it was properly titled), which had been available to them since 1640. Attendance was compulsory; the threat of a five-shilling fine convinced the recalcitrant. As only the freemen and admitted inhabitants were the active participants in the civil government, so only the regenerate had a voice in the church government. But everyone was subject to the authority of the church. The Sabbath was a holy day strictly kept for public religious services, private family worship, and study of the Scriptures and for receiving catechetical instruction. On Sundays daily chores were neglected. Fields went untended, and only the minimum amount of housework was permitted. But on Christmas and Easter daily routines proceeded as normal; these were not holidays celebrated by the Congregationalists.

The church of visible saints existed before its officers. The officers did not order the gathering of the church, but conversely could be called and ordained themselves only after the church had been organized. The church could exist without its pastor and teacher, but to be complete had to include both officers and brethren.[37] The Newtown Church, it should be recalled, was gathered one year before the arrival of Hooker and Stone. In contrast to Anglican practice, the officers of the Connecticut churches were divinely, not humanly, chosen. The Congregationalists felt that appointing the church's officers was the work of God, and therefore even the Pope, patriarchs, cardinals, archbishops, lord bishops, archdeacons, or other leaders in the church, if they had not been appointed by God, were interlopers, illegally chosen, and should be ousted immediately. This they applied directly to the Anglican hierarchy.[38] The ecclesiastical hierarchy of the Anglican Church had not been sanctioned by the Bible.

In Connecticut the officers chosen by God were subsequently called by the brethren of the particular congregation, not by civil magistrates, superior ecclesiastical officers, or patrons. "*The power of gift or election* is that which the people have, as the corporation hath power to choose a Major [mayor], and to give him authority to do that which they themselves cannot do: So it is with the Body of a congregation, who do elect and leave the impression of an Office upon men gifted, though they be not such formally themselves." [39] Once called, the officers of the Congregational churches of Connecticut, as ambassadors of God and interpreters of the Word, exercised the real authority within the church. They were its aristocracy.

The pastor and teacher were the teaching elders in each church. At the time of the settlement of the Connecticut towns, there was approximately one minister for every 260 or 270 people; by 1662, the ratio had increased to about one minister for every 430 inhabitants.[40] The increase was a reflection of the decline in vigor of Connecticut Puritanism as well as the growing difficulties in training the ministry. Regardless of whether or not they had been previously ordained in England by a bishop, the clergymen serving a Congregational church had to be full communing members of the church before they could be ordained by the saints. Hooker and Stone, for instance, after they had joined the Newtown Church, were probably proposed as pastor and teacher of the church by the ruling elder, Goodwin, and then approved by the congregation by a show of hands, not by the written ballot employed by the civil government. The ruling elder then asked them if they would accept the call, and after the affirmative reply, three or four of the leading members or elders from neighboring churches laid their hands on Hooker's head while the ruling elder prayed and declared him pastor of the church. In a similar manner Stone was undoubtedly installed.

Ordination was comparable to installing a magistrate in the Commonwealth. Therefore the Congregationalists felt it should not precede, but follow, election. The outward call was in effect a covenant between the pastor or teacher and his flock. The pastor, chosen by his people instead of by the elders or a bishop, was subject to them alone and could be dismissed by them only should "he prove pertinaciously scandalous in his life, or heretical in his Doctrine." [41] He had authority over no other congregation than that which had called and ordained him, nor could he perform the rites of baptism and the Lord's Supper anywhere but in his own church. The ordination by the members and the symbolic imposition of hands were reminiscent of apostolic practice.

It was the duty of the pastor and teacher to preach the Word, lead the church in prayer and in fasts and in feasts, administer the sacraments, and convene the church to elect any necessary officers or admit new members. Thomas Hooker also devoted one day a week to hearing the troubles of his people privately and spent much time in catechizing the children in his church. And he performed a multitude of miscellaneous duties like delivering the staff of office to John Mason in February 1637/38, when he took charge of Connecticut's militia. The pastor and teacher examined anyone desiring to join the church. They aided the elders in ordaining officers and preparing matters for the church and in explaining God's law to the church when offenders and offenses were to be discussed and sentenced.[42] Their voice was important in censuring members. Thomas Hooker opposed too harsh discipline; during his ministry there was only one member admonished and only Matthew Allyn was actually excommunicated. Hooker preferred meeting with his people and consoling or admonishing them privately to airing their problems and transgressions publicly. Others were not so conciliatory and compassionate with their flocks.[43]

Missionary work was not a significant part of their tasks, as it was of the Catholic priests in North America during the seventeenth century. The churches of Connecticut lacked the missionary zeal that they had proclaimed to be one of their foremost purposes in forming the United Colonies of New England. Their membership was too exclusive, and the demands put upon both the ministry and brethren in creating the new Commonwealth were too great. Included in the Code of 1650 was an order that one of the teaching elders of Connecticut go as a missionary twice a year to preach to the heathen Indians with the help of Thomas Stanton. In September 1654 the General Court accepted the responsibility of training John Mynor to go among the natives to interpret the Gospel being taught by one of the elders, as had Thomas Stanton previously. But the total missionary efforts were minimal.[44]

Originally there was a distinction between the offices of pastor and teacher, but it soon disappeared. It was too expensive for these nascent communities to support both. The pastor's primary duty was to use his training and ability "to attend to *exhortation:* and therein to Administer a word of *Wisdom*" to his church.[45] Hooker was beloved for his animated, forceful sermons and the quality of his prayers. The purpose of the pastor's sermon was to reach the unregenerate in his audience and to present to them the offer of grace and redemption. The blame for any man's refusing to accept the offer of salvation and to strive toward regeneracy rested solely on himself. Salvation was to come through faith, not works.[46] The pastor exhorted his saints to search their souls through continual introspection to prevent their relapse into unregeneracy. He explained the Bible to all and frequently discussed current civil issues. The sermons were lengthy, generally lasting two or even three hours, but the minister spoke without the aid of notes. Cotton Mather expressly pointed out that John Warham, of Windsor, was the exception and the first minister in New England to depend on them.[47]

The primary duty of the teacher was "to attend to *Doctrine,* & therein to Administer a word of Knowledg." [48] Employing images drawn from daily life in his sermons, he explained the Bible and taught the principles of Christian faith. He tried to interpret difficult concepts like predestination and salvation. He taught the best means to avoid temptation and guided his congregation in their struggles. From him the Congregationalists in Connecticut learned the necessity of referring to the Bible whenever they were in doubt about their daily behavior or routine problems. Samuel Stone was the most important teacher in Connecticut during the Commonwealth. He had been born in Hertford, Hertfordshire, in 1602, the son of a freeholder. He attended Emmanuel College at Cambridge from 1620 until 1627, receiving his Bachelor of Arts and Master of Arts degrees. In 1630, after having been suspended at Stisted, Essex, for nonconformity, he wholeheartedly joined the Puritan forces. He fell under Thomas Hooker's influence and agreed to migrate to Massachusetts Bay with him to become the teacher in the Newtown Church. When it resettled in Connecticut, he led one band. There he acted as teacher of the Hartford Church from 1635 until 1647 and as pastor in fact, even though not in name, from 1647 until his death in 1663. In these positions he examined the sinners in his church, advised the Commonwealth on civil issues, and at times even attempted to save the souls of convicted witches. He represented the Connecticut churches at the Synods of 1637, 1643, and 1646–1648 and at the end of the period sailed to England with Governor John Winthrop, the younger, on his quest for the Charter.

Samuel Stone was a godly, righteous, and sober man whose life was totally absorbed in his religion. In his younger days he had been liberal enough to smoke tobacco and sufficiently witty to save Hooker from the authorities, but as he aged, he became more engrossed in his mission and less tolerant of the moderate elements. He was sterner than Hooker and lacked his warmth in dealing with the people. His unrelenting and autocratic stand on the questions of baptism, church membership, and the rights of the brethren led him to the disastrous quarrel with the ruling elder, William Goodwin. He directed the majority of his sermons toward explaining Congregational doctrine and discipline to his congregation. With admiration, but not devotion, Cotton Mather wrote that as Stone

> had the *Art* of keeping to his Hour, so he had an incomparable Skill at filling of that Hour with Nervous Discourses, in the way of *Commonplace* and *Proposition*, handling the Points of *Divinity*, which he would

conclude with a brief and close *Application:* And then he would in his *Prayer*, after *Sermon*, put all into such pertinent Confessions, Petitions, and Thanksgivings, as notably digested his *Doctrine* into *Devotion*. He was a *Man of Principles*, and in the management of those Principles, he was both a *Load stone* and a *Flint-stone*.[49]

It was Stone who defined Congregational government as *"a speaking* Aristocracy *in the Face of a silent* Democracy." [50]

The Connecticut Puritans demanded a learned ministry to aid them in overcoming their sins. Before their ordination candidates had to pass an examination prepared by the elders covering theology, Hebrew, Latin, and Greek, as well as discourse on their personal beliefs and qualifications. So it is not surprising that the first generation of divines in Connecticut—Thomas Hooker and Samuel Stone in Hartford, Henry Smith in Wethersfield, and John Warham and Ephraim Huit in Windsor—products of the Universities of Oxford and Cambridge, should reveal their knowledge of Greek, Latin, and Hebrew, rhetoric, philology, grammar, and logic, in writings as well as in sermons. The sermons had to be reduced to the level of a congregation familiar with the current debates on Arminianism, Antinomianism, or Antipaedo-baptism, but not trained in the classics, in logic, or in rhetoric. In their written works they were free to examine these issues in all their complexities.[51] The list of works by Hooker was particularly lengthy. The pastors and teachers in the Commonwealth were its most educated element, respected by the people and by the General Court for their wisdom and experience.

In Connecticut, as in other parts of New England, the pastors and teachers were revered as the keepers of the Word and interpreters of it, but also as privileged citizens of the Commonwealth. Some became wealthy men; Thomas Hooker left an estate valued at over £1,136, and the inventory taken after the death of the Reverend Ephraim Huit, of Windsor, in 1644 included four silver bowls, one trencher, one salt cellar, four silver spoons, thirteen personalized children's spoons, and one additional silver dish—a vast amount of silver for those times. They were permitted certain civil rights not granted to laymen. Hooker, for instance, was exempted from the duty of performing highway work.[52] The ministers in Connecticut held a very important position, not equaled by the governor. The voice of the pulpit was strong.

The ruling elders were laymen chosen and subsequently ordained by the congregation to handle the disciplinary and administrative matters of the church. They questioned offenders before their trial in the presence of the congregation and at the hearing recommended discipline or leniency. They aided and comforted other members in their sorrows and misfortunes, settled differences among them, and protected the good name of the church. Examining candidates for membership and leading in the excommunication proceedings when necessary were part of their duties. They assisted the pastor and teacher in governing the church and in dealing with any problem which did not involve "labouring in word and doctrine, and is not a common act of rule," and in their absence led the congregation in prayer.[53] The office was a powerful one and consequently a difficult one. Strife within the Churches of Hartford and Wethersfield exploded after Hooker's death because of irreconcilable conflicts between the teaching elder and the ruling elder, between Stone and William Goodwin in Hartford, and between the succession of pastors in Wethersfield and Clement Chaplin, the ruling elder.

While the Newtown Church was without pastor and teacher in Massachusetts Bay, William Goodwin and Andrew Warner, the ruling elders, led the church in its religious exercises. Goodwin conducted the preliminary removal to Connecticut in the fall of 1635, arriving there many months before Hooker. He had been a follower of Hooker's since his days at St. Mary's in Chelmsford and he later married Hooker's widow, Susannah.[54]

Each Congregational church had deacons to care for its temporal affairs. It was their duty to act as treasurers of the church, to receive the offerings at the Sunday services, and to accept any other contributions and gifts that might be donated to the church. They then supplied the "tables" of the Lord by dividing the income among the officers and the poor.[55] Occasionally there were also "widows" who visited the sick to aid and comfort them. These officers of each church were chosen by the brethren, but thereafter were permitted to rule according to the Word of God, just as the officers of the Commonwealth were elected by the freemen and admitted inhabitants, but during their tenure of office ruled virtually without restraint. The theoretical restrictions were never invoked.

The Congregational churches in Connecticut were autonomous. They recognized the sovereignty only of God and not of any mortal being. They united at their own volition in the church covenant, admitted new members without outside civil or ecclesiastical coercion, and selected their own officers to serve the needs of their particular church alone. But they did recognize a bond of fellowship with the other Congregational churches. Even the early Separatist Robert Browne had favored mutual aid and synods.[56] The relations between the churches remained harmonious throughout the period in which the Fundamental Orders were in effect.

At the gathering of the Church of Salem, representatives of the Separatist church at Plymouth were present at the ordination of the pastor and teacher to extend to them the right hand of fellowship. According to tradition, Thomas Hooker and Samuel Stone from the Hartford Church similarly participated in the installation of John Davenport in New Haven.[57] This practice undoubtedly was repeated at the founding of the later Congregational churches. After a church was gathered, its minister might deliver a sermon to another congregation in the absence of its pastor or teacher or vice versa. Stone officiated in the Windsor Church on June 10, 1640,[58] as did Hooker on June 20, 1647. During the Pequot War, Stone acted as chaplain for the soldiers from the divers churches of Connecticut. The teaching elders of the churches could serve other congregations in these ways, but could not administer the sacraments anywhere but in their own church.

In another respect the New England churches helped their fellows. Whenever there were serious difficulties facing a church, a council, or synod, was called to discuss the issue and to present whatever advice or admonition it deemed necessary. Expressing his admiration of this practice, Captain Edward Johnson wrote that "these New-England Churches are neer one hundred miles distant one from another, and yet communicate, counsel, care, love, joy, grieve with, and for one another, dismiss some, and commend others (as occasion serves) to the Christian care and watchfulness, from one Church to another."[59]

Synods could be and were called by the magistrates or the General Court, although technically the organization of the synod was considered an act of the churches. Each synod was prorogued separately; there was no permanent body and no presbyterian union. Each was composed of representatives of both the officers and the brethren, as it would have been impossible to summon the churches in their entirety because of the perilous journey to the synod. Generally there were two moderators. The summoning of the synods was considered "a safe and wholesome and holy Ordinance of Christ," which men like Thomas Hooker favored, although they refused to recognize the councils as having any authority to coerce or censure a church or any of its members or to act as an appellate court for the particular congregations.[60] The purpose of the synods was to arbitrate troubled points of religion, whether personal or doctrinal, and to advise the church concerned in an effort to remedy errors and heresies and to restore religious tranquillity.

The first synod held in New England was the Cambridge Synod of 1637. Aid was sought by the General Court of Massachusetts Bay in settling the problems caused by Mistress Anne Hutchinson and the Antinomians. To the synod came the leading elders and brethren from all the churches. Hooker was chosen one of the moderators, while Roger Ludlow and Samuel Stone attended as delegates. The result of this meeting was that eighty-two opinions and several practices of the Antinomians were judged erroneous, and a reconciliation between John Cotton, John Wheelwright, and John Wilson was effected. Between 1646 and 1648 another synod was held at Cambridge, which adopted the Cambridge Platform. Councils were later called in Hartford from 1657 until 1659 in a futile effort to heal the schism in that church. The last synod called during the period of the Fundamental Orders was the Boston Synod of September 1662. Its purpose was to settle the troublesome issue of the Halfway Covenant which plagued the Commonwealth.

The churches in Windsor, Hartford, and Wethersfield were gathered and their officers installed before the Fundamental Orders were adopted, but they could not survive on the Connecticut River without a permanent civil government. The Puritans in Connecticut readily admitted the need for a temporal government to rule the body of man, just as the church guided his soul. In *A Survey of the Summe of Church-Discipline*, Hooker wrote, "Men sustain a double relation. As members of the commonwealth they have civil weapons and in a civil way of righteousnesse, they may, and should use them." [61] The civil government was designed to maintain the Congregational way in Connecticut by outlawing all other churches and by employing the civil police authority to punish idolatry, blasphemy, profanation of the Sabbath, heresy, or any other infringement on the Congregational code, even to the point of regulating excesses in dress. The churches depended on the law officers of the towns and Commonwealth to enforce God's ordinances and Puritan morality. The civil officers forced the entire populace to worship in the churches and to contribute toward their support. But they could not compel the churches to accept members, nor could they interfere with their internal affairs.

The Congregationalists who believed in a church guided by the written Word of God as found in the Bible, gathered by a covenant, ruled by God alone, and limited to saints who were free to select their own officers naturally sought to establish a civil government along similar precepts. It is not surprising that these Congregationalists on the Connecticut River should therefore incorporate into their political Utopia the written constitution, the covenant, and the autonomous but mixed form of government with Christ as its king, a select electorate as the people of its democracy, and the magistrates, deputies, and other officers as its aristocracy. The Fundamental Orders borrowed heavily from the polity of the Congregational churches, for they were a civil constitution designed to serve the temporal needs of a spiritual community. In England, Puritanism had been militant; in Connecticut, it was triumphant in church and state.

III

The Fundamental Orders

In January 1638/39 Connecticut's pioneers in the three tiny communities, Windsor, Hartford, and Wethersfield, adopted a constitution to insure the triumph of Congregationalism, despite the fact that they had lived and worked together in Connecticut for a maximum of only six years. Each settlement had a Congregational church to satisfy the religious fervor of its populace, and in each plantation the proprietors had divided the land into home lots, private farming strips, and common pasture and meadow. But only Hartford had achieved the status of a town with a functioning government.

Yet the men in Connecticut drew up a remarkable constitution, ratified it, and lived according to its law during the years when England was in turmoil. Many precepts espoused in the Fundamental Orders had been familiar in England, Holland, or Massachusetts Bay prior to 1639, but the precise synthesis of principles was unprecedented. The intentional creation of a civil government by the consent of its citizens and its formalization by a written organic law was unparalleled. The omission of any sovereign authority other than God was unique. As for the human governor, never had an executive been so limited by the legislature and the freemen. The Congregationalists had wisely perceived that their immediate need was a solid legal foundation for their political institutions to enable them to maintain order in their society. In concrete terms, unencumbered by extraneous detail, they therefore laid down the pattern for the Commonwealth government in the preamble and eleven orders of their constitution. The fathers of Connecticut combined the traditions they had known in the towns and villages of England with their experience in New England, first in Massachusetts Bay and then on the Connecticut River from 1633 until 1639, with a determination to move away from their past and improve on it by substituting more expedient practices for archaic forms in order that their state might conform more exactly to an ideal Congregational community.

Congregational thought readily accepted a close relationship between the churches and state. Thomas Hooker served as both the political and the religious mentor of early Connecticut, while Roger Ludlow, John Haynes, and other leading citizens were important members of the church as well as leaders in the Commonwealth. John Cotton wrote that "Mr. Hooker doth often quote a saying out of Mr. [Thomas] Cartwright (though I have not read it in him) that noe man fashioneth his house to his hangings, but his hangings to his house. It is better that the commonwealth be fashioned to the setting forth of Gods house, which is his church: than to accommodate the church frame to the civill state." [1] Chronologically, first appeared the churches in Connecticut, then the state. The purpose of the Commonwealth was to supplement and support Congregationalism.

The Fundamental Orders called for a civil government which borrowed heavily from Congregational polity. The Commonwealth, like the churches, originated in a covenant. The sovereign of both was Christ. The officers, whether civil or ecclesiastical, were men elected because of their education, ability, and godliness to serve in offices created by God. And the freemen and admitted inhabitants, like the brethren of the churches, were privileged citizens, permitted to elect their officers and to remove them if necessary, but otherwise reduced to obedience. Many residents of Connecticut had no vote, just as many who listened to the sermons on Sunday or lecture day could not have their children baptized. The churches and state served different functions, but remained as closely related as they were in England and Massachusetts Bay. Seventeenth-century thought could not conceive of their independent existence; it was not until the Constitution of 1818 that they became officially separate in Connecticut.

In the early seventeenth century, Europe was enjoying the paintings of Rubens, van Dyck, Hals, Rembrandt, Poussin, and

Velázquez, the architectural feats of Inigo Jones and Bernini, and the music of Monteverdi and Praetorius. Milton had just written his *Lycidas,* but not yet his *Paradise Lost,* and Harvey was conducting his experiments on the circulatory system. But Connecticut was only in the most primitive stages of settled society. At most there were ten plows in the three infant agricultural communities. Benjamin Trumbull remarked that after the Pequot War in 1637, those "who, in England, had fed on the finest of the wheat, in the beginning of affairs in Connecticut, were thankful for such coarse fare as Indian bread, for themselves and children."[2] Windsor, Wethersfield, and Hartford technically were not towns, but communities of men united as proprietors of the soil and brethren of the churches. The constable in each settlement was the sole law-enforcement officer until the ninety-man army was raised to thrash the Pequot Indians. There were collectors of rates, commissioners, and committees, but none of the river towns was incorporated until early 1638/39, when Hartford was formally organized as a political body.

Before the adoption of the Fundamental Orders the settlements had been laid out after the pattern of medieval towns. For defense against the Indians and Dutch the houses stood together along the one or two main streets, with the farm lands and woods encircling the cluster of homes. On each home lot besides the house there were barns and various outbuildings, a garden, and perhaps a small fenced pasture. The original temporary huts sufficed for only the moment. Soon the men in Connecticut began building wooden homes around a central chimney, in the traditional English style except that instead of leaving the beams and plaster exposed on the outside like the half-timbered houses so common today in Europe, they added a layer of clapboards to ward off the winter blasts. In the homes there was little furniture beyond the barest necessities; the antiques we treasure today come mostly from the eighteenth century. Running water and electricity naturally were unknown, but so were sewers and street lights. Even the main town and commonwealth streets were merely unpaved paths, dusty in the dry weather and rutted and muddy in the rain. Marriages in these communities took place at an early age, and infant mortality was high, as the number of gravestones marking the burial spots of babies and small children in the colonial graveyards attests.

Life was primitive on the river; yet from 1633 until 1639 through trial and error emerged the scheme of government confirmed by the Fundamental Orders. Under the Massachusetts Bay Commission and the "General Corte," [3] the plantations on the Connecticut River experienced actual, if not at first theoretical, independence from England and the Bay. The Massachusetts Bay Commission served its term of one year, holding eight recorded meetings from April 26, 1636, two months prior to the arrival of the Hooker party, until March 28, 1637. At each session five to seven of the eight commissioners named by the General Court of Massachusetts Bay were present. Henry Smith, William Pynchon's son-in-law, attended no meetings. The Commission at once took from the Bay's Court the right to swear in the constables for the plantations by naming Henry Wolcott, of Dorchester (Windsor), Samuel Wakeman, of Newtown (Hartford), and Daniel Finch, of Watertown (Wethersfield), to the office of constable in their respective towns. It initiated legislative action in Connecticut by granting permission to the dismissed members of the Watertown Church to form a new church at Wethersfield, by regulating trade with the Indians, by undertaking one case of probate (the extremely difficult one involving John Oldham's possessions in both Connecticut and the Bay), and by providing adequate defenses for the settlements.

Furthermore, the commissioners ordered that Samuel Wakeman and George Hubberd survey Dorchester (Windsor), that Samuel Wakeman survey Watertown (Wethersfield), and that the lines dividing the plantations be accurately drawn. They decided that the indentured servant John Reeves should return to his master, Francis Stiles, and held Stiles responsible for paying Reeves's passage to Connecticut. It later ordered Stiles to begin teaching his other servants the trade of carpentry. The three Stiles brothers were carpenters whose services Connecticut sorely needed. The commissioners also renamed Watertown, Newtown, and Dorchester as Wethersfield, Hartford, and Windsor, respectively.[4] On the Commission there were no deputies and no governor, other than John Winthrop, Jr., whose position was merely titular as far as the Connecticut communities were concerned.

By March 1636/37 the commission of John Winthrop, Jr., from the Warwick Patentees and the Massachusetts Bay Commission itself had expired. No new governor of the Connecticut River was appointed by the Patentees to replace Winthrop, but the settlers on the river immediately acted to replace the Massachusetts Bay Commission with an elected court, independent from outside authority. Between March and May 1637 an election must have been held by the inhabitants of Windsor, Hartford, and Wethersfield, although it was not recorded. At the first session of the new General Corte, held on May 1, 1637, "committees," the counterpart of the deputies in Massachusetts Bay, appeared for the first time. Three committees represented each of the settlements on the western bank of the river; Agawam (Springfield) sent no delegates until March 1637/38.[5]

Presumably, the committees from the plantations met prior to the May session of the Corte and elected two magistrates from each town to complete its membership. In the election of 1637 only William Westwood of the original Massachusetts Bay Commissioners was not named to the General Corte as a magistrate. To represent Hartford's Southsiders, the electorate replaced him with Thomas Welles. Welles, although not appointed to the Commission by the General Court of Massachusetts, had sat unofficially at the March 28, 1637, session.

Connecticut's first election took place in 1637, its second in 1638. The General Corte on February 9, 1637/38, dissolved itself by ordering "y^t the generall Courte now in being shalbe dissolved and there is noe more attendance of the members thereof to be expected except they be newly chosen in the next generall Courte."[6] Thomas Hooker, writing to John Winthrop in the fall of 1638, left a documentary letter referring to the 1638 election. To Winthrop he wrote that at "the time of our election, the committees from the town of Agaam came in with other towns, and chose their magistrates, installed them into their government, took oath of them for the execution of justice according to God, and engaged themselves to submit to their government, and the execution of justice by their means, and dispensed by the authority which they put upon them, by choice." [7]

The immediate cause of summoning the General Corte in May 1637 was the urgent need of Windsor, Hartford, and Wethersfield to unite against a common enemy, the Pequot Indians. The Pequots had harassed the English constantly since their first arrival in the Connecticut River Valley. In 1633 they murdered Captain John Stone, of Virginia, who had sailed from the West Indies to trade with the Dutch. But because their Narragansett enemies were threatening them, the Pequots hastily offered the pipe of peace to the white men. Peace lasted until July 1636, when some Block Island Indians, protégés of the Pequots, murdered John Oldham and several seamen near Block Island. They failed to escape before John Gallop spotted them swarming over the death shallop and quickly investigated the incident. Rather than ignore the outrage and leave the murders unavenged, Captain John Endecott, of Massachusetts Bay, with ninety or one hundred men hurried to Block Island, killed fourteen Narragansetts, and set fire to their homes and fields in retaliation, thereby stirring up the wasps around their ears that the Connecticut men complained of so bitterly.

The Pequots attacked Saybrook Fort without warning in October 1636, capturing one Butterfield and torturing him until he died. Again they struck. This time they caught Joseph Tilly up the river from Saybrook, cut off his hands and feet, and taunted him until he expired. Their hatchets and tomahawks fell on Wethersfield in April 1637. After killing six men and three women and kidnaping two girls, they rubbed salt into the wounds of the English by waving their victims' clothes as they sailed past Saybrook Fort. More than thirty Connecticut men had been ambushed, tortured, and murdered and countless buildings destroyed before the Congregationalists acted to reduce the constant menace. The three settlements on the Connecticut River united in the General Corte, waged war against the heathens, and emerged victorious.

The first four sessions of the Corte, from May 1 until November 14, 1637, were entirely devoted to the war. The problems involved in raising an army of 90 fighting men out of an entire population of 850 to fight on the offensive as well as defend the home front taxed the resources of the tiny communities inordinately and posed almost insurmountable logistical problems.[8] But the Corte acted swiftly and on Wednesday, May 10, had its tiny force ready to sail down the Connecticut River on a pink, a pinnace, and a shallop under the military command of Captain John Mason and the spiritual guidance of Hartford's teacher, Samuel Stone. The ships were laden with beer, corn, suet, butter, fish, and pork to feed the hungry men, as well as arms and ammunition for the attack. Uncas offered to reinforce the party with seventy of his Mohegan braves, hoping that their combined efforts would defeat Sassacus, the despised Pequot chief.

Instead of attacking the Pequots directly at their forts at Mystic and Groton, the Yankees, resorting to the cunning and strategy for which they have always been known, sailed from Saybrook past the Indian strongholds to Narragansett Bay. After dark they silently made their way back toward the main fort, camping for the night at Porter's Rocks. Early on the morning of May 26 Mason's men surprised Mystic Fort suddenly and without warning. Mason threw a burning brand over the walls, and the entire fort burst into flame, trapping between six and seven hundred Indians inside. The Connecticut soldiers next attacked the royal fort at Groton, but Chief Sassacus and his warriors escaped. Triumphantly Captain Mason and his men returned to Hartford little more than two weeks after their departure. In the meanwhile Uncas and his Mohegans pursued a fleeing Pequot sachem, Mononotto, and caught him trying to swim for safety. Uncas brutally beheaded him and wedged his severed head in the crotch of a tree, where it remained. Hence the origin of Sachem's Head, according to tradition.[9]

The final solution to the Pequot menace came in June, when Mason again sallied forth against the Indians, this time reinforced by Captain Israel Stoughton, of Massachusetts Bay, and his troops. The Puritans trapped the Indians in a bog thicket near Fairfield. After a furious fight in the swamp on July 13, Thomas Stanton persuaded two hundred old men, women, and children to surrender, but Chief Sassacus and sixty or seventy braves fought their way out and escaped. They took refuge with the Mohawks, only to be betrayed. Proudly, the Mohawks soon presented the English with Sassacus' head! Such were Indian promises.

The virtual annihilation of the Pequot tribe by the Connecticut Congregationalists in this brief war proved the superiority of the Puritan over the heathen. Formal peace returned with the treaty of September 1638. The two hundred prisoners were divided among Uncas' Mohegans, Miantonomo's Narragansetts, and Ninigret's Niantics. The survivors agreed to pay an annual tribute to Connecticut and surrender their lands to the English. Connecticut and the Bay quarreled over the division of the territory until the commissioners of the United Colonies many years later finally awarded the entire jurisdiction to Connecticut. While Connecticut never ceased to fear the Indians, the Pequot War eliminated all actual danger to the Commonwealth throughout the period of the Fundamental Orders. The victory also served to elevate the reputation of the Connecticut settlers in the eyes of the Dutch at New Amsterdam and the English in Massachusetts Bay and to cement the union of the three river plantations.

By the time the Fundamental Orders were adopted, the Commonwealth on the Connecticut River had had almost three years' experience in unchallenged self-government. In the twenty months of its existence, besides waging the war, the General Corte negotiated the treaty of peace with the Pequots in September 1638 and acted to settle the fiscal obligations incurred during the war by levying an enormous tax of £620 on the towns. The Corte managed Connecticut's economy to the best of its ability by awarding monopolies on the Indian trade to several of its citizens. It endeavored to deal fairly with the Indians, a problem Englishmen had never had to cope with in the Old World, by expressly forbidding the settlers' tying up, imprisoning, or whipping an Indian unless they had been assaulted by that particular one. It also hired Thomas Stanton to act as its interpreter.[10]

Because of the infancy of the settlements, the Corte faced tasks like building a road through the uplands between Hartford and Windsor capable of bearing horse and cart traffic; this included erecting a bridge over the swamp. The Corte created a permanent militia under the command of Captain Mason and voted him an annual salary of £40 for training each man in Connecticut ten days a year. It fixed the salary of common soldiers at 1*s.* 3*d.* per day for a six-day week, of sergeants 20 pence a day, and Lieutenant Robert Seely 20 shillings a week.[11]

It made an effort to arrange for the purchase of Indian corn for the hungry towns and established its right to control its own adjournment. The Corte heard lawsuits in the presence of a jury and saw that committees were elected by the plantations without a religious qualification to share the government with the magistrates. The Corte had proved itself capable of administering the civil affairs of the Commonwealth and emerged as the dominant political body on the Connecticut River. But the Connecticut Conregationalists felt the need for a more formal body politic.

It was during the period of the General Corte that the Fundamental Orders were formulated, but the *Public Records of the Colony of Connecticut* end abruptly with the minutes of the April 5, 1638, session and contain no further entries until January 14, 1638/39. Unfortunately Connecticut did not have a contemporary historian like Governor John Winthrop or Governor William Bradford, or even a Thomas Lechford or Captain Edward Johnson to record the framing and ratifying of the Fundamental Orders. Much mystery still overshadows the formulation of the constitution and will remain unsolved until someone discovers the missing minutes or a pertinent letter, perhaps in the lining of a bonnet, where one of Connecticut's priceless charters reappeared, or in an attic trunk. The dearth of documentary information has resulted in considerable conjecture by the historians and numerous interpretations of the few facts at hand.

Little is known of the steps taken in the creation of the Fundamental Orders because strict secrecy was imposed on the men attending the constitutional sessions. The right to secret debate became an integral part of Connecticut law in October 1639, when the General Court threatened that whatsoever "member of the generall Court shall reveale any secrett wch the Court inioynes to be kept secrett, or shall make knowne to any p^rson what any one member of the Court speaks concerning any p^rson or businesse that may come into agitacõn in the Court, shall forfeit for every such fault ten pounds, and be otherwise dealt withall, at the discretion

of the Court. And the Secretary is to read this order att the beginning of every generall Court." [12] A similar ultimatum that silence
be kept undoubtedly covered the constitutional sessions. The men
of Connecticut may have intentionally withdrawn from the notice
of hostile Englishmen in England and in Massachusetts Bay until
the Fundamental Orders could be correctly phrased and irrefu-
tably accepted as the firmly established law of a united people.

Worth considering, too, is the explanation that until several
months after its adoption the constitution was probably incomplete;
the records of the Commonwealth for September 10, 1639, speak
of its being "ripened." Important also is the possibility that human
frailty was responsible for the disappearance of any minutes that
may have been kept. This was the time when Edward Hopkins
replaced John Steele as secretary of the Commonwealth. At most
there was one copy of the proceedings; there was no press in Connecticut before the Charter, and it would have been disastrous for
the Congregationalists to send such minutes to England or even
to the Bay for publication. In the shuffle the records might easily
have been lost.

While the records kept their secrets, the leaders in Hartford,
Windsor, and Wethersfield wrote the constitution for the Commonwealth. The first hint that constitutional discussions pervaded
the plantations during 1638 appeared when Henry Wolcott's notebook was translated from his shorthand notes, revealing that
Thomas Hooker delivered a sermon to an unrecorded session of
the General Corte on May 31, 1638. In the sermon Hooker expounded many of the principles which were to reappear in the
Fundamental Orders in less than eight months. This much of the
sermon pertinent to the current civil issues fortunately has been
preserved in Wolcott's notebook:

> text Deuteronomy 1 13 choose you wise men and understanding
> and known among your tribes and I will make them heads over you
> captains over thousands captains over hundreds 50 10
> doctrine that the choice of public magistrates belongs unto the people
> by Gods own allowance
> 2 doctrine the privilege of election which belongs to the people it must
> not be exercised according to their humors but according to the blessed
> will and law of God

3 doctrine   they who have power to appoint officers and magistrates it is in their power also to set the bounds and limits of the power and places unto which they may call them

1st of 1   1 reason because the foundation of authority is laid 1stly in the free consent of people

2 reason   because by a free choice the hearts of the people will be more enlarged to the love of the person and more ready to yield obedience

3 reason   because of that duty and engagement of the people

use 3   fold 1   here is matter of thankful acknowledgment in the apprehension of Gods faithfulness towards us and the promotion of those mercies that God doth command and vouchsafe [13]

This was the first sermon recorded by Wolcott to substantiate the fact that Hooker lectured on civil matters from the pulpit.

As Perry Miller emphasized, Hooker was then offering the tenets of Congregationalism to the political leaders of the Commonwealth.[14] In the first and second points of doctrine Hooker reiterated the political reality in Connecticut. By May 1638 there had been two annual elections of civil officers, just as there had been elections in the churches. But his liberalism is beginning to become evident in his explanation of this privilege. Not even in the Bay Colony would it have been admitted that "the foundation of authority is laid 1stly in the free consent of people." His bold explanation of the psychology practiced by the Congregational churches in allowing the brethren to select their officers with God's guidance "because by a free choice the hearts of the people will be more enlarged to the love of the person and more ready to yield obedience" is more consistent with the times.

It was in this third point of doctrine that Hooker advocated a more advanced philosophy of government. Here he made a plea for a government where the magistrates were limited by the people. At the time of the sermon there had been no instances of an electorate's imposing restrictions on magisterial powers and no instances of its actually removing any officers, civil or ecclesiastical. Hooker emphasized this point only as a warning to the magistrates. It should not be taken out of its seventeenth-century context and construed as a plea for democracy. The membership of the churches was limited, as was the membership in the Commonwealth, and at no time during the period of the Fundamental Orders was this measure invoked to impeach a civil or ecclesiastical officer and remove him from office.

Only two hints of the constitutional events occurring in 1638, aside from Wolcott's sermon notes, have survived. One is a letter written by Roger Ludlow to Governor Winthrop on May 29, 1638, two days before Hooker's address. The letter deals primarily with the proposed union of the New England colonies, but in it Ludlow reveals the information that recently had met "a generall assembly of these plantacõns in this River, & fallinge into consideracõn of divers p̄ticulers that might or may concerne the generall good of these p̄ts." This session of the General Corte is not mentioned in the *Public Records of the Colony of Connecticut,* but the letter bears the signature, "R. Ludlowe, in the name of the whole," undoubtedly meaning "in the name of the General Corte." [15]

The other hint is Thomas Hooker's heated reply to Governor Winthrop, which has already been mentioned. Hooker's letter provides the additional information that committees had been elected in the four towns and that they in turn had chosen and installed the magistrates. These committees and magistrates met as the unrecorded session of the Corte, which Ludlow included in his signature and Hooker addressed on May 31.

The points emphasized in the Hooker sermon, Ludlow's comments on the unrecorded session of the General Corte, and Hooker's letter describing the election of 1638 provide the only evidence that the men on the Connecticut River were meeting during the summer and fall of 1638, much less that they were drawing up a constitution. Governor Winthrop recorded nothing relevant to the creation of the Fundamental Orders in his *Journal,* nor did Governor Bradford. The *Records of the Governor and Company of the Massachusetts Bay in New England* answer none of the questions regarding the origin of the Fundamental Orders, nor do the extant letters written during 1638 and 1639 by John Davenport, Roger Williams, Edward Hopkins, John Haynes, George Fenwick, William Pynchon, John Winthrop, Jr., and Thomas Welles. The official silence during the period of the framing and adoption of the Fundamental Orders is understandable, but it is indeed strange that no one should discuss its merits or the wisdom of its precepts once it was adopted. Did no one in England or New England know of its creation, or was its significance not appreciated? The mystery has exasperated many a historian.

Differences of opinion have long existed among scholars concerning the formulation of the Fundamental Orders. George Leon Walker wrote that at "some time in 1638 a General Court was elected for the purpose of framing a body of laws for the permanent government of the Colony." [16] Others disagreed, interpreting the facts to prove that not the Corte, but a committee composed of Roger Ludlow, John Haynes, Thomas Welles, John Steele, and Edward Hopkins framed it. They based their premise on the fact that committee action was then being employed in the Bay to prepare a legal code.[17] John Haynes had actually served on the committees appointed on May 6, 1635, and May 25, 1636, to draft a code of law for the Bay. Furthermore, the men suggested had all served on the Connecticut Corte of April 5, 1638, the last recorded before the adoption of the constitution. The General Court appointed Hopkins, Welles, and Steele, together with William Spenser, on September 10, 1639, "to ripen some orders that were left vnfinished the former Court, as about p'vition of settling of lands, testaments of the deceased, and recording spetiall passages of P'vidence." These orders were never attached to the original eleven, but the naming of these particular men would indicate that they had played a part in drafting the constitution.[18]

Historians Andrews, Coleman, Adams, and Stiles, however, concluded that Roger Ludlow was the only man in Connecticut with sufficient legal training to provide the final polished legal phraseology to the committee's draft of the Fundamental Orders. Ludlow was born in Wiltshire about 1590 and grew up in a west-country gentry family. He matriculated at Balliol College, Oxford, in 1610 and in 1612 entered the Inner Temple. His legal training there led to his being elected an assistant by the Massachusetts Bay Company in February 1629/30, the last meeting of the Company held in England. He sailed to New England on the *Mary and John* with the Winthrop Fleet when he was forty years old and was one of the founders of the town of Dorchester. His wife was Mary Endecott, sister of Governor Endecott of the Bay.

For four years he continued to be re-elected an assistant there, until in 1634 he became deputy governor. He was respected and recognized as one of Dorchester's leading citizens, one of its three stockholders in the Company, and a major landowner. In 1635 he was not re-elected to the General Court of the Bay, because by then he was determined to participate in the removal to Connecticut. In April 1636 he could be found in Connecticut presiding over the first meeting of the Massachusetts Bay Commission. Throughout its existence his name was listed first on the roll, indicating that he served as its presiding officer. He also presided over the first session of the General Corte in May 1637. In the fall of 1638 it was he who, with John Haynes, signed the treaty with the Pequots.

Roger Ludlow was a controversial figure in both Massachusetts and Connecticut. He was stern, passionate, and demanding of his peers as well as of his subordinates. His temper was quick and his tongue sharp, but his religious convictions were as sincere as they were fervent. In 1638 and 1639 he was the only man in Connecticut trained in the law. In addition to this he had had almost five years' experience in colonial government in the Bay, another one in Connecticut as a member of the Massachusetts Bay Commission, and still another on the General Corte.[19] Samuel Eliot Morison, John M. Taylor, and Roy V. Coleman attributed the framing of the constitution to him without mentioning the aid of a committee, and even Benjamin Trumbull referred to him as "a principal in forming its [Connecticut's] original civil constitution."[20]

It would seem most plausible that Connecticut would imitate the Bay and employ several minds, working collectively or singly, to draw up the Fundamental Orders, particularly when in September 1639 a committee was called on to polish them. It is entirely logical that Ludlow would then synthesize the several plans into the finished constitution. Many of the phrases in the preamble of the Fundamental Orders resemble those in the Massachusetts Bay Commission. Perhaps he drew up both. His absence from the September committee is explained by his involvement in the founding of Uncoway (Fairfield), which required his temporary departure from the river towns.[21] Roger Ludlow was the leading citizen of Connecticut before the constitution. Thomas Hooker was its foremost pastor. In all probability the constitution of this Congregational Commonwealth was inspired by the religious spokesman and then transformed into the language of the courts by its legal authority.

The identity of the ratifiers of the Fundamental Orders poses a similar problem. Herbert Parker wrote that the constitution "was adopted on the 14th of January, 1638–39, by the freemen in church congregations, of Windsor, Hartford and Wethersfield." Just as positively Benjamin Trumbull stated that on "the 14th of January, 1639, all the free planters convened at Hartford, and, on mature deliberation, adopted a constitution of government." His opinion was upheld by John Fiske. Other historians were convinced that it was ratified by representatives of the towns, but were not more specific, while Breckinridge Long, Dwight Loomis, and J. Gilbert Calhoun concluded that the constitution was approved by a popular assembly. The Reverend Joseph H. Twichell even asserted that all the adult males of the towns had gathered to adopt it.[22] There is no agreement on whether it was adopted by the freemen, the free planters, the committees, the Corte, or all the adult males in the Commonwealth.

The records of the General Court contribute nothing toward resolving the mystery. For January 14, 1638/39, the *Public Records of the Colony of Connecticut* bear only the following irrelevant entry:

> It is Ordered that the tresurer shall deliuer noe mony out of his hands to any p^rson w^thout the hands of two Magistrats if the som̄ be above 20s.; if it be vnder then the tresurer is to accept of the hand of on; but if it be for the payment of some bylls to be alowed, wch are referred to some Com̄ittes to consider of whether alowed or not, That such bylls as they alowe & sett there hands vnto the Tresurer shall accept & give satisfactñ.[23]

No mention whatsoever is made of the ratification of the Fundamental Orders. This note was not even recorded by Edward Hopkins, who was secretary of Connecticut in 1639; instead, it was inserted by Thomas Welles, who in January 1638/39 was treasurer of the Commonwealth, but did not become secretary until April 1640. Nevertheless, the entry substantiates the fact that the General

Court met on the date that the Fundamental Orders are thought to have been approved.[24]

If considered in the seventeenth-century context, it becomes apparent that the constitution must have been adopted by the General Corte, rather than by all the freemen in the churches or by the town meetings. This is the opinion espoused by Edwin Stanley Welles, George M. Dutcher, and Sherman W. Adams and Henry R. Stiles. It was the General Court that on April 11, 1639, suggested that a committee be appointed "to ripen orders formerly in agitaĉon against [the] next meeting of the Court" and on September 10, 1639, chose that committee.[25] The language of the Fundamental Orders, "It is ordered, sentenced and decreed . . . ," is typical legislative jargon. The General Court recorded the constitution in its minutes eventually as if it were an integral part of its action, and in most instances it was the Court that amended the orders. All the subsequent orders or statutes of the Commonwealth, the capital crimes codified in 1642, and the Code of 1650 were passed by the Court. We, "the Inhabitants and Residents of Windsor, Harteford and Wethersfield" in the preamble can easily be interpreted in its figurative sense, indicating that the magistrates and committees in the General Court had ratified it in behalf of their constituents, the inhabitants and residents. The preamble speaks of "successors," but mass meetings cannot have successors and people generally have heirs, while the General Court, because it was an institution, could exist in perpetuity through its successors.[26]

The Fundamental Orders of Connecticut were not recorded properly under the date of January 14, 1638/39, in the original records of the Commonwealth, "Book Number A. or the First Book of the Records of the Colony of Connecticutt;" instead, they were entered between pages 220 and 227 of the manuscript as it is now paged.[27] Pages 11 through 22, where they and the minutes of the preceding nine months should have been entered chronologically, are blank. Obviously, these pages were being saved for the constitution in its final form. Proof that the constitution was adopted on January 14, 1638/39, rests on the date affixed to these sheets when they were finally entered in the records. Furthermore, in the minutes of the General Court for May 20, 1647, there is an order which begins, "Whereas, by an Order of the 14th of January, 1638[/39], it was Ordered, that euery Generall Court, . . ." It continues by quoting from the tenth fundamental.[28] The date given in this reference and the date ascribed to the constitution when it was recorded substantiate the fact that the Fundamental Orders must have been adopted on January 14, 1638/39.

The ratification of the Fundamental Orders marks the beginning of Connecticut's constitutional life. Charles Borgeaud once defined a constitution as "the fundamental law according to which the government of a state is organized and the relations of individuals with society as a whole are regulated. It may be either a code, a well-defined text, or a collection of such texts promulgated at a certain time by a sovereign authority, or it may be the result, more or less definite, of a series of legislative acts, ordinances, judicial decisions, precedents, and traditions of dissimilar origin and unequal value." [29]

The Fundamental Orders were a formal written constitution, established by the sovereign authority in Connecticut to delineate the body politic in statute form. In many ways the government they defined was similar to the trading corporation which Massachusetts Bay technically was. It also resembled the Netherland Republic which originated in the Union of Utrecht of 1579, as it was the governing body of several independent provinces or plantations which had united for purposes of defense and taxation. The office of governor was new to Connecticut, and the freemen rather than the deputies now elected the magistrates, but otherwise the constitution was of paramount importance in providing written authority for the facets of administration which had already existed as unwritten law from 1633 until January 1638/39.

The purpose of the Fundamental Orders was to provide a legal guide for the government of the holy and regenerate in the river towns during the years when the Commonwealth existed without the authority of the Great Seal of England. The Massachusetts Bay Commission had little actual legal standing and the General Corte none. Taking matters into their own hands, the Connecticut Congregationalists now laid the authority for their existence as a political entity on a divine covenant and united the three river towns into a functioning state. United, the Commonwealth could better defend itself against the Dutch or Indians or against the invasion of a governor-general like Sir Edmund Andros, who in 1687 intruded so blatantly into their affairs.

Under the Fundamental Orders the Puritan ideal became a reality. Church and state were virtually synonymous. The leaders of the state were the brethren of the Congregational churches, and the leaders of the churches were freemen of the Commonwealth. The individual was not permitted great freedom, except to be saved from himself by the rule of the saints. The Commonwealth was autonomous and Congregationalism supreme under the constitution. With the adoption of the constitution the records of the General Court acquire a more formal, orderly note. They seem to exude the new confidence and authority that Connecticut had attained in becoming a commonwealth, complete with constitution.

The Fundamental Orders are divided into a preamble and eleven orders. In the preamble may readily be seen the covenant of grace and the church covenants transposed from the religious aspect of the lives of the Puritans on the Connecticut River to the political. The covenant represents an agreement between God and the Congregationalists and also a written social compact in which the settlers publicly proclaimed their intention of uniting into a political society. The idea of a voluntary national or plantation covenant between God and a body of believers is as old as God's covenant with Noah. It recurred frequently in the Old Testament as a means of organizing a stable community under the rule of God's law, in spite of man's frailties.[30] The theory of the covenant had been expounded by Plato in the fourth century before Christ. It formed a vital part of the thinking of George Buchanan in Scotland and Richard Hooker in England, of the Separatist Robert Browne, and then of the generation of nonseparating Puritans which included William Perkins, John Preston, Richard Sibbes, and William Ames. In New England it became an integral part of the polity advocated by the federal theologians like Thomas Hooker, John Cotton, and John Davenport and lay leaders like John Winthrop.[31] Previously in New England, covenants had appeared in the Mayflower Compact and in the Congregational churches of Plymouth and Massachusetts Bay and Connecticut.

Civil covenants formed the basis of the towns of Exeter, New Haven, Providence, Portsmouth, and Newport.[32] The covenant theory was not original in Connecticut.

In the preamble of the Fundamental Orders, Connecticut's first citizens agreed to

> assotiate and conioyne our selues to be as one Publike State or Comonwelth; and doe, for our selues and our Successors and such as shall be adioyned to vs att any tyme hereafter, enter into Combination and Confederation togather, to mayntayne and p^rsearue the liberty and purity of the gospell of our Lord Jesus wch we now p^rfesse, as also the disciplyne of the Churches, wch according to the truth of the said gospell is now practised amongst vs; As also in o^r Ciuell Affaires to be guided and gouerned according to such Lawes, Rules, Orders and decrees as shall be made, ordered & decreed, as followeth.[33]

This was a covenant between the godly property owners of Hartford, Windsor, and Wethersfield, not between all the residents on the Connecticut River, just as the church covenants were the agreement between the saints only. Civil rights were the privilege of the few.

Intentionally, Springfield did not enter into the covenant. It had been settled in 1636 about twenty-five miles up the river from Hartford by William Pynchon. At first it seemed logical that it should become the fourth Connecticut town; such it had been under the Massachusetts Bay Commission and the General Corte. But instead of lying on the western bank of the Connecticut River, it was on the eastern, and rather than depending economically on agriculture, it was primarily a trading center. Pynchon's Calvinism was stricter than Hooker's, and the differences ran deep. The estrangement became complete after the Pequot War, when the General Corte commissioned Pynchon to supply the settlements with five hundred bushels of Indian corn, a responsibility he had neither requested nor desired. The offer of a monopoly on the corn trade failed to change his attitude. On April 5, 1638, the Corte fined Pynchon forty bushels of corn for not carrying out his duties, thereby incurring the wrath of this independent Puritan. He promptly severed all ties with Connecticut. As Perry Miller emphasized, Pynchon's breach of an unwritten covenant, which wounded Hooker so, was directly responsible for the covenant in the Fundamental Orders being explicit and in written form.[34]

In the plantation covenant of the Fundamental Orders the Congregationalists of Connecticut recognized God as their sovereign. He had guided them to the river, had explained the need for an orderly civil government to preserve the churches and the gospel, and was then aiding them in creating their government and providing a law for it. In accordance with His teachings, the rest of the constitution was designed to provide a civil environment compatible with His Congregational churches.

What was not included in the preamble and what made the covenant of Connecticut unique was any reference to an earthly authority. Plymouth and New Haven were founded without a charter from the King or Parliament, but Plymouth in the Mayflower Compact recognized the supremacy of the King; New Haven, which like Connecticut ignored the temporal authority of the English monarch, was founded later than the Connecticut Commonwealth. The preamble of the Fundamental Orders ignored the King of England absolutely. It did not reserve for him the traditional fraction of all precious metals discovered, it did not plead for the customary liberties and immunities of Englishmen, nor did it even declare Connecticut's independence from the Crown. Charles I was too far away from Connecticut and too troubled with his own affairs. He was detested by the Connecticut Congregationalists almost as much as by the Puritans in England, who soon dethroned and beheaded him. God, instead of the King, wielded sovereign authority over the Congregationalists of Connecticut, just as He exercised His rule over their churches.

Following the preamble in the constitution are the eleven fundamentals, or statute laws, which delineate the form of government approved by the covenanting inhabitants to regulate their society from January 1638/39 until October 1662. In concrete terms the constitution set forth the role each of the component parts of the government—the electorate, the officers, and the General Court—was to play. The active participants in Connecticut under the Fundamental Orders were the freemen of the Commonwealth and, to a lesser extent, the admitted inhabitants of the towns. The freemen were the citizens of Connecticut.[35] The first

The first page of the Fundamental Orders of Connecticut, showing the preamble and first fundamental. *Courtesy of the Connecticut State Library, Hartford, Connecticut.*

fundamental required that to become a freeman an individual must be an admitted inhabitant of one of the towns and an actual resident of Connecticut. He then had to be approved by the General Court, or in certain instances by a magistrate. Just as no one was admitted to the membership of a Congregational church without a vote of approval by the brethren, no one was permitted an active voice in the Commonwealth without the General Court's sanction. Women, children, apprentices, indentured servants, and the few Indian slaves were not eligible to become freemen in seventeenth-century Connecticut. There was no stipulation that to become a freeman a man had to be a member of a Congregational church, although in practice most, if not all, freemen were at least sympathetic to the Congregational principles. Massachusetts Bay prior to May 18, 1631, Plymouth, and the Providence Plantations likewise made no explicit religious qualification the basis of freemanship.

Connecticut never outrightly denied a man the privilege of the vote because of his religious convictions, although on February 26, 1656/57, in response to rumors of a Quaker invasion, the General Court ordered that "those that shall hereafter bee made free, shall haue an affirmatiue certificate vnder the hands of all or the major part of the deputies in their seuerall townes, of their peaceable and honest conuersation, and those and only those of them wch the Gen: Court shall approue shall bee made free men." [36] The Reverend John Higginson, of Guilford, referring to Connecticut, retorted with the provocative comment that "since the time of the Counsell that power and p^{r}uiledge wch the Eld^{rs} of that Jurisdiction had before, to judge of the fitnesse of men for freedome in that Comonwealth, hath bene taken from them and transferred vnto other hands." [37] Here is a hint that the elders and pastors of the churches had actually had considerable influence in the admission of freemen in Connecticut. Even though there was no religious qualification set by the first fundamental, there may well have been one in practice.

The Commonwealth of Connecticut, like Massachusetts, gradually tightened the restrictions on its franchise. On April 9, 1646, Connecticut's General Court ordered that "if any p^{r}son wthin these libertyes haue bine or shalbe fyned or whippen for any scandalous offence, he shall not be admitted after such tyme to haue any voate in Towne or Comon welth, nor to searue on the Jury, vntill the Court shall manifest their satisfaction." [38] This order applied to admitted inhabitants as well as freemen. Then on February 26, 1656/57, the Court stipulated that to become a freeman of the Commonwealth, the candidate must first have a letter of recommendation from a majority of the deputies in his town and then receive a vote of approval from the Court itself. On March 9, 1658/59, the condition was added that no one could be eligible to become a freeman until he had reached twenty-one and possessed a personal estate valued at £30, unless he had held office in the Commonwealth. Future candidates could be considered for election only at the October Court in an effort to avoid public pressure.[39] All the freemen regularly attended the Court of Election in the spring, whereas none but the magistrates and deputies met at the October Court. A popular but troublesome candidate might turn the freemen against the Court.

The change from a requirement of £30 in real estate to the greater £30 in personal estate was intended to reduce the number of qualified applicants. Between 1657 and 1659 one hundred and thirty-five admitted inhabitants advanced to the rank of freeman, but during the next three years only three new freemen were added to the list, proving the effectiveness of the measure.[40] Both in England and in Massachusetts Bay there were age and property qualifications, and already in Connecticut, in April 1657, they had been added to the prerequisites for becoming admitted inhabitants. No official tabulation of the number of freemen in Connecticut under the Fundamental Orders is extant, but Albert E. McKinley conservatively counted only 229 between 1639 and 1662, out of what he estimated was a total population of over three thousand. Less than one-third of the admitted inhabitants of the towns achieved freemanship.[41]

The freemen in Connecticut were entitled to attend the Courts of Election in the spring and there to cast their ballots for the magistrates. Occasionally they voted on pending issues. Subsequent to the formation of the United Colonies of New England, they were also authorized to vote for the commissioners to represent the Commonwealth for the ensuing year, but frequently they delegated the choice to the General Court. Ordinarily the freemen came in person to the spring Courts of Election, but at some time prior to 1660 those living in the distant towns began voting by proxy because of the difficulties of transportation. They cast their ballots at a freeman's meeting in their respective towns. The ballots were then sealed, sent to Hartford, and there counted.[42] Only freemen could be elected magistrates or deputies. They were comparable to the stockholders in a joint-stock company and the brethren in a church.

The body of freemen enjoyed a unique privilege. When the Fundamental Orders were being ratified, there had been no Parliament in England for ten years and an oligarchy ruled Massachusetts Bay. Both situations led directly to the insertion of the provision into the sixth fundamental permitting the freemen to convoke the General Court under certain circumstances. If the governor and majority of the magistrates should fail or refuse to call either of the two standing courts or any other considered necessary, a majority of the freemen could present a petition to the magistracy, requesting a session of the Court. If it were denied, the majority of the freemen could then issue a warrant to the constables in the towns, ordering them to summon the freemen to meet; they could choose their own moderator and act with authority equal to that of any General Court. This section of the fundamental was never applied, but served to discourage any overpowerful alliance of the governor and magistrates.

The second echelon of voters in Connecticut at this time comprised the admitted inhabitants. They were the electors in the towns, rather than in the Commonwealth. The only requirement that the Fundamental Orders imposed for becoming an admitted inhabitant was that the candidate subscribe to the oath of fidelity. To do this he had to be a Trinitarian. All other prerequisites were left to the discretion of the towns. Windsor, Wethersfield, and Hartford originally required that admitted inhabitants be resident householders and landowners, but there was no expressed religious qualification.

In the later years of the Fundamental Orders the conditions set for admitted inhabitants also became more strict. As Connecticut's population increased and its composition changed, church and state became less identical. Newcomers and the growing number of servants and apprentices disturbed the Commonwealth with their drunkenness, tobacco-smoking, moral infractions, and multitude of petty crimes. To prevent them from attaining the status of admitted inhabitant, on November 10, 1643, the General Court ordered that whereas the Fundamental Orders had formerly permitted any admitted inhabitant who had subscribed to the oath of fidelity in the Commonwealth to cast his vote for the deputies, in the future the admitted inhabitants also had to be approved by a majority vote in their town meeting. An adjourned session of the General Court held in April 1657 required that admitted inhabitants be "housholders that are one & twenty yeares of age, or haue bore office, or haue 30*l.* estate." The "or's" spelled the difference between the requirements for the admitted inhabitants and the freemen. The freemen had to be over twenty-one *and* have a personal estate worth over £30, which was far greater than an all-inclusive one of the same value. This automatically excluded most bachelors and many of the poorer people in Connecticut. On May 17, 1660, the Court added that "none shalbe receaued as Inhabitant into any Towne in the Collony but such as are knowne to be of an honest conversation, and accepted by a maior part of the Towne." [43] This latter order was the result of a desire, particularly in Hartford and Wethersfield, to restore peace and uniformity in the towns which had witnessed traumatic crises in the churches during the previous six or seven years by excluding the discordant elements from the voting population. At the end of the period the average man was less dedicated to the original purposes of the Commonwealth and less willing to abide by its laws.

Hartford, and probably Windsor and Wethersfield too, approved new voters by a majority vote of the admitted inhabitants. The Hartford town meeting retained the privilege of rejecting prospective inhabitants in the later days of the Fundamental Orders and on at least one occasion exercised its right to revoke the privilege of the franchise when it voted "that Jeams Blor should not continue wth us as an Inhabitant." [44] In Connecticut the admitted inhabitants of the towns participated in the Commonwealth government to the extent that in the town meetings they elected the deputies to represent them in the General Court, but they could not serve as deputies or magistrates themselves.

The freemen and the admitted inhabitants constituted the electorate under the Fundamental Orders, but the constitution specifically recognized the General Court as the supreme power of the Commonwealth. It was Connecticut's parliament. Each General Court sat for one year and was divided into two sessions, the Court of Election and the September or October Court. The Court of Election, which all the freemen of the Commonwealth attended, was held on the second Thursday in April to elect the governor, deputy governor, at least six magistrates, a secretary, and a treasurer. The autumn session was primarily a legislative assembly.

The most important order of business in the Court of Election was the choice of magistrates. The third fundamental specifically required that any new candidate for the magistracy had to have his name proposed at a meeting of the General Court held prior to the Court of Election. This was to prevent the choice of a magistrate without an adequate consideration of his qualifications and explains entries like "Mr. Fenwicke, Mr. Whiting, Mr. Hill and Mr. Ward are nominated by the Court to be presented to the vote of the Cuntrey for magistratts att the Court in Aprill next, p'vided Mr. Fenwicke and Mr. Whiting shall be freemen by that tyme." [45] The newness of the Commonwealth demanded a certain amount of flexibility in the system. The deputies from each town were granted the right to nominate two men for magistrates at the Court of Election, and the General Court could supply additional candidates. In Connecticut, but not in Massachusetts Bay, a man did not have to be a member of a Congregational church to be eligible for the magistracy. It was sufficient that he be a freeman and reside in the Commonwealth.

As each candidate's name was read by the secretary at the Court of Election, the freemen presented their ballots, blank if they voted "Nay" or inscribed with the nominee's name for "Aye." The men who received more written ballots than blanks became magistrates for one year; the one with the most ballots became governor. Roger Ludlow, in writing this point in the Fundamental Orders, had mellowed—or had been outvoted—since the day in Massachusetts Bay when he heard the suggestion

that the assistants might be chosen anew every year, and that the governor might be chosen by the whole court, and not by the assistants only. Upon this, Mr. Ludlow grew into passion, and said, that then we should have no government, but there would be an interim, wherein every man might do what he pleased, etc. This was answered and cleared in the judgment of the rest of the assistants, but he continued stiff in his opinion, and protested he would then return back into England.[46]

Before the Fundamental Orders the "committees" had selected the magistrates; after the adoption of the constitution, the freemen assembled at the Court of Election chose them.

If at least six magistrates were not elected in addition to the governor by this method, the candidates who had received the next highest number of written ballots were added to the magistracy until the complement of six was reached. Cotton Mather counted only thirty-seven different men who served as magistrates in Connecticut between 1636 and 1662; Roger Ludlow was elected first, Samuel Sherman last.[47] The use of the written, and presumably secret, ballot had first appeared in New England on July 20, 1629, in the election of the Reverend Francis Higginson as teacher of the Salem Church and Samuel Skelton as its pastor. Thomas Dudley was chosen governor in the Bay Colony by written ballot in 1634, but the practice did not become common in England until 1872. Connecticut voted by secret ballot in its civil elections throughout the period of the Fundamental Orders. Once the new Commonwealth officers had been elected by the freemen, they were joined by the deputies sent by the admitted inhabitants from the towns to fill out the ranks of the legislative body. The duties of the freemen and admitted inhabitants were then completed, and they played no further role in the legislative session.

In the Fundamental Orders the powers of the magistrates thus selected in the Court of Election were not explicitly stated, but in practice, once they had taken the oath of office, they exercised tremendous authority, serving in legislative, judicial, and even executive capacities. They advised the governor, sat on the General Court, and with the governor, deputy governor, and jury became the Particular Court, Connecticut's answer to a common, canon, and local law court. They performed marriages, granted divorces, admitted freemen, administered oaths, represented Connecticut in the meetings of the New England Confederation, swore in juries, and in the distant towns often served as judges. They could not be called into account personally for their official actions. But their powers were limited by the rights reserved to the freemen and deputies and by their lack of a veto over the acts of the deputies. Newtown had been thwarted in its attempt to remove to Connecticut by the assistants' vote in 1634; consequently, Connecticut was never allowed to become an oligarchy, although the power of the magistrates actually increased toward the end of the period, as the fear of their seizing control decreased.

The greatest change introduced by the Fundamental Orders was the creation of the office of governor. John Winthrop, the younger, technically had been Connecticut's first governor under the Massachusetts Bay Commission, but had never exercised his authority. During the period of the General Corte there was no executive. But at least a titular head of the Commonwealth was requisite in handling Connecticut's intercolonial relations, even though the governor was considered in the Fundamental Orders as little more than another magistrate. Little emphasis was placed on his executive capacity. To be eligible for the office of governor a candidate had to be "a mēber of some approved congregation." He had to have served previously as a magistrate in Connecticut and could not have held the office the preceding year. There was no precedent for this provision in the Fundamental Orders that no governor could succeed himself in office; its inclusion in the constitution reveals the Congregationalists' innate distrust of the executive. Their purpose was to prevent a situation like that in Massachusetts, where John Winthrop was elected governor for twelve years between 1630 and 1648 and deputy governor or an assistant the remainder of his life. But the result in Connecticut was that John Haynes, of Hartford, a pious, humble, and well-bred gentleman, according to Cotton Mather,[48] and Edward Hopkins, also of Hartford and a man of wealth, position, and equal devotion, alternated as governor and deputy governor from 1640 until Haynes's death in January 1653/54. George Wyllys, an original proprietor of Hartford, whose tree became the famous Charter Oak, was elected governor in 1642 instead of Hopkins, but only he broke the Haynes-Hopkins succession. The prohibition of two successive terms was repealed by vote of the freemen immediately before the second term of John Winthrop, the younger, expired. Thomas Welles, with whom Winthrop had alternated as governor and deputy governor, had died in Wethersfield on January 14, 1659/60. The freemen and the General Court were then anxious that Governor Winthrop, their "Worshipfull governor," present their petition for the Charter to Charles II. Following the repeal, Winthrop was re-elected on May 17, 1660, and continued in office until his death in 1676.

The other three prerequisites for the governorship originated in the experience of the settlers in Massachusetts Bay. The governor had to be a member of an approved congregation, that is, a Congregational church. This required church affiliation was the only religious qualification in the constitution of Connecticut. He also had to be a freeman of Connecticut, and he had to take the oath of office.

The governor chosen at the Court of Election called the General Court to order and acted as its presiding officer, recognizing speakers, keeping order, putting questions to the vote, and casting the deciding vote in a tie. But his authority was limited. He possessed no veto, and the tenth fundamental specifically denied him the right to adjourn or dissolve the Court without the approval of a majority of its members. The governor of Connecticut acted like the presiding officer of any English corporation; he could not arbitrarily dissolve the Court as Charles I had dissolved his Parliaments. Nor had he any patronage to disperse to augment his influence. Originally the governor did not even receive payment for his services, but on March 9, 1647/48, the General Court voted an annual stipend of £30 to both the governor and deputy governor as compensation for their expenses.[49]

The Fundamental Orders provided for moderators to substitute for the governor in the event of his absence or the refusal of the governor or magistrates to summon a Court, but on only two occasions did moderators preside over the General Court. The first occurred early in 1653/54 when Governor Haynes died in office while the deputy governor, Edward Hopkins, was in England, leaving Connecticut without either a governor or a deputy governor. The freemen met in Hartford on February 16, 1653/54, and chose Thomas Welles as moderator for the adjourned session of the Court, vesting in him the power to summon the next Court, which was to be a Court of Election. This crisis forced the Court to act at once, and on May 18, 1654, it amended the tenth fundamental to permit a majority of the magistrates, instead of a majority of the freemen, in the governor's absence to summon the General Court. The Court with a majority of magistrates and deputies present could select a moderator and then proceed as usual.[50] The second instance took place at the Court of Election on May 17, 1660. In anticipation of the absence of Governor Winthrop, who was about to sail for England to obtain the Charter, the Court chose Matthew Allyn as moderator "to supply the place of ye Gouerno^r and Dep: in case of their occasional absenc from ye Gen: Court." [51]

The remaining officers in the Commonwealth were the secretary and treasurer. Both were magistrates and served in that capacity as well as in their special roles. The secretary was responsible for keeping the minutes of the General Court and for sending copies of the laws newly enacted to the constables in the various towns to be proclaimed publicly and then written into the towns' lawbooks. The secretary also filed, searched, and recorded wills and inventories presented to the Court and served warrants. The amount of his compensation depended on the value and type of action. Thomas Welles, Captain John Cullick, and Daniel Clark acted as Connecticut's secretaries during most of the period of the Fundamental Orders.[52]

William Whiting, Thomas Welles, and John Talcott were Connecticut's most important treasurers. The treasurer dealt with the fiscal affairs of the Commonwealth. He collected the taxes levied on the towns from each town's collector of rates and made certain that the Commonwealth's own obligations were met. But the Congregationalists kept tight hands on their purse strings. The treasurer could pay out only 20 shillings, and then it had to be in payment of a bill that had already been authorized; otherwise, he had to have the signature of one magistrate. For anything over that amount two signatures were required. Often he paid Connecticut's debts out of his own pocket. In August 1639 the General Court found that it was £16 10s. 6d. indebted to Treasurer Thomas Welles. The treasurer's task was compounded by the lack of a monetary currency. His payments had to be equilibrated in wampum, beaver skins, peas, or corn and delivered in kind. In October 1657 the General Court voted to pay the treasurer £10 annually for his labors. Both he and the secretary served terms of one year.[53]

The Fundamental Orders decreed that following the election of the officers of the Commonwealth, deputies could join the newly appointed governor, deputy governor, secretary, treasurer, and magistrates and sit as the General Court. The deputies were elected in the towns by the admitted inhabitants. The seventh fundamental required the constables, upon receiving notice of a forthcoming Court of Election, to inform the admitted inhabitants of their respective towns that there would be a town meeting to elect the deputies for the General Court. Only freemen were eligible to serve as deputies. The two, three, or sometimes four men who received the greatest number of written votes became the town's delegates to the General Court for the year. The names of the deputies were then written on the back of the original warrant which had ordered the constable to call the meeting of the admitted inhabitants, and the list was endorsed by the constable and returned to the Court. In June 1640 the General Court added the provision that if a deputy could not attend a meeting of the General Court or should die in office while the Court was adjourned, the governor could send out a warrant to his town, ordering a special election.[54]

From the May 1, 1637, session of the General Corte until the adoption of the Fundamental Orders, Hartford, Windsor, and Wethersfield had each been represented by three "committees." Under the Fundamental Orders the original towns usually sent four deputies, but only one or two came from the newer towns. The number was determined by the General Court in accordance with the number of freemen living in the particular town.[55] On October 3, 1661, the General Court recommended that because of the growth of the Commonwealth the number of deputies sent by each town should be reduced by half, but it is doubtful if this suggestion was approved by the freemen, as twenty-four deputies were named as newly elected in the Court of Election held on May 15, 1662, compared with the twenty-three recorded at the Court of Election held in 1661, one year before the suggestion.[56]

Only after the Charter was granted was the number of deputies reduced to two for all the towns.

The constitution guaranteed the deputies the right to meet before the General Court assembled to discuss among themselves matters pertinent to the welfare of the Commonwealth or to challenge the credentials of any colleague. If a majority of the deputies agreed that an irregularity had occurred in an election, they could present the case to the whole Court, which could then fine the intruder and his town and order a new election if he were found guilty. The deputies were also granted the right to fine any of their number for disorderly conduct or absenteeism. If they could not collect the fine, they could refer the problem to the treasurer of the Commonwealth. Shortly after the adoption of the Fundamental Orders, the General Court voted to free the deputies from watches, warding, and training—onerous but necessary duties under the circumstances.

Under the Fundamental Orders the magistrates and deputies sat and debated together as a unicameral body, but voted separately. The deputies were specifically granted an equal voice with the magistrates in Connecticut on February 5, 1644/45, when the Court voted that "no act shall passe or stand for a law, wch is not confirmed both by the mayor part of the said Magistrats, and by the mayor p^{r}te of the deputyes there p^{r}sent in Court, both Magistrats and deputyes being alowed, eyther of thē, a negatiue voate." [57] In Massachusetts Bay the General Court was divided into two houses in 1644, but Connecticut retained its unicameral legislature until 1698, long after the Charter had replaced the original constitution.

The first Court of Election was held under the Fundamental Orders on April 11, 1639, and at it the freemen chose John Haynes governor, Roger Ludlow deputy governor, Edward Hopkins secretary, and Thomas Welles treasurer. Three men were elected to the magistracy besides the governor, deputy governor, secretary, and treasurer. They were joined by twelve deputies, or "committees," as they continued to be called through January 1639/40.[58] Throughout the period of the Fundamental Orders legislation always resulted from the Courts of Election; it was recorded under the list of the newly chosen officers. The Courts of Election continued to be held in April until the order was amended on April 9, 1646, when the "Freemen finding yt inconuenient to attend the Court of Election the second Thursday in Aprill, haue ordered yt for hereafter to be keept the third Thursday in May." [59] The Courts had undoubtedly conflicted with spring planting.

The General Court of Connecticut, thus composed of the officers of the Commonwealth, the magistrates, and the deputies, possessed the exclusive power to

> make lawes or repeale thē, to graunt leuyes, to admitt of Freemen, dispose of lands vndisposed of, to seuerall Townes or pʳsons, and also shall haue power to call ether Courte or Magestrate or any other pʳson whatsoeuer into question for any misdemeanour, and may for just causes displace or deale otherwise according to the nature of the offence; and also may deale in any other matter that concerns the good of this cor͂mon welth, excepte election of Magestrats, wᶜʰ shall be done by the whole boddy of Freemen.[60]

The General Court was the supreme power in Connecticut throughout the period of the Fundamental Orders. It outranked all of its component parts. In it rested the combined authority of England's Parliament, King's Bench, Common Pleas, Chancery, High Commission, Star Chamber, and the High Court of Admiralty and the multitude of lesser courts. From the first settlements, not the towns, but the General Court of the Commonwealth, the federal government, predominated over the local institutions.

The General Court inherited the authority formerly wielded by its predecessors, the Massachusetts Bay Commission and the General Corte. Before the Fundamental Orders they had been entrusted with Connecticut's legislative and judicial powers and their moderator served as the Commonwealth's executive. Uniting the three branches of government into a single body and endowing it with extensive prerogatives was in strict accordance with the philosophy of government that Thomas Hooker had expounded in his letter to Governor Winthrop of Massachusetts in the fall of 1638, when he wrote that, reserving "smaller matters, which fall in occasionally in common course, to a lower counsel, in matters of greater consequence, which concern the common good, a general counsel, chosen by all, to transact businesses which concern all, I conceive, under favour, most suitable to rule and most safe for relief of the whole." [61]

The General Court of the Commonwealth possessed virtually the same powers the General Court of Massachusetts Bay had enumerated for itself on May 14, 1634, which is not surprising when the membership of the Connecticut Court is compared with the Bay's Court sitting in the spring of 1634. Roger Ludlow, John Haynes, William Goodwin, George Wyllys, George Hull, William Spenser, John Talcott, and William Phelps sat on the 1634 Court in the Bay. By 1638 Ludlow, Haynes, Phelps, Hull, and Talcott were serving on the last General Corte recorded before the Fundamental Orders were adopted, and in April 1639, Phelps, Wyllys, and Spenser were elected to the first General Court authorized by the new constitution.[62]

In the Fundamental Orders the inhabitants and residents of Connecticut bestowed on the General Court the authority to pass the requisite laws for the Commonwealth and to repeal them. The Court regulated the economy of Connecticut by approving monopolies of the trade in Indian corn and beaver and by establishing the day on which the weekly market should be held in Hartford. It provided for the defense of the Commonwealth by arming the inhabitants whenever the Dutch or Indians became menacing and saw that Connecticut sent representatives to the meetings of the United Colonies. It admitted individual freemen or expelled them. In certain cases the General Court also acted as a court of justice in civil and criminal causes. There was no clear line dividing the judicial jurisdiction of the General Court from that of the Particular Court. The first fundamental empowered the governor and the magistrates, without the deputies, "to administer iustice according to the Lawes here established, and for want thereof according to the rule of the word of God." A court comparable to the Particular Court had already been held on November 1, 1636, under the Massachusetts Bay Commission.

The General Court reigned supreme over both towns and individuals. It fined Saybrook and Norwalk each 40 shillings in 1655 for failing to submit their grand lists. Individuals living in the Commonwealth of Connecticut fell under its watchful eye. On several occasions the Court took action against persons living outside its jurisdiction. A man's position in the Commonwealth did not protect him from the wrath of the General Court. Roger Ludlow, Connecticut's first citizen under the Massachusetts Bay Commission and the General Corte, the probable author of the constitution and in the fall of 1639 deputy governor of Connecticut, was fined 5 shillings that September for leaving Connecticut without the Court's permission. At its next session the Court refused to accept his apology and in a huff sent a committee to Uncoway (Fairfield) to investigate his attempts at establishing a settlement there.[63]

Again striking at famous names, the General Court in May 1649 ordered a warrant issued for the arrest of William Hallet and Mistress Elizabeth Feake, whom it considered guilty of the "fowle sin of adultery," and ordered that they appear in Hartford before the next session of the Particular Court. That Mistress Feake was the niece of John Winthrop, governor of Massachusetts Bay, and the first cousin of John Winthrop, Jr., made little difference. Nor did the fact that her first husband was insane and that no court in Connecticut would grant her a divorce on these grounds. Their questionable marriage offended Puritan morals.[64]

The Fundamental Orders thus in concrete terms defined the electorate, the officers, and the General Court. The final fundamental then provided a method for dividing the taxes levied by the General Court equitably among the towns. The concluding notation on the constitution was simply "14th January, 1638, the 11 Orders abouesaid are voted." The Fundamental Orders were not signed, and no means of amendment was specified.

Following the constitution, the oaths of office for the governor, magistrates, and constables were written into the colonial records. Thomas Hooker regarded the oath as a covenant between the officer, the Commonwealth, and God. It was a further extension of the covenants of the churches and the civil covenant and was customarily required both in Massachusetts Bay and Connecticut of an officer-elect before he was permitted to perform the duties of the office to which he had been chosen. In these covenants there was no allegiance sworn to any outside authority. The constables, for instance, specifically swore to uphold the peace of the "Commonwealth." There was no reference to the King, Parliament, or General Court of the Bay. The oaths excluded Jews, Quakers, and atheists, as non-Trinitarians, because of the allegiance sworn in the oath of fidelity, thus enforcing the Congregational domination.[65] The oaths of office formed a logical complement and also conclusion to the Fundamental Orders of Connecticut, re-emphasizing the covenants which united the Commonwealth.

Although no means of amendment was prescribed by the constitution, the Fundamental Orders were altered several times between 1639 and 1662. The majority of the amendments were effected by act of the General Court. The first by the Court, in November 1643, redefined the requirements of the admitted inhabitants by insisting that they first meet the approval of a majority in their own towns. The second, in February 1644/45, revised the order regarding the composition of the General Court to permit the governor or deputy governor, three magistrates, and a majority of the deputies to conduct business; the tenth fundamental had required the presence of four magistrates. To this amendment was added a third, in February 1644/45: the provision that no law was binding unless it had the vote of a majority of the deputies as well as of the magistrates, thereby giving both bodies veto power. The fourth amendment, in April 1646, forbade anyone's voting in a town or the Commonwealth if he had been fined or whipped for a scandalous offence unless reinstated by the Court. The fifth, in May 1647, modified the membership requirements for each Particular Court by providing that the governor or deputy governor, plus two magistrates, or three magistrates alone could sit as the Court. In February and April 1656/57 the constitutional requirements for both freemen and admitted inhabitants were made more explicit. The freemen had to have the approval of a majority of the deputies in their town and then the vote of the General Court; the admitted inhabitants were required to be of age, to have held office, or to possess an estate worth £30. The final amendment by the General Court came in March 1658/59, when the Court made the qualifications for freemanship more stringent by adding the age and personal-estate qualification.[66]

Three times the freemen themselves amended the Fundamental Orders. First, in April 1646, they in effect changed the date of the Court of Election from the second Thursday in April until the third in May. Then in May 1654, faced with an emergency situation, they acted to provide for the election of a moderator by the magistrates in the absence of the governor and deputy governor. In the spring of 1660 the freemen at the request of the General Court again voted to amend the constitution by removing the provision that no man could succeed himself as governor.[67] The constitution served as Connecticut's fundamental law from 1639 until 1662, but it was not rigidly immutable.

This was the form of government that the Congregationalists in Connecticut, drawing upon their experience in England, in Massachusetts Bay, and on the Connecticut River from 1633 until early 1639, wrote into their constitution in an effort to maintain the religious, social, and political cohesion of the river towns and to insure a harmonious environment for their churches. The general form of government had been in existence since the creation of the Massachusetts Bay Commission, but informality gave way to formality with the adoption of the Fundamental Orders.

The new constitution of the Commonwealth sanctioned an advanced, but not what would have been considered a radical, form of government in the seventeenth century. Connecticut conformed to tradition by having its church and state closely associated. The Congregational churches were state churches, even though their status was not made explicit in the Fundamental Orders. More novel were the responsibility of the civil officers to their constituencies and the uniting of three independent settlements into a federation. In preserving the rights of the freemen and deputies and omitting the religious qualification for all officials except the governor, Connecticut progressed one step further toward democracy than had Massachusetts Bay.

But the government sanctioned by the Fundamental Orders was not the democracy that has been portrayed by historians attempting to find precedents for the Constitution of the United States or commemorating two- or three-hundredth anniversaries of the Fundamental Orders. The role of "the people" has been misinterpreted too often. In Connecticut between 1633 and 1662 many persons possessed no civil rights except those expressly granted them by the constitution or the General Court. There was

no consideration of the equality of all men, nor was there toleration of any religion except Congregationalism. True, the officers
were elected from below, rather than being the appointees of the
King or Lord Protector or their staff; but when two-thirds of the
admitted inhabitants in Connecticut were not allowed to become
freemen, the Commonwealth could hardly be considered a democracy in the modern connotation.

To those ruled by the government defined by the constitution,
but not allowed to participate in it, Thomas Hooker taught obedience. In no uncertain terms on December 26, 1638, only nineteen
days before the adoption of the Fundamental Orders, he preached:

> doctrine   that men should be carried out of conscience to yield subjec-
> tion unto superior power
>
> 2 doctrine   that this conscientious subjection is marvelous useful
>
> use of instruction   those that are in subjection should take the oath of
> fidelity   here were multiple arguments to prove this
>
> 2 use of exhortation   1 to governors   2ly to all
>
> 1st to 1st   they should punish those that are opposite to subjection
>
> 2ly   to all they should be subject for conscience sake.[68]

The individual was subordinate to the community and its governors and bound by the law of the towns and the Commonwealth.
Not his rights and liberties, but his obedience to society, were
stressed in these Congregational communities.

The government ordered by the Fundamental Orders, like the
government of the Congregational churches, was a mixed institution composed of democratic, aristocratic, and monarchical elements closely aligned with the churches. The admitted inhabitants
of the towns and the freemen of the Commonwealth constituted
the democratic aspect of the political state. They were the "people"
of Connecticut. Just as the body of the churches was composed
only of visible saints until the acceptance of the Halfway Covenant, so the body of the state included only men of property,
honest in their actions, righteous in their attitudes, and acceptable
to this Congregational community. It was they or their representatives who had united in the civil covenant. The admitted inhabitants were permitted by the Fundamental Orders the privilege of
choosing deputies in their own town meetings to send to the General Courts. The freemen were granted the right to attend the

Courts of Election and cast their ballots for the magistrates. Occasionally they could vote on certain issues and in an extreme situation act as a General Court. Following the election, the power of the electorate was delegated to their representatives. The common people in Connecticut had no more voice than had they in England or the Bay. It would have been inconsistent for Calvinists to be democrats and permit more power than this to reside with the people.

The political aristocracy of Connecticut under the Fundamental Orders consisted of the magistrates and deputies sitting in the General Court. They exercised the executive, legislative, and judicial powers of the Commonwealth. The real power resided in the hands of this minority. The governor was prevented from serving two successive terms throughout most of the Commonwealth period, and the new candidates for the magistracy had to be nominated at a session of the General Court prior to the Court of Election, but year after year the same names appeared in the leading offices of the Commonwealth to govern Connecticut.

God was recognized in the covenant of the Fundamental Orders as the sovereign of the Commonwealth; from Him the Commonwealth derived its authority. Neither did the Puritans of Connecticut pledge allegiance to Charles I, as had their contemporaries in Plymouth and Massachusetts Bay, nor was their state the creation of a joint-stock company and consequently subject to the orders of a nonresident corporation. God alone guided the men of Connecticut in their state and in their churches. He had urged them to unite in a civil covenant, aided them in the choice of their civil officers, and assisted their officers in conducting the government. He directed them in the development of their church polity, and He had guided them in creating a comparable temporal government to preserve their Congregational churches. They felt that He would then teach them to enact a law to govern the community and to create a judicial system capable of interpreting the law of the Commonwealth.

IV

Law and the Courts

EVEN in the tiny God-fearing, morally oriented communities of
Connecticut in the middle of the seventeenth century, law and
justice were essential. Living in the wilderness, the Congregationalists could not survive in a state of nature, unbound by law other
than natural law, totally unrestricted in their actions by a known,
written law. Laws regulating the cultivation of the land were immediately necessary to transform forests into fields and to prevent
the greedy from encroaching on his weaker neighbor. Laws were
necessary to enforce the Puritan code and to uphold the supremacy
of the Congregational churches. Connecticut's law during the Commonwealth era evolved as an amalgamation of positive law, immutable law revealed to man directly by God, divine law found in
the Bible, and the selected parts of English and Massachusetts Bay
law that suited the demands of the Congregationalists. The law,
both public and private, that emerged was kinetic in character,
adaptable always to the changing needs of the maturing state.

When the inhabitants and residents of Windsor, Hartford, and
Wethersfield agreed in the preamble of the Fundamental Orders
to unite, they recognized the necessity of having a sympathetic
but effective government to protect their union and the churches
for whose sake they had immigrated to the Connecticut Valley. To
implement the governmental institutions the constitution provided
for both a legal and a judicial system to meet the exigencies of
the Commonwealth. It invested the General Court with the exclusive right to enact the requisite laws for the Congregational communities. The Fundamental Orders not only provided for a court
of magistrates, the Particular Court, to administer justice but also

supplied the means to enforce the laws and the court decisions. The Puritans appreciated man's frailties and understood the need for statute as well as organic law.

Connecticut is fortunate because the records of the General Courts, the Particular Courts, and many of the town courts are extant. This has not always been the case. The records of the General Court have always been available, but not of the Particular Court. Until 1861 the original Volume II was nowhere to be found. Today the records of the Particular Court through the December 6, 1649, session are interspersed between the minutes of the General Court in the *Public Records of the Colony of Connecticut*, Volume I. But when J. Hammond Trumbull edited the first volume in 1850, he believed that the records of the Particular Court from January 1649/50 to 1663 were irretrievably lost. However, Charles J. Hoadly by chance discovered them in 1861 in New York City. Many years later, the Society of Colonial Wars in the State of Connecticut, in conjunction with the Connecticut Historical Society, published the complete set of minutes of the Particular Court from 1639 until 1663 as Volume XXII of the *Collections of the Connecticut Historical Society* (Hartford, 1928).

Unfortunately, *A General History of Connecticut, from its First Settlement Under George Fenwick, Esq. to its Latest Period of Amity with Great Britain*, "that most unscrupulous and malicious of lying narratives," [1] has also survived. It was written anonymously by the Reverend Samuel Peters, a graduate of Yale University who was later ordained as an Episcopal clergyman. Peters fled to London as a Tory during the American Revolution and there published his attack in 1781 with all its acrimony and all its inaccuracies. Peters' fictions have damned the reputation of the laws of Connecticut under the Fundamental Orders. It was Peters who dubbed them the "Blue Laws," implying that they imposed a Hawthornesque discipline and enforced a stern and gloomy way of life, rigidly ruled according to a prim and proper code of behavior. True, the laws of the General Court were intended to preserve the Puritan way of life, but Puritanism was not devoid of pleasure and happiness. Many of the infractions of the moral code were punished with only minimal sentences, particularly when the sinner was willing to repent publicly. The standards of Connecticut's Puritans should not be construed as vastly different from those generally accepted in contemporary England.

Upon their removal from the jurisdiction of Massachusetts Bay, the planters of Connecticut suddenly found themselves outside the law which had been laid down by the General Court of the Bay to bind and regulate the community there, just as they and the other settlers in the Bay had previously found themselves outside the jurisdiction of English law. During the first few years of the Commonwealth the General Court of Connecticut enacted orders at random to satisfy the immediate needs of the river towns. Then, in 1642, the Court adopted a list of twelve capital crimes. A complete code of existing law, the Ludlow Code, was ratified in 1650. In these enactments the men of Connecticut borrowed heavily from the Bay's Body of Liberties of 1641 and its Laws and Liberties of 1648, from Mosaic Law and from English civil and ecclesiastical law; but empirically and sparingly they adapted their heritage to the demands of the wilderness.

On December 1, 1642, the General Court of Connecticut enumerated the twelve crimes that warranted the death penalty: idolatry, witchcraft, blasphemy, murder with malice aforethought in two forms, bestiality, sodomy, adultery, rape, kidnaping, perjury with the intent to cause a man to lose his life, and treason. All but the twelfth, "If any man shall conspire or attempte any inuasion, insurrection or rebellion against the Com̃on welth, he shall be put on death," were accompanied by specific references to the Pentateuch.[2] Alexis de Tocqueville, writing in the middle of the nineteenth century, was unable to comprehend the significance of the biblical references. Puzzled, he commented that the "legislators of Connecticut begin with the penal laws, and, strange to say, they borrow their provisions from the text of Holy Writ."[3] This was not at all strange for men of the seventeenth century; it was perfectly logical that Puritans who depended so completely on the Bible as a guide for every phase of their lives should turn to it to justify taking a man's life. The Fundamental Orders had explicitly stated that the courts should "administer iustice according to the Lawes here established, and for want thereof according to the rule of the word of God."[4]

For its capital laws Connecticut was directly indebted to the

Bay. Only the ninth crime, "Yf any man shall forcebly and w^{th}out consent rauishe any mayd or woman that is lawfully maried or contracted, he shall be put to death," was not copied from the capital crimes enumerated in the Bay's Body of Liberties of 1641. The Connecticut list differed by omitting the Bay's punishment of manslaughter in anger or passion with death, and the second part of its law against treason.[5] Worthy of special note is the fact that in Connecticut an act constituted treason only if it threatened the Commonwealth of Connecticut. The English King, Parliament, and nation had been excluded from the covenant of the preamble of the Fundamental Orders; they were therefore omitted from the jurisdiction of Connecticut's legal and judicial systems.

At the time when the capital laws were being enacted the General Court had recommended a harsh term in the house of correction for any child or servant convicted of incorrigibleness, but hesitated to suggest the death penalty. At the same time it requested that Governor Wyllys and Magistrates Haynes, Hopkins, Welles, and Phelps together with the elders of the churches investigate the sins of cursing parents, incorrigibleness, ravishment, contempt of the ordinances, lying, and breach of promise and present a draft of their suggestions at the next session of the Court.[6]

With the adoption of the Code it became a capital crime for any youngster over sixteen to curse or strike his parents unless it could be proved that the parents had neglected his education or had provoked the insult. The death penalty could also be imposed on a son over sixteen who refused to obey his parents and on a triple offender for burglary committed on Sunday. Such apparent harshness added spice to Peters' assault on Connecticut's Congregationalists, but in fact the death penalty was never served on any child during the period of the Fundamental Orders. The laws stood as a threat to reinforce parental discipline over a rebellious younger generation.

The three supplementary crimes, added to the original twelve by the Code of 1650, brought the number of capital offenses to fifteen by the end of the period of the Fundamental Orders. John Cotton had suggested twenty-four crimes punishable by death in his "Moses his Judicialls" of 1635,[7] while in England at the beginning of the reign of James I there were thirty-one. By 1819 the number in England had increased to 223, 176 of which were without benefit of clergy. The practice in New England was a marked improvement over that in old England, where even larceny involving twelve pence was a capital crime.[8]

In spite of there being twelve capital crimes between 1642 and 1650 and fifteen after the adoption of the Ludlow Code, the death penalty seldom was pronounced before 1662. There are no recorded hangings of murderers during the period of the Fundamental Orders, although there were several trials involving suspects. At some time between February 14, 1643/44, and April 1644, an undated session of the Particular Court found John Ewe guilty by misadventure in the death of Thomas Scott. This was the first heard under the new code. Instead of the death penalty, Ewe received a fine of £5 to be paid to the Commonwealth and another of £10 payable to Scott's widow.[9] The unsavory Aron Starke escaped with his life only because his trial before the Particular Court was heard in July 1640, over two years before bestiality became a capital crime. This character had previously been brought before the Court for "vncleane practises" and sentenced to stand in the pillory, be whipped, and have an "R" branded onto his cheek for attacking Mary Holt. The Court ordered Starke to pay £10 to Mary's parents or to the Commonwealth and then marry her. John Nubery was found guilty of buggery by the jury in the Particular Court in December 1647, but the records do not reveal his sentence. At that time it should have been to the gallows.[10]

The leading families of Connecticut became involved in the next trial for homicide. In December 1651 the grand jury found Thomas Allyn, the son of Matthew Allyn, responsible for the accidental death of Henry Stiles. The question put to him asked if he did "suddenly negligently, Carelessly Cock thy peece, and Carry the peece Just behinde thy neighbo^r, wch peece being Charged and going of in thine hand slew thy neighbo^r to the great dishono^r of God, breach of the peace, and loss of a member of this Comon wealth." The jury found Allyn guilty of homicide by misadventure, fined him £20, and put him on probation for twelve months, during which time he could not bear arms. His father was bound in a recognizance of £10 for his good behavior. One year later, in December 1652, the Particular Court freed the

Allyns from their recognizance and allowed Thomas to attend training, watching, and warding once more.[11]

Again, in June 1655 the Particular Court met and a jury was sworn for the trial of William Taylor. Taylor was indicted for beating James Graves to death. The jury found him guilty of inflicting the beating, but not of causing death. Three years later, in October 1658, the Particular Court met specifically to try Katherin Boston, of New London, on the grounds that she had poisoned her husband, John Boston, the previous June. The jury found her not guilty, but fined her £10. The number of trials for murder during the Commonwealth period is surprisingly small.[12]

Alleged witches were the only other suspects brought to trial in Connecticut for a capital crime. Before 1662 there were twelve indictments. In each case the trial was to the jury. The General Court in Massachusetts Bay had ordered in 1634 that no trial involving a capital crime should be heard without the presence of a jury. Connecticut adopted this rule in practice, although it was not required by law.

The first trial for witchcraft was held on May 26, 1647. Alse Young, of Windsor, was tried, but there is no documentary evidence of the Court's decision. Next accused of "familliarity with the Deuill" was Mary Johnson, of Wethersfield, who was arraigned in Hartford the following year, found guilty, and promptly hanged. John Carrington, a carpenter from Wethersfield, and his wife, Joane, were brought to trial on February 20, 1650/51. Joane's indictment, delivered in March, charged that "not hauing the feare of God before thine eyes thou hast Interteined familliarity with Sathan the great Enemy of God and mankinde and by his helpe hast done workes aboue the Course of Nature for wch both according to the Lawes of God, and the Established Lawe of this Common wea[lth] thou deseruest to dye." John Carrington's indictment was separate, but in virtually the same form. Both Carringtons were executed.[13]

Later in 1651 Governor Haynes and Magistrates Cullick and Clark went to Stratford to try Goody Bassett. They found her guilty of witchcraft. In 1653 Goodwife Knapp was tried and executed in Fairfield. The next poor woman hounded as a witch was brought to trial on November 28, 1654. Lydea Gilburt, of

Windsor, was found guilty by the jury of conspiring with the devil to cause the death of Henry Stiles, whom Thomas Allyn had accidentally shot, and she was sentenced to die. Over three years later, in March 1657/58, Elizabeth Garlick, a servant of Lion Gardiner and the wife of Joshua Garlick, was arrested in Easthampton. She was held by the local magistrates until the town meeting could determine whether the town authorities had the power to hear a capital offense. At the meeting it was decided that capital crimes were outside the jurisdiction of the local court. A committee was then appointed to escort Goodwife Garlick to Hartford for trial. The Particular Court of Connecticut acquitted her because of insufficient evidence on May 5, 1658. The jury on October 9, 1661, reported that it strongly suspected that Nicholas and Margaret Jennings, of Saybrook, were guilty of conspiring with the devil to cause several deaths, but could not reach an agreement. Finally, the Particular Court indicted Andrew and Mary Sanford on June 6, 1662, but the jury, unable to prove Andrew guilty, decided on June 13 that only Mary was guilty as charged.[14]

The Puritans in Connecticut succumbed to the witchcraft mania that spread throughout the Christian world during the seventeenth century. The Congregationalists believed that the powers of the devil could be executed by human witches. Had not the Bible commanded in Exodus 22:18, "Thou shalt not suffer a witch to live"? Although witchcraft constituted a deadly sin, Connecticut's juries acted rationally, acquitting several of the accused because of inconclusive evidence. The death sentences were carried out mercifully by hanging; there were no burnings at the stake in early Connecticut. Not until 1692 did Connecticut yield to the malicious gossips in its midst and permit the fear of witches to get out of proportion.

Eight years after the compilation of the capital crimes, the entire body of Connecticut law was codified. On October 10, 1639, soon after the Fundamental Orders had been ratified, the General Court took the first steps toward providing the Commonwealth with a code when it ordered "that Mr. Willis, Mr. Webst[r] and Mr. Spencer shall review all former orders and lawes and record such of them as they conceave to be necessary for publique con-

cernement, and deliver them into the Secretaryes hands to be published to the severall Townes, and all other orders that they see
cause to omitt to be suspended vntill the Court take further order."
Later in the same session the Court requested its secretary to provide a copy of all the existing penal and general laws within
twenty days after its adjournment.[15] Recognition of their right to
a known law had not yet been won by the deputies in Massachusetts Bay.

By April 9, 1646, the General Court had determined that the
laws of Connecticut should actually be codified and an end put
to the handing down of arbitrary sentences by itself and the Particular Court, determined at their own discretion. On that date it
voted that "Mr. Ludlowe is desiered to take some paynes in drawing forth a body of Lawes for the gouernment of this Comon
welth, & p^rsent th̄e to the next Generall Court, and if he can
prouide a man for his occations while he is imployed in the said
searuice, he shalbe paid at the Country chardge." But Ludlow was
busy in Fairfield and had not accomplished his task by the October
session of this Court. The Court was growing impatient, and to
prod him along added to its records of May 25, 1647, that when
"Mr. Ludlowe hath p^rfected a body of lawes as the Court hath
desiered him, it is the mynd of the Court that he should, besids
the paying the hyer of a man, be further considered for his
paynes." [16]

Sometime before May 1650 Roger Ludlow did complete the
code. In its February 5, 1650/51, session, the General Court ordered that "the Secretary [John Cullick] shall bee allowed and
paid the sum̄ of six pounds, being in p^rt of payment for his
great paines in drawing out and transcribing the country orders,
concluded and established in May last." [17] However, there is no
written record of the debates over the Code and its final ratification
in the minutes of the General Court for May 1650. The minutes
of the sessions of the Court held on the sixteenth and twenty-first
of the month infuriatingly make no reference to the Code.

Because Roger Ludlow had been requested by the General
Court to draw up a code of the Commonwealth's laws, he has long
been known as the "Father of Connecticut Jurisprudence." He was
lauded for his originality and for his great service to Connecticut

in the biography written by John M. Taylor in 1900. Charles W. Burpee, misreading the records of February 1650/51, lamented the fact that for four years' efforts Ludlow received only £6. William A. Beers made the same error and used this quotation to prove that Ludlow was the author of the Code, not noticing that the man paid was the secretary of the Court, John Cullick, rather than Ludlow.[18] There is no evidence that Ludlow received any compensation for his labors.

Ludlow's reputation was dealt a blow in 1929, when Max Farrand discovered the Massachusetts Bay Laws and Liberties of 1648. Until 1929 the Laws and Liberties were unknown to modern historians; they had not been carefully preserved in the records of the General Court of the Bay. After they came to light, Haskins and Ewing compared the Ludlow Code with the Massachusetts code and found that not only the capital crimes had been taken from the Massachusetts Bay Body of Liberties of 1641 and the remainder was original but twenty-two provisions were virtually identical to those in the Massachusetts code, thirty-six had been used with only slight variation, and of the seventy-eight provisions in the Ludlow Code only twenty were original. Sixty-six of the titles in the Bay Code were omitted.[19] Even the alphabetical arrangement of the sections in the Ludlow Code was borrowed from the Body of Liberties and the Laws and Liberties.

Ironically, William Pynchon, of Springfield, had written to Governor Winthrop of Massachusetts Bay on October 19, 1648, that when "Mr. Ludlo lay at my howse he tould me that he saw two sheets of the orders printed, & he did much blame the meanesse of their framing & contriuinge, & wished they might be corrected before any coppies were sent into other parts. But often tymes it fals out that a man may be one of the 20 that will find fault, & yet be none of the 20 that will mend them."[20] Pynchon underestimated Ludlow. Ludlow, while copying extensively the Massachusetts Bay precedents, did do something about the law of Connecticut.

The Ludlow Code is now found at the end of Volume II of the *Public Records of the Colony of Connecticut*.[21] Prefixed to it is a copy of the Fundamental Orders. New laws were recorded as they were passed either under the proper title or at the end of the Code. Ludlow's classification was retained until the middle of the nineteenth century, and in 1900 fifty-eight of the original seventy-eight provisions still remained in effect in Connecticut. That Connecticut should produce a code soon after its founding was entirely in keeping with the practice in the other English colonies. Bermuda and Virginia each had a code; Plymouth codified its laws in 1636, followed by Massachusetts Bay in 1641 and 1648, Rhode Island in 1647, and New Haven in 1655. As Benjamin Trumbull said, with the adoption of the Ludlow Code in 1650 "Connecticut now had the appearance of a well regulated commonwealth." [22]

The English heritage of the Connecticut Puritans was as obvious in the Ludlow Code as were the Law of Moses and the Massachusetts Codes. Common-law terms like "barratry," "escheat," "primer seizin," "specialty," "wardship," and the recognition of the individual's right to due process, an open trial, trial by jury, and decisions based on precedent appear in the Code of 1650 in Connecticut. Court procedure followed the common-law example of the declaration, the plea, and then the answer. Connecticut's methods of providing for the poor also came to a great extent from England's Statute of Artificers of 1563 and its Poor Law of 1601.

But English common law and statute law were not transported across the Atlantic Ocean *in toto*. In Connecticut, common law was improved on by eliminating many of the obsolete technicalities, avoiding the expenses of attending court for petty suits, and requiring that trials be held without delay. Primogeniture was abolished, and debtors were not arbitrarily imprisoned. Civil liberties were preserved to a greater extent than in England; servants, Indians, and freemen enjoyed equal protection under the law. Double jeopardy and confessions obtained by torture were illegal, the testimony of several sworn witnesses in the presence of the accused was necessary before a person could be convicted of a capital crime, and appeals from convictions for small or major crimes were more readily granted. Connecticut's debt to the Law of Moses is particularly obvious in the capital laws and moral code in general. In many instances the Bay had adapted its biblical and English heritage to its own needs, and its solutions were in turn transformed to meet the demands Connecticut's Congregationalists imposed.

The Code of 1650 begins with a preamble stating the necessity for preserving the tranquillity and stability of both churches and Commonwealth by protecting "the free fruition of such Libberties, Immunities, Privileges, as Humanity, Civillity and Christianity, call for, as due to euery man in his place and proportion, without Impeachm^t and infringement." [23] Then follows the remarkable passage guaranteeing

> that no mans life shall bee taken away, no mans honor or good name shall bee stained, no mans person shall bee arrested, restrained, banished, dismembered nor any way punnished; no man shall bee deprived of his wife or children, no mans goods or estate shall bee taken away from him, nor any wayes indamaged, vnder colour of Law or countenance of Authority, vnless it bee by the vertue or equity of some express Law of the Country warranting the same, established by a Generall Courte, and sufficiently published, or in case of the defect of a Law in any perticular case, by the word of God.[24]

Here in essence is a written guarantee of life, liberty, and property for each member of the Congregational community promulgated forty years before John Locke's *Two Treatises of Government* (1690) and over one hundred and twenty-five years before Thomas Jefferson and the Declaration of Independence. But it is not the work of Ludlow. This passage was copied verbatim from the Massachusetts Bay Body of Liberties of 1641, written by the Reverend Nathaniel Ward, of Ipswich, in accordance with the deputies' determination to limit the power of the assistants over the individual. A similar fear of a dominant oligarchy prevailed on the Connecticut River.

The seventy-eight sections of the Ludlow Code were arranged alphabetically, but they may be examined more easily if considered topically. Each section is titled and contains a paragraph or even a page detailing the responsibilities of an office or the nature of a particular crime. Where infractions of the law are involved, specific fines, prison terms, or penalties like disfranchisement, banishment, or branding are clearly stated. Each settler in Connecticut knew in advance the risk he took when he broke the law.

The capital laws of the Commonwealth were united in the

Code under the obvious title, "Capitall Lawes." The first twelve
were identical to those proclaimed in Connecticut in December
1642, but to them were added the three already discussed: a third
conviction of burglary on the Sabbath; cursing or striking his parents by a child over sixteen, unless the parent had been negligent
in educating him or had provoked him; and refusal to obey his
parents by a "stubborne and rebellious sonne of sufficient yeares
and vnderstanding." These latter, like the original capital laws,
were followed by biblical references.[25]

Some of the sections defining the constitutional law of the Commonwealth are "Abillity," "Age," "Magistrates," "Marshall,"
"Oaths," "Records," "Secretary," "Treasurer," and "Voates." Unlike the capital laws, they are scattered throughout the Code.
These sections serve to describe the powers and responsibilities of
the branches of Connecticut's government in greater detail than
was possible in the Fundamental Orders. Of interest is the fact
that the legal age in the Commonwealth then as now was twenty-
one, while the age of understanding was sixteen and, particularly
in cases of lying, the age of discretion was considered fourteen
years.[26]

In Connecticut, as in England and the New England colonies
in the seventeenth century, the central government retained broad
regulatory powers over the economic life of the Commonwealth,
controlling everything from weights and measures to land tenure,
inheritance practices, agriculture, taxes, and debts. Economic reg-
ulation is not a phenomenon peculiar to the twentieth century. It
is a particularly obvious feature of the Code. Of special note, however, because it marked an epoch-making decision in Connecticut's
economic history, is the provision in the Code that "oure Lands
and Heritages shall bee free from all fynes and lycenses vppon
Alienations, and from all Harriotts, Wardships, Liveries, Primer
seizins, yeare, day and waste, escheats and forfeitures vppon the
death of parents or ancestors, bee they naturall, vnnaturall, casuall
or juditiall, and that for euer."[27] The medieval feudal economy
was not imported into Congregational Connecticut. This provision
sounded the death knell for any nobleman's dreams of migrating
to Connecticut and establishing himself as a hereditary landgrave
or baron, as happened in South Carolina. The King owned no

enormous tracts of land in the Commonwealth that he could disperse to his favorites, and during the Interregnum no one was interested in imposing such a system. To a great extent the disintegration of the feudal system in England had been directly responsible for driving many gentry, yeomen, and tenant farmers to Connecticut. At the dawn of the era of capitalism it was inconceivable that such an archaic economic system should be imposed. The leaders of the Commonwealth were determined that it should not be resurrected. Land in Connecticut was held without feudal restrictions, without even the token quitrent Virginia's landholders owed.

The first proprietors had purchased the title to the lands at Windsor from the River Indians in 1633 and 1635 and at Hartford and Wethersfield in 1636 and again in 1640, when Governor Haynes negotiated the purchase of Tunxis (Farmington) for the proprietors. These arrangements had to be renewed regularly because the Indians consistently misunderstood the terms of the original treaties and because the leadership in the tribe changed frequently. The King of England and Parliament had no share in these agreements and consequently no rights and privileges. Nor had any feudal lords power to exact feudal dues.

It is surprising that in the Ludlow Code more was not said about the inheritance practices in Connecticut than was covered in "Escheats." It was the other major divergency from the economic policies of England. Only mentioned in the section on escheats was the provision that if no heirs could be found, the goods and chattels were to be taken into the public treasury and kept until claimed.[28] In Connecticut both real and personal property bequeathed in wills fell under the jurisdiction of the Particular Court, not the ecclesiastical courts as in England. The first case of probate was recorded in September 1636; it concerned the difficult settlement of John Oldham's estate. Unlike the English courts, the Particular Court recognized wills presented by word of mouth, although as early as September 10, 1639, the General Court ordered that wills be recorded. Generally in Connecticut when a will existed, the townsmen were appointed by the Court as executors to take an inventory of the estate of the deceased and to identify his children and legatees. But the system was flexible. Thomas Hooker, for instance, made his wife, Susannah Hooker, the executrix of his estate. The executors and the Court insured that an estate was not wasted while the will was being probated, but like the Widow Hudgison, executrix of her husband's estate, they were liable for the estate's outstanding debts.[29]

Primogeniture in cases of intestacy never was practiced in Connecticut as it was in the South and in England, where large landed estates were more common. The Congregationalists had observed the practice of partible inheritance in Amsterdam and Leyden, on some manors in England, in Plymouth, and finally in Massachusetts Bay and felt it a more suitable solution to their needs.[30] After the townsmen had taken the inventory of the estate and paid the debts of the deceased, the Court determined the most equitable distribution of the remainder among the wife, children, and kindred. The method of division varied. It was not a hard and fast rule that the eldest son should receive a double portion when his father died intestate, but frequently he did, just as the eldest son had done in biblical times. Younger sons usually received a greater share than daughters in the division of an estate, the amount and percentage depending on the relative ages of the children and the size of the estate. Sometimes when young children were involved, the widow was awarded the power to administer the entire property with the proviso that she educate the children and leave the residue of the estate to them in the event of her death.[31]

The laws in the Ludlow Code provided that the economic needs of the churches and Commonwealth should be met by rates levied on the towns by the General Court and passed on by them to their inhabitants. Each resident, even though not a member of the church nor a voter in the Commonwealth, was expected to contribute his share voluntarily to satisfy the fiscal demands of the community. Anyone reluctant to donate what was considered his just proportion was subject to an assessment. Each town had a commissioner to evaluate the real and personal estate of every man over sixteen to determine whether he was contributing to the Commonwealth according to his ability. All men were also subject to a poll tax of two pence. Connecticut at this early date knew the justice of a graduated tax; artisans were taxed more heavily on their real and personal estate than were common laborers and workmen, while the sick, lame, and infirm were exempted altogether.[32]

The Code covered the very practical problems of collecting fines and taxes. The General Court levied the fines, assessments, and rates on the towns for the local officers to collect. The constables in the towns had blanket permission to enter houses or other buildings in order to secure a payment or to arrest an offender. They could also attach lands or persons. But they were warned not to seize the minimum requirement of bedding, tools, arms, household goods, or clothes from the offender and were liable for damages should they injure the person fined.[33]

The Congregationalists in Connecticut during this period had emigrated from England largely because of their opposition to the ecclesiastical policies of Archbishop Laud. Most of them had removed from Massachusetts Bay to Connecticut with the body of a church. The express purpose of the Fundamental Orders was to provide a civil government to preserve the Congregational churches. Therefore, as may be expected, the role of the government as the law-enforcement agency of the churches is plainly visible in the Code. The Commonwealth government was just as responsible for the First Table (the first four of the Ten Commandments, which defined man's duties to God) as for the Second Table (the last six commandments, covering man's responsibilities toward his fellow man). This obligation is clearly acknowledged in the section of the Code where the General Court had ordered

> that the Civill Authority heere established hath power and libberty to see the peace, ordinances and rules of Christe bee obserued in euery Church according to his word; as allso to deale with any Church member in a way of Ciuill [justice] notwithstanding any Church relation, office or interest, so it bee done in a Ciuill and not in an Eclesiasticall way: nor shall any Church censure degrade or depose any man from any Ciuill dignitye, office or authority hee shall haue in the Commonwealth.[34]

Conversely, this order also served to limit the churches' authority over the officers of the Commonwealth.

In the records of the Particular Court the language is infinitely more vehement in cases involving offenses against God's ordinances or His ministers than in cases of debt or trespass, for instance, and crimes committed on Sundays were treated with greater severity than those committed on weekdays. For contempt of the ministers or interruptions during the services, a first offender faced discipline by a civil magistrate at the lecture. His second offense merited a fine of £5 or punishment by standing in public for two hours on lecture day with a paper on his chest reading AN OPEN AND OB-STINATE CONTEMNER OF GODS HOLY ORDINANCES. The slanderous accusations against Mistress Hooker, Thomas Hooker's widow, and Elder William Goodwin, of the Hartford Church, so infuriated the members of the Particular Court in 1654 that the Court forced Mrs. Hooker's servant to confess to Webster and Stone that his report was nothing but lies and then to repeat his statements before the whole Court. The Court ordered him to post the enormous bond of £100 for his good behavior until its next meeting, to be whipped publicly immediately after the close of that day's session and on the next lecture day in Hartford, and to stand in the pillory.[35]

Absence from church on the Lord's day or on fast or feast days drew a fine of 5 shillings. For burglary committed on Sunday the criminal received in addition to the usual penalty for his first offense the loss of one of his ears. His other ear was cut off for his second theft, and for a third he could be put to death. Thomas Willkenson was committed to prison until the Court should see fit to release him for his disorderly conduct in the meetinghouse on the Sabbath. Peter Bussaker was sentenced to remain in prison until the next sermon, when he was to stand in the pillory, and, when the sermon was over, to be severely whipped in the presence of all the townsfolk. The Court further ordered the attachment of his entire estate for the payment of his creditors. Bussaker had raised the ire of the Puritans "for his fillthy and prophane expressions (viz. that hee hoped to meete some of the members of the Church in hell ere long, and hee did not question but hee should)!"[36]

The Commonwealth and towns exercised considerable authority over the affairs that might easily be considered within the realm of the churches. It was the General Court that ordered days of humiliation or of thanksgiving. The town meeting in Hartford saw that a new gallery was built on the meetinghouse in February 1644/45. When Matthew Allyn was excommunicated from the Church of Hartford, he petitioned the General Court for redress. The Hartford Church was sued on at least one occasion: for impounding the hogs of Henry Wolcott's father.[37] The General Court had the right to call synods, and it interceded repeatedly in the disputes in the Hartford, Middletown, and Wethersfield Churches between 1653 and 1659. Near the end of the period of the Fundamental Orders this tendency toward civil interference in ecclesiastical affairs increased. It was a reversion to the practice in the English parishes and was coincident with the coming of age of the second generation.

In Connecticut the civil courts, rather than church courts, dealt with the intellectual problems of the Commonwealth. The Ludlow Code specified that the townsmen were responsible for seeing that all children and apprentices could read the English language and were cognizant of the capital laws. The townsmen were accountable if the heads of families failed to catechize their servants and children weekly or if any masters and parents neglected to provide the children with an honest calling. Education was one of the basic concerns of the Puritan communities. The section "Schooles" begins:

> It being one chiefe project of that old deluder Sathan, to keepe men from the knowledge of the Scriptures, as in former times keeping them in an vnknowne tongue, so in these latter times by perswading them from the vse of Tongues, so that at least the true sence and meaning of the originall might bee clouded with false glosses of saint seeming deceiuers; and that Learning may not bee buried in the Graue of o^r Forefathers, in Church and Common wealth, the Lord assisting our indeauors,———.

The Court therefore ordered that every town of fifty householders provide a teacher for its children and that the parents or masters pay his salary. Every town of one hundred families or householders was required to maintain a grammar school, supported by land grants and taxes in order to prepare its boys for Harvard College.[38]

The Commonwealth collected funds for the support of Harvard, realizing the necessity of training a new generation of ministers in rhetoric, oratory, Greek, Latin, moral and natural philosophy, and the Bible to keep away "that old deluder Sathan." There were also dame schools for the girls. Books were so scarce at this time that it was rare for anyone except the ministers, the few professional people, and the wealthiest of its citizens to own any except the Bible.

The sections of the Code prescribing the white man's dealings with the Indians are also significant. The Indians were explicitly taken under the wing of the courts and their rights defended against infringements by the English. But in turn, they were severely punished for theft, murder, or trespass. Oddly enough, nowhere in the Code, except in the Capital Laws, is the reliance on the Law of Moses so great as in the sections dealing with the heathen Indian. The General Court warned its Indian neighbors that "if any hurte or injurye shall therevppon follow to any persons life or limbe, (though accidentall,) they shall pay life for life, limbe for limbe, wound for wound, and shall pay for the healing such wounds and other dammages. And for anythinge they steale, they shall pay double, and suffer such further punnishment as the Magistrates shall adiudge them." [39]

The Courts dealt fairly if strictly with the Indians when they came into conflict with their white neighbors. For example, the jury on the Particular Court of March 7, 1649/50, handed down its verdict that Nathaniel Ward and Andrew Warner pay Thomas Lord for caring for the squaw whose ear their dogs had bitten off. They were also ordered to pay the squaw two bushels of Indian corn. But, the Court added, the next Indians who clapped their hands at English dogs or threw stones at them to provoke them would have to pay the exact amount of corn back to Ward. The Particular Court settled spats between Indian and Indian, as when it ordered Papaqueeote to pay six fathoms of wampum to Jackstraw "for his Iniurious pulling of his haire from his head p the Roots." Again mediating in Indian quarrels, it ordered Petusho to pay Sepus three fathoms of wampum "for his Cruell Stamping uppon him to the efusion of blood at his mout." No Puritan ever dreamed that this would be one of the results of his crossing the ocean. [40]

The growing population increased the crime rate and the moral problems of the Commonwealth. To preserve the Puritan concept of morality, one of the first orders passed by the Massachusetts Bay Commission and in 1650 incorporated into the Ludlow Code was that young men could not visit families for extended visits without permission from the town, nor could bachelors live alone without the town's permission. Servants were not allowed to "giue, sell or truck, any commodity whatsoeuer" without permission from their master, and workmen were ordered to work the entire day. Men and ships could be impressed to apprehend runaway servants. Stubborn, "refrectary and discontented Seruants and Apprentices" who ran away from their masters were punished by having their term tripled or lengthened by adding three times their absence to their original term. Young bachelors and servants constituted the most disturbing elements in the community. All too frequently the Particular Court found itself troubled with discordant members of the society like John Bartlitt, whom it fined 40 shillings in June 1651 "for his great missdeameno^r in frequenting the howse and Company of goody Parsons of Wyndsor vnseasonably and dissorderly on the Sabath dayes and other times." Besides the young swains, idle persons troubled the Court, "common Coasters, vnproffitable fowlers, and Tobacko takers." [41]

In England marriages had been solemnized by the clergy, but in Connecticut they were performed by the civil magistrates. Not until 1694 did the ministry begin to officiate at weddings. Marriages fell under the jurisdiction of civil law, as they had in Holland since 1580 and Plymouth since 1621. Both John Robinson and William Bradford had attacked marriage by the clergy.[42] To prevent hasty decisions the General Court as early as April 10, 1640, had ordered that banns be posted at least eight days before the wedding. No marriages or even courtships were permitted in the Code without the approval of the parents, masters, or guardians if the couple were minors or servants. As a result, Will Chapman was sued in March 1653/54 for having "trespessed aginst the Saide order in an high nature going aboute to gaine the affectyons by way of marraid[ge] of one Elizabeth Bateman Sarvant to Cap: John Cullick & hath the Same laid diuers unsufferable Scandalls & reproaches upon the Said Cap: & his family & severall others." At the time Captain Cullick sat on the Court as a magistrate. The Court fined Chapman £5 for his breach of the order, for his other misdemeanors sent him to prison for fourteen days, and then had him post a recognizance of £40 for his good behavior until the next session of the Quarter Court.[43]

Divorce in the Commonwealth was so rare that it did not merit a section in the Code, but it did occur. In May 1655 the Court sympathetically voted to grant Goody Beckwith, of Fairfield, a divorce from her husband, Thomas, provided that the magistrates about to hold court at Stratford could be convinced that her husband had deserted her. In August 1657 the Court freed Robert Wade, of Saybrook, from his conjugal bonds because of his wife, Joan's, "vnworthy, sinfull, yea, unnaturall cariage towards him." She had refused to live with him either in Connecticut or in England for almost fifteen years. In another case the General Court on March 14, 1660/61, provided that if Sarah North did not hear from her husband by the end of the seventh year, she should be free from her marriage. In March 1661/62 it ordered a committee to examine a letter sent to Bridget Baxter by her husband to check on the authenticity of the handwriting. Her husband had deserted her and was then living in England. In May the Court granted Bridget the divorce and forbade her creditors to trouble her further, since they had reduced her to her last bed and the clothes on her back. With two countries to call home and the difficulties of communication, a husband could easily disappear. But Jasper Clemens, of Middletown, got caught. The General Court on May 17, 1660, learned that Clemens had a wife in England, even though he was about to marry Ellin Browne in Connecticut. The Court ordered that Ellin and Clemens not see each other until proof could be brought that his former marriage had been dissolved.[44]

Gaming, that is, playing shuffleboard in public, was penalized with a maximum fine of 20 shillings, as after February 1656/57 were the use of cards and dice. All were frowned upon as a waste of precious time. Innkeepers had to be licensed by the Commonwealth and were responsible for preventing drunkenness in their establishments. The river towns were each ordered to appoint an innkeeper and provide an ordinary and stable for strangers, but the sale of "wyne and strong water" was restricted to licensed retailers.[45] A limit at a sitting of a half pint of wine per person was set, and no drinking was allowed after 9 P.M. The restrictions were temporarily lifted for seamen who had just landed or were to embark early the next morning and for visitors to the Commonwealth. The penalties for "tipling" were severe. Thomas Newton was fined £5 for giving wine to Phillipe White when he had already had too much. In 1654 the General Court prohibited the importation of all liquor from Barbados, regardless of whether it was labeled "Rum" or "Kill Devil." Complete confiscation was the penalty, two-thirds going to the public treasury and one-third to the person who seized the booty. One wonders what the latter would do with his loot! Prohibition never covered wine and beer, although they were heavily taxed. They were more important in the Congregationalists' diets than water and milk.[46]

Condemned liars in Connecticut had to sit in the stocks, pay a fine, or suffer up to forty lashes if they were multiple offenders over fourteen years old. The Court ordered John Rushell, convicted of lying on two counts, to sit in the Hartford stocks for two hours and then in the Wethersfield stocks for another two hours on the next lecture day. He also had to provide security for his good behavior. Shaming the guilty proved to be an effective penalty. The younger children were reprimanded by their parents or masters. Swearing was considered a sin punishable by sitting in the stocks, and smoking was forbidden without either a doctor's permission or a license from the Court. This latter order seems more lenient than might be expected.[47]

Personal morals became the problem of the state because not all the population could be disciplined within the churches. Misdemeanors concerned with behavior like this of June 14, 1661, cluttered the records of the Particular Court: "Georg Burls for his Gross miscarriages in being drunk severall times and for swearing curseing and fighting and absenting from yᵉ ord: and taking Tobacco in time of ordnances is adiudged to goe forthwith to prison and to abide there til next Lecture and then to be put in yᵉ Stocks vntil aftʳ Lecture and then to be whipt on yᵉ naked body to yᵉ numbʳ of 15 stripes." There are countless entries like "John Drake complaines against John Bennett for saying he had intised and drawne away the affections of his daughter" and "John Griffin complaines against John Bennett for slaundering and defaming of him, by charging him with giuing in to the Courte false euidence and testimonye." Frequent are the entries, "Josiah Wilkinson P^t contr Georg Tong et his wife in an action of Sland^r accuseing him to be a whoremaster a Rogue and a liar to ye damadge of 200^l." The jury awarded Wilkinson £50 plus costs of court and shortly thereafter fined Tong another 10 shillings for cursing.[48] Plaintiffs and defendants minced no words even before the bench.

Even in Puritan Connecticut there were illegitimate children. The Particular Court applied its own form of preventive medicine when it ordered that "Mr Chest^rs Blackmore (hauing had a second base child) that shee shall bee this day corrected, and againe vpon a lecture day at Wethersfeild." [49] Little sympathy existed for such offenders. The well-being of the family was vital to the Puritans, and the desire to protect it prompted many of these laws.

The Ludlow Code contains numerous provisions for the protection of the individual in the community. In February 1643/44 the General Court forbade selling corn at less than the established price, to the detriment of the poor. The Particular Court made an early attempt to regulate the practice of medicine when the jury decided that Henry Wolcott was guilty of practicing "phisick" upon the son of Bray Rossiter, a doctor himself, and fined him £3 and costs of court. The General Court had the welfare of wives in mind when in September 1651 it ordered John Lord to provide his wife with clothes, as he had "left her destitute of a bed to lodge on, and very bare in apparell, to the indangering of her health." The Particular Court fined John Brookes 40 shillings for his inhumane carriage toward his wife. Similarly children were protected by the law. The Particular Court fined Skipper Richard Goodale 20 shillings payable to John North and 40 payable to his son for the cruel beating the skipper inflicted on the boy. Nor were servants to be abused by their masters. The Particular Court sentenced Edward Messenger to a severe beating in 1653 for unmercifully whipping his servant and then lying to extenuate his brutality. All men received equal treatment before the law, regardless of their station in life, just as all were equally eligible to join the churches.[50]

Individuals in the Congregational Commonwealth had rights, but they also had responsibilities. All men were required to perform watches and wards and to serve on juries when called. They also had to serve in the militia. Even after the 1638 treaty with the Pequots, Connecticut remained an armed camp. Round-the-clock watches were kept, and guards came armed to the meeting-house while others stayed outside to warn of attack. Each man over sixteen had to have a musket in constant readiness (or a suit-able substitute), half a pound of powder, two pounds of bullets or shot, and two fathoms (six feet each) of match for every match-lock, and to train ten days each year. It is only necessary to read the sections, "Guards at Meeting," "Millitary Affaires," and "Watches" to realize the fear of attack that never left these Puri-tans in peace.[51]

These and the remainder of the seventy-eight sections of the Ludlow Code provide a clear picture of the way this Congrega-tional community was intended to function after more than four-teen years' experience on the river. But law itself was not sufficient to regulate the Connecticut Commonwealth. To insure that the laws were obeyed and that justice prevailed, the Fundamental Orders provided for two courts: the General Court and the Par-ticular Court. The supreme court in Connecticut was the General Court. Below it ranked the Particular Court. The lower courts were the Commissioners' (or Magistrates') Courts and the Town Courts, which the constitution had not mentioned. Just as the Com-monwealth maintained its separation from England in its churches and in its constitution, so it did in its judicial system; there were no appeals from Connecticut to any of England's courts before 1662.

The courts in Connecticut represented a marked improvement over those in England which were far removed from the average Englishman by distance and expense. The Connecticut courts never quarreled over the type of law a case should be judged by, nor within whose jurisdiction it should lie. Each had its own specific realm where suits could be tried with a maximum amount of speed and care. The judges in the river towns never enjoyed the se-curity of a seat on the bench with life tenure. The judges in the General and Particular Courts, because they were magistrates, held office for only one year, while the commissioners retained their seats during the pleasure of the General Court. The town judges, as townsmen, served a term of one year unless re-elected.

The forms of action and procedure were a simplified version of contemporary English practice; the men making the laws and outlining court procedure were not familiar with the complex forms of English law. There was no necessity of importing the English processes for so tiny a society. In Connecticut, after an action was entered with the secretary of the Court according to common-law designation, such as debt, trespass, slander, case, or occasionally as an action of trovers, the secretary issued a warrant for the defendant to appear at a specific time and place. Often the accused was freed under bond pending trial; if he could not post one, he was imprisoned at his own expense until the trial. If he failed to appear at the trial, the Court served a warrant for his arrest.

To prevent the annoyance of a multitude of minor suits the General Court ordered that the plaintiff had to prosecute his case within a given time or pay damages. He also had to pay the costs of court unless the defendant failed to appear or the judges determined that they should be assumed by the defendant. The Court possessed the right to refuse to hear any case brought by a common barrator and fine him for his nuisance.[52] In their judicial system the Connecticut settlers revealed a conscious desire to improve on their heritage and to provide a system where justice could be dispensed as rapidly and as inexpensively as possible.

But the Puritans frequently abused the system where legal redress was so convenient with vexatious suits. The Particular Court was plagued with claims and counterclaims. In March 1655/56 Robert Munroe sued John Bissell for a misdemeanor in taking the lock from his cellar door, thereby endangering his liquor supply. Bissell in turn sued not only Munroe but also a Mr. Williams and William Heydon for breaking open his cellar door. The dockets became overloaded. In March 1660/61 Simon Lobdell brought Jared and Hannah Spencer into court. He charged Hannah with breach of promise for refusing to marry him and Jared for breach of promise. The damages claimed were £150. Theirs was only one of about forty actions heard that day. The jury first awarded Lobdell costs of court and then reviewed the case in a special session and delivered its verdict in favor of the plaintiff as a special verdict. Lobdell then appealed to the

General Court, which in upholding the verdict drawn by the Particular Court answered that it would not review the case again.[53]

For a few years toward the end of the Commonwealth period the Gibbs family cost the Particular Court endless time. In exasperation the Court in March 1650/51 ordered that Sarah Gibbs be put into service for having "Carried her selfe very sinfully and disorderly." It warned her mother, the Widow Gibbs, that if a job that met the approval of the Windsor magistrates were not found for Sarah, she would have to appear at the next court, and if she could not prove to it that "Shee hath seene and reformed her euill wayes," she would be sent straight to the house of correction. Sarah, however, failed to mend her ways. Finally, thoroughly vexed with her for bringing action against Nicholas Wilton in September 1659 "for defameing her in a high nature," perhaps justly, the Particular Court turned the whole case over to the magistrates at Windsor to examine and determine. By nature the Puritans were prone to litigiousness.[54]

In Connecticut during the seventeenth century there was only Connecticut law and only one court system. Instead of courts of the hundred and the shire, courts-leet and courts-baron, city and borough courts, Courts of Star Chamber, Chancery, Kings Bench, Exchequer, ad infinitum, Connecticut's pioneers established a simple, straightforward, and efficient system. The judicial hierarchy here was never complicated. The General Court was the highest court of the Commonwealth, and from it there was no appeal. As with the tribunals in the other settlements in America, its composition was the same whether it acted as a court of justice or a legislative body. In both instances it was composed of the governor, the deputy governor, the magistrates, and the deputies.

The occasions when the General Court heard cases were few. It served as a court of appeal on September 12, 1650, when Matthew Allyn resorted to it in hopes that it would alter the judgment handed down by the Particular Court, which had fined him 10 shillings and costs of court for "deteining Certeine specialties," £60 and costs of court for the "vniust molestation" of his brother, Thomas Allyn, and £45 and costs of court "for not satisfiing of seuerall disburssm's about his Cattle." The General Court upheld the decisions in the first and third instances, but lowered the fine in the second to twenty "marke" plus costs of court.[55] In the session of October 6, 1651, the General Court reviewed a verdict handed down at Stratford, presumably by a Magistrate's Court. The higher court affirmed the lower court's decision that Thomas Barlowe and Jehu Burr be required to pay 40 shillings in damages "for a colte of Leiftennant Wheelers." The General Court heard John Cooper's appeal from the jury in Southampton in May 1652 and Simon Lobdell's appeal to it from the Particular Court in March 1660/61, mentioned above.[56]

The General Court served as a court of original jurisdiction for serious infringements, but not for capital crimes. For example, on June 11, 1640, Richard Gyldersly was summoned before the Court for "casteing out p^rnitious speeches, tending to the detriment & dishonnor of this Comonwelth." He was fined 40 shillings and bound in a recognizance of £20 to appear at the next session of the Court. At the same time Matthew Mitchell, of Wethersfield, was fined 20 nobles "for vndertaking the office of Towne Clarke or Recordor, notw^thstanding his vncapablenes of such office by censure of Courte." The town of Wethersfield was also fined £5 for electing him in spite of the censure.[57] In other cases the General Court decided what persons should be freed from training, watches, and wards; it determined boundaries between towns and occasionally ordered inventories of estates.

The conscientiousness of the Court may be seen in the case of John Blackleich. On March 13, 1661/62, Blackleich was accused of speaking contemptuously about several leaders of the Commonwealth. The Court, after deliberating the case, ordered that he pay a fine of £30, apologizing for the light fine by explaining that it was in consideration of his "weaknes." The Court added its opinion that the transgression should ordinarily deserve one of £100.[58] But the Court had doubts about its decision. In the minutes of the same session is the record that the Court, upon reconsidering the matter, felt that undue prejudice had appeared in the witnesses' testimonies and that the evidence had been acquired by indirectness. Therefore, it acquitted Blackleich, revoked the fine, and delivered its opinion that it suspected that Loveridge and Burnam, Blackleich's accusers, were in fact the guilty parties.[59]

The vast majority of both criminal and civil causes were handled by the Particular Courts. The purpose of the courts was to settle specific differences between individual citizens in the Commonwealth. Originally each Particular Court was composed of at least the governor or deputy governor, who presided, and four other magistrates on the bench, but in April 1643 the provision was modified to permit Magistrate Ludlow to preside over the Court, or if he and both the governor and deputy governor could not attend, then the eldest magistrate should moderate. Still the presence of four magistrates in addition to the moderator was requisite. In February 1644/45 the Fundamental Orders were amended to permit the governor or deputy governor with three other magistrates to constitute a quorum. Then on May 20, 1647, it was again amended to allow the governor or deputy governor and two magistrates, or three magistrates alone, to sit as the Particular Court. It was not always feasible to summon five magistrates.[60]

The first recorded meeting of the Particular Court was held on the first Thursday of May 1639, but the consensus is that the tribunal was already an established institution by that time.[61] The Particular Court met at irregular intervals until April 1642, when the General Court restricted its meetings to one every quarter. In January 1642/43 the Particular Court set its meetings for the first Thursdays of March, June, September, and December. At these times it was referred to as the "Quarter Court"; at its intervening sessions it was titled the "Particular Court." In 1646 the order was amended to require the Particular Court to coincide with the spring and fall sessions of the General Court, expressly so that Roger Ludlow could attend. Later as the agenda increased this was again changed to order that the meeting be two days before the convening of the General Court. Instead of rotating from one town to another, the Particular Courts met at Hartford, either in the home of one of the magistrates or in the meeting-house.[62]

The Particular Courts had a petty jury of twelve sworn jurors in attendance in addition to the magistrates on the bench.[63] The performance of jury duty was obligatory, except in special cases like Robert Haywood's. Haywood was freed from the duty because it was vital that he run the Windsor mill. When any of the jurors were prejudiced in a case, as in the dispute over the possession of the Hartford mill in March 1658/59, they were removed and substitutes sworn in their places. The first trial to the jury in a civil action occurred at the session of November 7, 1639, although juries were mentioned on November 1, 1636. Under "Juryes and Jurors" the Ludlow Code endorsed the practice of trying to the jury all cases involving 40 shillings or more, regardless of whether they concerned civil or criminal actions. The purpose in not having jury trials for minor suits was to prevent the petty suits from jamming the dockets of the Commonwealth courts. The jurors, including the foreman, each received 6 pence for any action heard. The fee was paid by the plaintiff if the action were nonsuited; otherwise it was charged to the loser.[64]

The jury determined by a two-thirds majority all cases pending before that particular session of the Court. In the event of a hung jury, the case could be returned to the Court with an attached explanation, and after deliberation there, the new verdict could be handed down by a majority of the magistrates. No instances of hung juries were recorded until June 3, 1658, but then in May 1659 and May 1661 two additional suits were returned to the magistrates. Of the latter cases the first was the trial of Matthew Griswold, plaintiff, against Reynold Marvin, defendant, in an action of review involving a mare and her colt. The plaintiff sought damages of £60. The jury reported "that they cannot agree on a verdict but returne the case to ye Bench." The second case was that of William Thomson, plaintiff, against Peter Blachford, defendant, in an action of the case. Thomson charged Blachford with unjust molestation and defamation, an illegal protest, and with refusing to give security for some land sold to one Burlingham. He claimed £150 damages. The jury again surrendered the decision to the magistrates.[65]

The Particular Court could be found reconsidering a verdict of the jury as early as January 2, 1639/40. The previous December, Richard Westcoat had sued Jonathan Plum in an action of trespass on the grounds that some of Plum's cows and pigs had gotten into his cornfield. The jury first awarded Westcoat six bushels of corn plus costs of suit. The Particular Court reviewed the suit on January 2 and decided it on February 6. It upheld the verdict of the jury, but ordered Jeffery Ferris and Mr. Chester to share the fine with Plum. Ferris' fence was broken, and his cows too had trampled Westcoat's corn. Nor could Chester's boar resist his share of the corn.[66]

If the magistrates disagreed with a verdict or felt that the jury had not proceeded according to the evidence, they could twice return the verdict for reconsideration. If they disapproved of the final verdict, they could either impanel another jury or alter the damages, provided they did so in open court.[67]

The Ludlow Code called for a special coroner's jury of six or twelve men to be summoned to investigate any unnatural death and to present its findings under oath to a magistrate. It also authorized a grand jury of twelve or fourteen men to investigate other breaches of the law and to present its findings to the Particular Court annually before the autumn session, or more frequently if necessary.[68] The grand jury was first mentioned in July 1643. Jury duty was a difficult and unpopular task.

The jurisdiction of the Particular Courts was broad in Connecticut. They ruled in virtually any legal controversy which arose between individuals in the Commonwealth, whether it involved a capital crime or a minor criminal cause, damages incurred by wandering cattle or pigs, a question of a title to a parcel of land, insolvency, slander, or any other action over 40 shillings. The Court fined Puritans for not prosecuting their suits and disposed of lands in the Pequot territory. It regulated its own proceedings and swore in constables for the towns. The minutes of each session include the date, the names of the magistrates and members of the jury present, and a review of the suits. This entry for June 2, 1653, is typical:

> A perticuler Courte June the 2, 1653
> John Heynes Esqr Gou^r Mr: Webster Mr: Woolcott Mr: Clarke Mr:
> Wells
> Jury John Pratt Junr Natha: Ward Rich: Goodwin Junr George Graues
> Mathu Grant Tho: Buckland Junr Benia: Nubery John Demon John
> Ryly Luke Hichcock Junr Sam: Hale:
> Nickho: Disborne plt: agt: John Androwes defendt in an Actyon of
> slander to the damage of 20*ll*

John Latimore plt: agt James Whetly Defendt in an actyon of the case to the damage

Mathu Allen plt: agt: Tho: Ford defendt: as Atterny to Rob Nash in an Actyon of reveue wherin the said Math: Allen was damnifyd 30*l*

In the actyon of Nich: Disborne plt: agt: John Androws defendt: the Jury find for the plt: 1*ll* 16*ss* damge & cost of Courte & for wittnesses 4*ss* execution was dd for 41*ss* 4*d* the 14 of March 16$\frac{53}{54}$

In the Actyon of John Latimore plt: agt: James Wheatly defendt: the Jury find for the plt: 5*ll* 5*s* damages & Cost of Courte

In the Actyon of Reuewe by Mathue Allen plt: agt: Tho: Ford defendt: as Atturny to Rob Nash the Jury find for the defendt: cost of Courte:

John Nott for his miscariedg with the widdow Mudg is find 5*ll*

Edward Messenger for his unmercifullnes towards his Seruant & lying to extenuet his fault is to be severly whipped when he shall be cauled forth by the Governor

Liberty is granted that the land belonging to the widdow Mudge at Pequet may be sould for the paing of debts & the Bettering the Childrens portyons [69]

As is evident from the quotation, the Particular Courts served as appellate courts as well as courts of original jurisdiction. They heard appeals from their own decisions and from those of the town courts. For example, the Particular Court sitting on July 8, 1650, heard the quarrel between Thomas Dammon, plaintiff, and John Packer, defendant, in an action of the case concerning the sinking of a ship for which the plaintiff was seeking damages of £100. The jury awarded Dammon 20 shillings and costs of court. In a rehearing of the case on September 5, 1650, in an action of review, the Court awarded him £10 and costs of court in lieu of the £40 he was then seeking.[70] There are numerous other instances of cases being reviewed and adjusted by the Particular Court.

In the Particular Courts, as in the common-law courts of England, trained lawyers had little part. The magistrates were not men educated in the law, nor were the members of the jury.[71] The legal profession was one disliked and distrusted by the Puritans. Thomas Lechford, himself a lawyer, had nothing but difficulties during his brief stay in Massachusetts Bay, and Roger Ludlow faced constant opposition. Thomas Hooker expressed the general opinion of lawyers when he said, "if a Man will follow every wrangling Lawyer at every impertinent *Quibble* or Out-leap, he must never look for an end of lawing: And it is the Fashion of many Attornies, rather to breed Quarrels, than to kill them in the Conception." [72] Attorneys appeared in the records of both the General and Particular Courts as early as June 1, 1643, but Thomas Bull, Matthew Allyn, Henry Wolcott, and John Hudshon, for example, were not attorneys-at-law, but men granted a written power of attorney by the plaintiff or defendant requesting his services as a representative in court.[73]

Below the Particular Courts were the Courts of Magistrates and the Town Courts. The former were held by a magistrate either sitting alone or with an assistant in the distant towns of Stratford, Fairfield, Norwalk, New London, and later Easthampton, Southampton, and Huntington on Long Island. The rutted roads and hazardous crossings of Long Island Sound prevented the members of an entire Particular Court from traveling to each town or all the witnesses, plaintiffs, and defendants from journeying to Hartford. The authority to hold these courts was delegated to the magistrate or someone chosen as an assistant by the General Court as the necessity arose. The Courts of Magistrates were comparable to the Inferior Quarterly, or County, Courts in the Bay. The magistrates could determine criminal and civil processes involving less than 40 shillings, impanel juries, and summon witnesses.[74]

The first occasion of the appointment of a Magistrate's Court occurred in June 1640, when the General Court appointed William Hopkins, of Cupheage (Stratford), commissioner to serve with Roger Ludlow, by now of Uncoway (Fairfield), in executing justice in the towns along the seaboard. In April 1643 the Court again ordered two magistrates, Captain Mason and Mr. Welles, to travel to Stratford and Fairfield later in the month and made arrangements for one or possibly two magistrates to make the circuit again in September to sit with Ludlow in executing justice. Instances of the authorization of Magistrates' Courts appeared frequently during the 1640's and 1650's. Acting on the motion of Ludlow, the Court of Election on April 10, 1645, granted its

permission to Governor Haynes or a magistrate of his choice to go
to the seaside towns twice a year to hold court. Subsequently, on
May 17, 1649, Captain John Mason was ordered by the General
Court to administer the oath of magistracy to John Winthrop, Jr.,
at New London. The Court then vested in the latter and two
assistants the power to hear small cases without a jury and provided that redress could be sought by appeal to the General Court
itself. In June it instructed Magistrate John Webster to go to
Stratford to aid Roger Ludlow in holding court there.[75]

As Connecticut expanded, the magistrates journeyed to the
distant towns with increasing frequency. On October 6, 1651, three
deputies, Andrew Ward, George Hull, and William Beardsly,
were chosen to assist the magistrates in dispensing justice in the
towns along the shore of Long Island Sound. In 1652 Fairfield
and Stratford were granted permission to elect their own assistants
for one year. The General Court specifically provided that when
any question of legality arose, appeals could be made to Connecticut (that is, Hartford) or other magistrates could be sent to the
distant town to help settle the controversy. Connecticut was just
beginning to rear its first fledgling settlements along the shore of
Long Island Sound. Wherever Connecticut's Congregationalists
set their roots, law and order sprang up soon after.[76]

In addition to the General Courts, the Particular Courts, and
the Courts of Magistrates, there were the Town Courts. The General Court on October 10, 1639, when it was enumerating the
rights of Windsor, Hartford, and Wethersfield, had decreed that

> each of the aforesayd Townes shall haue power by a generall consent
> once every yeare to choose out 3, 5 or 7 of their cheefe Inhabitants,
> whereof one to be chosen moderator, who having taken an oath prouided
> in that case, shall haue a casting voice in case they be equall; wch sayd
> p^rsons shall meett once in every 2 monthes & being mett together, or the
> maior part of them, whereof the moderato^r to be one, they shall haue
> power to heare, end and determine all controversies, eyther trespasses or
> debts not exceeding 40*s*. provided both partyes live in the same Towne;
> also any two of them or the moderato^r may graunt out sumons to the
> party or partyes to come to their meetings to answere the actions; also to
> administer oath to any witnesses for the clearing of the cause, and to giue
> judgment and execution against the party offending.[77]

Each member served for one year. Appeal to the higher courts was recognized, but it was accompanied by the warning that if no grounds for the appeal could be found, the appellant would be subject to fine. The Town Courts without a jury dealt with the majority of the small claims originating within the town, leaving the more important actions to the Commonwealth courts.

The punishments inflicted when the Commonwealth was without a code were handed down according to the whims of the Court, General or Particular. In 1642 the capital crimes became written law. Then in 1650 the multitude of felonies which could and did plague the Commonwealth were organized into the Ludlow Code, each with a specific punishment or punishments attached. The penalties ranged from the five-shilling fine imposed on Henry Curtis for "neglecting of his watch" to the sentence of Elizabeth Buckly, who on December 7, 1654, "for her horrid wikedness in willfully Burning the Barne of Will Lord of Seabrooke is adiudged to be forthwith seveerely whipt & to suffer imprisonment during the pleasure of the Court & next Lecture day in Hartford to be seveerely whipt againe & when the Courte Shall see Cause to release her from prison Shee Shall put in suffitient security for her good behauio^r while Shee remaines in this Jurisdictyon." [78] Beyond this were banishment and the death penalty.

The majority of the crimes merited fines, sitting in the stocks, whipping, or a term in the house of correction. Fines were the most common form of punishment. For "vnseasonable and imoderate drinking" Thomas Cornewell, Jonathan Latimer, Mathew Beckwith, Samuel Kittwell, and Thomas Upson were fined 30, 15, 10, 10, and 20 shillings, respectively, in August 1639. The General Court fined Samuel Ireland 10 shillings for contempt of court when he failed to appear after a warrant had been served on him. Nicholas Olmstead "for his laciuious caridge & fowle mysdemenors at sundry tymes wth Mary Brunson" was fined £20 and ordered to stand in the pillory at Hartford during the next lecture. Thomas Walston had to pay 20 shillings "for inuegling the affections of Mr. Alcocks mayde." The same amount was imposed on Baggett Egleston, who bequeathed his wife to a young man! Theft was considered a more serious crime; John Carpenter had to pay £10 for breaking into Will Gybbins' house and drinking his wine.[79]

The Courts resorted to biblical practice on occasion and made the guilty party return in kind double, triple, or even quadruple the amount of his theft. The Court ordered Samuel Allen to return to Mistress Hooker triple the amount of wood he stole from her. Joane Sipperance was ordered to return double the lace she had taken and had three times the length of time she neglected her duties added to her service.[80]

The Particular Court showed great leniency in the case of Walter Fyler. Fyler had charged the Reverend Samuel Stone with the breach of an undisclosed fundamental law and the elders in general with sin and wickedness. The elders brought him to court in March 1654/55. The Court found that his actions were "all togeather Insufferable, & that they Desarve a greater punishment then hee is well able to beare yet hoping god will helpe him to see his great Evill & Sinn therein & hould forth repentance Suitable to the Nature of the fact." It fined him £5 because he could afford no more and ordered him to find securities for his good behavior.[81]

Branding on the forehead with the letter "B" was the specified punishment for burglary, but it was rarely resorted to. On one of the few occasions when branding appears in the records, the Court ordered James Hallet to restore quadruple the amount he stole and be branded on his hand the next training day in Windsor. Again, Robert Bedle was ordered to restore double the amount of his thefts and sentenced to be severely whipped and branded on his hand. More humane were the sentences to sit in the stocks that the Court imposed on Garret Spike and John Kelley for drunkenness and Thomas Smith, William Brinkley, and Jacob Cole "ffor ye horrible neglect and contempt of Gods Ordnances in lying abroad in Mrs Coles orchyard in time of publique worship on ye ffast and some of them vpon ye Sabbath." They had to sit in the stocks on lecture day from the ringing of the second bell until the end of the lecture.[82]

One of the severest sentences handed down by the Court was its order that John Dawes be banished from the Commonwealth. Dawes threatened Edward Hopkins, one of Connecticut's most revered citizens, while he was governor because of a sentence

Hopkins had imposed on Dawes's wife. The Court ordered him to leave Connecticut within ten days and not to return on peril of his life.[83]

Whippings occurred more frequently. Public humiliation proved to be an effective deterrent to future crimes in many cases. Ruth Fishe, for fornication, was sentenced to be whipped twice, once in Hartford following the lecture and again in Wethersfield. John Ranolds was fined £5 and whipped for harboring in his mistress' house the "rouges that brake pryson." He was also to give security for his appearance in court in three months, when he was to be corrected again unless he could convince the Court that he had mended his ways. For libeling Mrs. Chester and other misdemeanors the Court sent Danyell Turner to prison and ordered that he be brought out and whipped on the next lecture day and then returned to prison. After a month he was to be publicly whipped again and then give security for his good behavior. Virtually the same sentence was imposed on John Jennings "for his filthy and prophane speeches and carriages." Robert Bedle succeeded in arousing the wrath of the Court. For "his loathsū and beastly demeanor," Bedle, who had been branded for theft three months before, was ordered brought out on the next lecture day and severely "scourdged," and then to remain in the house of correction for a fortnight longer and then again whipped. The Court ordered him to appear at every session of the Quarter Court for a whipping until it could see sufficient improvement to justify releasing him.[84]

Whipping and even branding were simple punishments. Elizabeth Johnson, former wife of Peter Johnson of Fairfield, caused the authorities in Connecticut greater consternation. In May 1650 the Particular Court, in the presence of a grand jury of life and death as well as a petty jury, found Elizabeth guilty "of the fact." No details concerning her sin appear in the record, but Thomas Newton was also found guilty of the same crime. Goody Johnson apparently received a long sentence in the house of correction, for when William Rescue, keeper of the house of correction, presented his bill for her care through the first Thursday in June, she had already spent twenty-four weeks in prison. The expenses for that period were £6 10s., which had to be paid out of her estate. Elizabeth already had one son, whom she bound out as an apprentice to a master in Stratford before her trial, but raised Puritan eyebrows when she bore another child in prison. Faced with this ward, the General Court gave the baby to Nathaniell Rescue to keep as an apprentice until he reached twenty-one. Ten pounds from Newton's estate were allowed Rescue for the child's care. But it proved expensive to raise a child even in the seventeenth century, and in October 1651 the Court had to order the sale of the remainder of Peter Johnson's estate to pay for nursing the baby. Finally in May 1652 the Court ordered £5 more to Rescue for the support and education of the ward, but it forbade any further demands on Goody Johnson or the Commonwealth. No more was heard from Rescue or the child.[85]

During the period of the Commonwealth, Connecticut had one house of correction. It stood in Hartford's meetinghouse yard. In April 1640 the General Court had ordered that a building, approximately 16 or 18 feet wide and 24 feet long, be built either of wood or stone. In 1649/50 it appointed Will Rescue its keeper at a salary of £10 a year. This house of correction served to shelter alleged criminals pending trial and proven delinquents following their conviction and sentencing. Susan Coles, for instance, was sentenced to the house of correction at hard labor and coarse diet for her rebellious carriage toward her mistress. She also faced public whipping weekly on lecture day until the order of the Court should be rescinded.[86]

The house of correction rarely served as a debtor's prison; long terms in jail were too expensive for Connecticut's meager treasury, and the pauper was responsible for his own expenses. In the Ludlow Code under "Arrests" provision was made that no man be arrested and imprisoned for debt or fine if any possible satisfaction could be found from his estate. While the trial was pending, and even afterward, debtors were temporarily protected from their creditors by the Court's findings of *non soluant* or *non liquet*. If the obligations could not be canceled, the debtor had to remain under lock and key until he could raise the necessary funds. If the court had suspicions that he were concealing some resources, it could refuse to let him take the "Poor Debtor's Oath." Prisoners for debt could be sold as servants to pay their obligations. But the poor were not a significant problem in Connecticut. The laws against strangers kept foreign parasites out of the towns, and there was work enough for all able-bodied persons. The unfit depended on their families or the towns or occasionally received bequests in wills from generous men like George Wyllys, who left small amounts to the poor in Hartford, Windsor, Wethersfield, and Tunxis Cepus (Farmington).[87]

At times the Courts had difficulties in having their orders consummated. Sometimes they were deceived, sometimes ignored, and the exasperation can still be read in the records over two hundred years later. In September 1660 Henry Wolcott outrightly refused to accept the office of lieutenant of the Company of Windsor. Reluctantly the Particular Court installed Walter Fyler in his stead. In another case Nicholas Olmstead petitioned the General Court to free him from military training, and his request was granted in September 1651. Less than a month later he was back on the list of trainees. The Court discovered that he had falsified the plea in order to dodge his obligations. Again, when the General Court ordered that one member of every family come armed to the Sunday and lecture day sermons, its order was ignored. Vexed, it set a fine of 12 pence for every failure, half to be paid to the informant.[88]

These sentences and infinitely more were executed by the constable in each town. The constables had been the first law-enforcement officers provided for Connecticut by the General Court of Massachusetts Bay, when it established the Commission to govern Connecticut in 1636. Later they were chosen annually by the General Courts to serve as the link between the Commonwealth and the towns. They kept the peace by carrying out the punishments ordered by the courts, much as the petty constables in the English villages did. They executed the warrants from the magistrates and apprehended drunks, Sabbath-breakers, vagrants, and other offenders. They could detain any undesirable foreigner until he could be passed safely beyond the town's limits to the constable in the next town or until a magistrate of Connecticut could try him. They oversaw watches and wards and raised the hues and cries after criminals in the absence of the magistrates. It was their duty to summon the inhabitants of their towns for the annual drawing up of the grand lists for taxation purposes, to post the new laws as they were enacted, to see that the capital laws were read publicly once a year, and to keep the town's lawbook up to date. At the other extreme their duties included rounding up stray animals. It was they who enforced the law of the Commonwealth and the judgments of the courts.[89]

The office of constable was not without personal hazard even in Puritan Connecticut. In September 1645 the Particular Court saw fit to fine George Chappell £5 for abusing the constable and drinking excessively and Mr. Chester 40 shillings for resisting the constable. Later it ordered that William Wyatt and Thomas Carter be publicly whipped and then imprisoned until they could give sufficient security for their peaceable and good behavior to the governor. They were convicted of "Insufferable abusive Carriage" against Constable John Ryly. In each town the constable had a marshal to assist him in serving executions and attachments. In the Congregational communities the constables held a thankless job, but they were indispensable functionaries.[90]

The Fundamental Orders of Connecticut had provided the authority for the General Court to enact individual orders governing the criminal, constitutional, economic, ecclesiastical, social, and moral aspects of the community. In 1642 the General Court extended its authority and voted into law the twelve capital crimes. In 1650 the statutes previously enacted by the Court, together with others borrowed from the Bay, were then codified by Roger Ludlow and the entire code was approved by the Court. The constitution also called for a judicial system to interpret the law of Connecticut. When the General and Particular Courts proved unable to determine justice in the distant towns, because of the difficulties of transportation, the system was again amended to establish the Magistrates' Courts and the Town Courts.

Law and authority are vital to the survival of any society. Congregational thought recognized this. Thomas Hooker spoke of magistrates and ministers as the "two great meanes of safety." He expressed his conviction that the

> arguments are cleare, the Saints maintaine God in his ordinances, the want of which is under the penalty of death and condemnation. Gold cannot feed a hungry man, but bread he would have, because that he

hath need of: so the Saints of God are marvellous importunate to keep God in his Ordinances, so that though they weare a ragged coat, or be pinched with hunger; yet he wants God more then these, either food or rayment.[91]

The survival of Connecticut's churches was directly dependent on the ability of the Commonwealth's civil structure to maintain law and order.

The settlers in Connecticut, relying heavily on their biblical and English heritage as well as the precedents set in the Massachusetts Bay Body of Liberties and the Laws and Liberties of 1648, produced both statutes and a judicial system for their Commonwealth. Both contained many traditional features, but both also represented the solutions the men of Connecticut felt would best satisfy the individual needs of their churches and towns. As George Lee Haskins wrote, "the law of a particular civilization is a compound of past as well as of present forces; it is both an anchor to tradition and a vehicle for change." [92]

V

From Commonwealth to Colony

On October 9, 1662, the freemen assembled at the General Court for a formal reading of the Charter granted to Connecticut by Charles II. They enthusiastically voted their approval. For over a year the General Court and its governor, John Winthrop, Jr., had endeavored to have the constitutional status of the Commonwealth regularized by letters patent from the King of England. The acceptance of the Charter did not signify the failure of the Fundamental Orders as a constitution; it indicated, instead, the inability of the Englishmen of the second generation in Connecticut to exist under the anomalous legal status sanctioned by the Fundamental Orders. Because of changed external circumstances, they were no longer able to maintain that the authority for their state derived from God alone. To preserve their Congregational churches and state the men of Connecticut were forced to admit the King into their covenant and to accept the position of a charter colony.

Except for the failure of the concept of authority agreed on in the preamble, the Fundamental Orders had satisfied the majority of the demands of the river towns for over twenty years. The constitution had permitted the towns sufficient local autonomy to manage their own affairs, had provided for the admission of the new towns settled within its jurisdiction, and had allowed the Commonwealth to unite with Massachusetts Bay, Plymouth, and New Haven into a regional confederation. The General Court proved reasonably capable of coping with the Dutch at Fort Good Hope and conducting its infrequent relations with England. However, in interfering with the Churches of Hartford and Wethersfield, the civil legislature fanned the flames of contention, rather than extinguished the sparks ignited by the Halfway Covenant.

Under the Fundamental Orders there were no quarrels between the towns and the Commonwealth over their respective jurisdictions. The towns were unquestionably subordinate to the Commonwealth. Even for their incorporation they had to have the Court's permission. Each town was the local political unit, united by one church comparable to the English parish. Its voters were divided into admitted inhabitants and freemen. Some of the admitted inhabitants had been original proprietors of the land; others had had the political and economic privileges conferred on them as "Newcomers"; but all the admitted inhabitants could participate in the town meetings and vote for the deputies to represent them in the General Court. Some were also freemen of the Commonwealth, entitled to vote for the magistrates at the Court of Election, but the majority were allowed to vote only in the town meetings.

Summoned to the monthly meetings by drumbeat, trumpet call, or the cry of the warners carrying the message from house to house, the admitted inhabitants gathered at nine o'clock in the morning during the period of the Fundamental Orders to levy taxes for their minister's salary, for maintaining the school, and for other routine expenses. They listened to the laws recently enacted by the General Court.[1] They authorized the building of mills and warehouses and ordered that roads be constructed and kept in repair and fire laws and curfews be obeyed. They regulated hours and wages for day laborers, enforced the regulations against entertaining strangers, and even set a minimum depth below the surface for graves. The admitted inhabitants ordered watches and wards to preserve the peace and provided armed guards during the church services. One of the more important functions of the town meetings was to regulate agricultural affairs. The men attending the meetings voted bonuses for killing the dreaded wolf and restricted the felling of precious trees. They decided when cattle and swine should enter particular meadows, ordered pounds and fences built and repaired, and enforced the medieval practice that each man should contribute a certain number of hours in laboring for the common good. The town meetings could pass any local law, provided that it was not contrary to the law of the Commonwealth, and make the necessary arrangements for its enforcement.

In the meetings officers were chosen to govern the town. Usually four or six and occasionally seven of the leading men were chosen as townsmen, and from them a moderator was selected. The first recorded election of townsmen occurred in Hartford on January 1, 1638/39. The early records for Windsor and Wethersfield are not extant, but undoubtedly they, too, soon elected townsmen. The townsmen were the most important local officers. As a body they were vested with the power to execute the instructions delivered to them by the town meeting, to manage the town's finances, and to sit as the Town Court in actions of debt, trespass, or probate not over 40 shillings. The only powers specifically denied them in Hartford, for instance, were approving new voters, imposing certain levies, granting more than two acres of the town's land, altering highways already laid out, calling cattle into the service of the whole town, and acting independently without the knowledge of the other townsmen. Except for the last, these actions were specifically reserved for the body of admitted inhabitants assembled in the town meeting.[2]

In addition to the townsmen there was the town register, or recorder, who kept the house and land records, copied the orders of the General Court into the town's lawbook, and preserved the vital statistics. There were also public whippers, surveyors of fences, fence and chimney viewers, haywards, cowherds, shepherds, pounders, perambulators, town criers, listers, and the collectors of rates. Bell ringers aroused the sleepy populace each day one hour before the sun rose, and surveyors of the highways called each able-bodied man and team of horse or oxen two days a year to mend Connecticut's roads. Later, in accordance with orders from the General Court, meat packers, horse branders, leather sealers, sealers of weights and measures, examiners of yarn, and ordinary-keepers appeared in the towns. Finally there were the essential constables, whom the Court appointed, but who served in the towns. The town officials usually held office for one year, for which all except the townsmen received wages commensurate with the duties performed. Acceptance of a town office was obligatory.

In the towns attempts at public health laws were made, particularly after the epidemic of 1647 that killed Thomas Hooker and many others. The General Court ordered the towns to provide meat inspectors, and efforts were made to prohibit the practice of throwing the garbage into the streets for the hogs to consume. Most babies were delivered by midwives, although there was a handful of men in the Commonwealth trained in medicine. The first licensed by the General Court was Bray Rossiter, of Windsor, who performed the first autopsy in New England. John Winthrop, Jr., whose letters contain abundant advice concerning the health of his correspondents, actually practiced little medicine in Connecticut. The Court officially hired Dr. Thomas Lord of Hartford as the Commonwealth's physician in June 1652. The contract offered advantages to both sides. Connecticut could depend on having a doctor to set bones and practice general medicine, while Dr. Lord had a chance "to improue his best skill amongst the inhabitants of the Townes vppon the Riuer within this Jurissdiction." He received 12 pence for house calls in Hartford, 5 shillings for calls in Windsor, 3 shillings for Wethersfield, 6 shillings for Farmington, and 8 shillings for calls in Mattabeseck (Middletown). Furthermore, he was freed from watching, warding, and training and received an annual salary from Connecticut's treasury of £15. The Court hired Danniell Porter as surgeon in October 1655, authorizing him a salary of only £6 from the public treasury, but permitting him to charge 6 shillings for each call. His contract was renewed for another year the following February and extended indefinitely in March 1661/62. Connecticut's fifth doctor was Jasper Gunn, whom the General Court freed from watching, warding, and training in May 1657, while he practiced "phissicke." The medicine these men practiced was primitive, but it is remarkable that Connecticut's people had this much medical care.[3]

The Puritans in the towns frowned on dancing, cards, and the theater, but they were not an unsociable group. There were as many picnics, fairs, husking bees, house raisings, hayrides, and quilting parties as the labors of the new settlements and the demands of the churches allowed. Swordplay was discouraged, but it occurred, and eating and drinking at the ordinaries were thoroughly enjoyed. The townsfolk took pride in the military nature of the Commonwealth when a troop of horse was established by the General Court in March 1657/58 in Windsor, Hartford, and

Wethersfield. The horsemen were exempted from certain taxes
as well as from the usual militia training, and provision was made
for compensating them for the value of any horses killed in defense of the Commonwealth. In May 1660 permission was also
granted to Fairfield, Stratford, and Norwalk to form a troop of
eighteen men and two officers.[4]

Under the Fundamental Orders the jurisdiction over the land
was divided between the towns and the General Court. In an order
of October 10, 1639, the Court confirmed the right of the towns
to distribute the lands within their bounds.[5] Technically, not the
towns but the proprietors who had purchased the land from the
Indians retained the right to parcel it out in home lots, meadow,
or field. But in fact the town meeting and the proprietors were
virtually synonymous, because the town meetings were composed
of the landowners. The proprietors retained the common lands as
pastures and timber, stone, and wood reserves for the whole community, but they doled out individual parcels in fee simple, ignoring all feudal tenures. The range in landholdings in Connecticut
was not wide, as it was in the southern colonies. In Hartford the
largest holdings recorded in March 1640/41 belonged to John
Haynes and George Wyllys, who each owned two hundred acres,
while some "proprietors by courtesy" held four acres. Not until
late in the period did men begin to accumulate extensive acreage.
There were few nonresident proprietors; local ownership of the
land was enforced by the law that the land had to be improved
or a house built on it within six or twelve months after the original grant or it would be forfeited.[6]

The General Court nevertheless regulated lands within the
towns' boundaries as well as the unsettled areas. The Court's order
that all lands acquired, sold, or mortgaged be recorded caused the
flood of entries by the Hartford registrar in February 1639/40.[7]
England as a whole had no comparable law, although land regis-
try was required in certain manors and boroughs. The Court decreed that future purchases from the Indians could be made only
by authority of the Court itself and forbade purchases by individuals. It granted almost 30,000 acres of uninhabited lands to veter-
ans of the Pequot War and to prominent citizens as rewards for
their services. There were no arguments between the town meet-

ings and the General Court over the control of the land. The towns distributed the lands within their boundaries, while the Court passed the comprehensive regulations for it and parceled out unsettled territory.

The Fundamental Orders provided a workable method for enlarging the Commonwealth of Connecticut. The eighth fundamental decreed that "Wyndsor, Hartford and Wethersfield shall haue power, ech Towne, to send fower of their freemen as their deputyes to euery Generall Courte; and whatsoeuer other Townes shall be hereafter added to this Jurisdiction, they shall send so many deputyes as the Courte shall judge meete, a resonable p^r^por-tion to the nūber of Freemen that are in the said Townes being to be attended therein." [8] This was an act of foresight. When the Fundamental Orders were drafted and ratified, the only towns in Connecticut were Hartford, Windsor, and Wethersfield; by the time of the Charter, Connecticut had grown to include fifteen towns, the fifteen vines on its seal. Roger Ludlow began settling Fairfield and Stratford in 1639, and they were soon admitted to the Commonwealth. In 1644 Saybrook by purchase and Southampton, Long Island, by vote of the commissioners of the United Colonies fell under the jurisdiction of Connecticut. In 1645 Farmington was recognized as a town. The commissioners of the United Colonies in 1646 decided that John Winthrop's settlement, Pequot (New London), belonged by right to Connecticut instead of Massachusetts, and so that year it too joined the Commonwealth. The decision was reviewed the following year and upheld. Easthampton on Long Island in 1649, Middletown and Norwalk in 1651, Norwich about 1661, Setauk (Ashford) in May 1661, and Huntington on Long Island in March 1661/62 became part of Connecticut, entitled to send their deputies to the General Court. [9]

Some of these towns were founded as the result of divisions within the original churches of Connecticut, their population being later augmented by new settlers from Massachusetts Bay or England. If a minister became dissatisfied with the practices in a church, or if the town increased substantially because of new immigrants, a minority would leave. As soon as the town meeting voted to request permission to be recognized as a town, it petitioned the General Court. Upon its acceptance by the Court it

was admitted to the Commonwealth, even though it had not
originally participated in the covenant in the preamble of the Fundamental Orders, and was granted privileges of representation
similar to the three covenanting towns. But because of the paucity
of roads, the lack of bridges, and the necessity of traveling from
one town to another on foot or horseback, communication between
the faraway towns and the General Court remained a problem.
The towns on Long Island had to be allowed to keep their own
laws, provided that they were not outrightly contrary to Connecticut's. They had to rely on the judicial decisions of the Magistrates'
Courts to a greater extent and had to provide their own defenses.
Connecticut's growth was a mixed blessing. The cohesiveness and
homogeneity of the Congregational settlement were shattered by
the admission of the remote towns and less dedicated peoples.

The Congregational churches united in synods in times of
doubt and disagreement. Similarly, the Fundamental Orders permitted the Commonwealth of Connecticut to join with Massachusetts Bay, New Haven, and Plymouth in forming the United
Colonies of New England to solve regional problems when England could provide no support. This was the first instance of a
voluntary union of independent states in America, but it was a
weaker alliance than that effected by the Articles of Confederation
in 1781. The New England Confederation, unlike the synods, was
a permanent body which held regular annual meetings from 1643
until 1665. It survived until 1684, but was impotent after New
Haven's surrender to Connecticut. When Thomas Hooker and
Samuel Stone attended the Hutchinson Synod at Newtown in 1637,
they had proposed a union of the Puritan colonies of New England
to combat the threatening Dutch and Indians as a united front.[10]
The movement was defeated because of rivalries between the Bay
and Connecticut, particularly over the jurisdiction of Springfield
and the Pequot territory, and the unwillingness of the Bay, the
larger, wealthier, and older settlement, to recognize Connecticut
as an equal. Subsequent proposals for a union were offered in 1638
and 1639, but the jealousies were insurmountable.

Even though they had just defeated the Pequots in battle, the
Connecticut Congregationalists lived in constant fear of a new con-
spiracy. On September 8, 1642, the General Court forbade all

John Winthrop, the younger (1606–1676), portrayed by George F. Wright after the original by an unidentified artist in the possession of the New York branch of the Winthrop family. *Courtesy of the Connecticut State Library, Hartford, Connecticut.*

trade in weapons with the Indians and ordered at least two men to stand watch in each town to warn of attack. On September 17 the Court ordered the clerk of the band in each town to prepare a list of all men between sixteen and sixty, and on October 4 it decreed that Hartford, Windsor, and Wethersfield each provide ninety coats thick enough to repel Indian arrows.[11] Terror in Connecticut mounted. The power of the Dutch at New Netherlands was growing, and there was widespread suspicion that they were instigating an Indian attack on their English neighbors.

It was therefore with relief on May 19, 1643, when England was utterly unable to support the New England towns, that the Articles of Confederation were finally signed by Massachusetts Bay, New Haven, and Connecticut. Plymouth joined the Confederation four months later.[12] The union had been effected with great difficulty. Connecticut and the Bay quarreled over the distribution of the Pequot lands and fought over Springfield's claim to be free from the jurisdiction of Connecticut. The Confederation had to be loose. Its board, composed of two commissioners from each of the four participating colonies, possessed consultative and advisory powers only; each colony refused to relinquish its autonomy. The Confederation in no way challenged the independence of Connecticut, although on numerous occasions the General Court voluntarily adopted the recommendations of the commissioners.

The first avowed purpose of the Confederation was to spread the gospel among the Indians, but Connecticut did little missionary work during the period of the Fundamental Orders. It did send Thomas Stanton among the Indians, but his efforts did not produce significant results. The second, and obviously more important, purpose of the Confederation was mutual defense against the alliance of the Indians and the Dutch.[13]

Hardly a year passed without a skirmish with the Indians. The Commonwealth's loyalty to Uncas, chief of the Mohegans, because of his support during the Pequot War dragged it into the Indian feuds. When in 1643 Uncas quarreled with Sequassen of the River Indians and Miantonomo of the Narragansetts, Connecticut feared an attack because it protected Uncas. Massachusetts Bay refused to send soldiers. But in the battle at Sachem's Plain, near Norwich, Uncas, despite overwhelming odds, defeated Miantonomo. Later in September, Uncas presented his prisoner and the case to the commissioners of the New England Confederation at Hartford. The commissioners, advised by the ministers, recommended that Miantonomo be put to death. They delivered the prisoner to Uncas and turned their backs. Uncas marched him back to the spot where he had been captured. Then suddenly one of his men attacked the captive from behind and split his head open. Uncas then proceeded to devour a piece of his shoulder.[14]

Uncas again brought Connecticut into conflict with the Indians in September 1645 because he refused to return the ransom paid to keep Miantonomo alive. At that time the commissioners resolved to send three hundred men from the four settlements against a coalition of Niantics and Narragansetts. Cowed, Uncas' enemies sued for peace and agreed to give Uncas hostages, canoes, and 2,000 fathoms of wampum and to submit any future quarrels to the New England Confederation for mediation. In 1646 the irate River Indians plotted to murder John Haynes, Edward Hopkins, and William Whiting, because Connecticut continued to protect Uncas. Their chief, Sequassen, hired Watohibrough, a Waranoke Indian, as the assassin and planned to frame Uncas for the murders. But the Waranoke betrayed the River Indian, and the plot failed. By 1648 the Narragansetts and Niantics had become so enraged with Uncas that they raised an army of eight hundred braves and prepared to unite with the Mohawks and Pocomotocks to wipe out the Commonwealth. Their attack failed only because the French, for reasons of their own, happened to attack the Mohawks first, preventing their arrival, and the Pocomotocks refused to join the campaign without them. Once more, in 1654 the commissioners were forced to send out an expedition of soldiers from Connecticut and New Haven under Major Willard to Long Island. The New England Confederation almost dissolved at this juncture because of the Bay's continual refusal to comply with the votes of the other three member colonies, but at the last moment the Bay ate humble pie and agreed to co-operate. One uprising after another occurred until after the end of the period. The Confederation never actually supported Connecticut against the Indians. In each crisis Massachusetts Bay refused to send its soldiers, and the war aims of Connecticut were frustrated. Thus, in spite of Connecticut, intermittent peace with the haughty heathen endured until King Philip's War in 1675.

Nor did the New England Confederation help Connecticut in acquiring the House of Good Hope from the Dutch. Under a charter from the States-General, the Dutch West India Company had erected its blockhouse immediately adjacent to the eventual site of Hartford before the arrival of the English settlers. The fort retained its independence from the jurisdiction of Connecticut and proved to be a constant irritant to the Congregationalists. They complained to the Confederation after the Dutch refused to return an Indian woman to them for punishment and when they harbored other fugitives from Connecticut justice. They argued that the Dutch were fomenting a rebellion and selling liquor and guns to the Indians. They complained when the Dutch refused to pay their debts and purchased goods stolen from them, but to no avail. In 1650 the Dutch governor, Peter Stuyvesant, sent delegates to Hartford, who were successful in arranging a truce with representatives of the United Colonies. The truce fixed the Dutch-English boundaries on Long Island and the mainland and recognized the Dutch rights to the land in Hartford that they actually occupied. But Dutch cattle and hogs trampled more English corn. The incidents recurred, and tension mounted.

Finally, in exasperation on June 27 and 28, 1653, Captain John Underhill, acting under a commission from the Providence Plantations, and with only the alleged approval of Connecticut, seized Fort Good Hope and the lands belonging to the Dutch West India Company, thereby totally ignoring the treaty of 1650. The excuse was that they were enemies to the Commonwealth of England, but the real cause was the longstanding fear of an attack. Because England and Holland were waging the first Anglo-Dutch War in Europe and on the high seas, the General Court of Connecticut in April 1654, without sanctioning Underhill's action of the previous year, sequestered the fort and its adjoining lands and buildings from Captain Underhill in the name of the Commonwealth of England and ordered that no one was to improve or rent the property without its consent.[15] From that date it remained within the jurisdiction of Connecticut.

In desperation in 1653 Connecticut had sought to persuade the commissioners of the New England Confederation to declare war on the Dutch, but its proposal was vetoed once again by Massachusetts. Connecticut and New Haven decided then to appeal directly to England. They appointed Captain Astwood their agent and instructed him to petition Cromwell and Parliament for men and ships. Deputy Governor Hopkins was already in England. Before April 1654 the Court had received a letter from the Council of State, sent by authority of the Commonwealth of England, promising support. It was followed by three or four ships under the command of Major Robert Sedgewick and Captain John Leverett. The General Court in June 1654 ordered Major John Mason and Captain John Cullick to meet with the agents sent by the Lord Protector and representatives of the other colonies and authorized them to commit as many as five hundred soldiers from Connecticut. But before the expedition against the Dutch could set out, news of the English victory and the restoration of peace between the mother countries arrived. Cromwell's forces had to be sent against the French at Penobscot and St. Johns instead.[16] The United Colonies had given no more aid to Connecticut in removing the Dutch from Fort Good Hope than they had in subduing the Narragansetts.

The efforts of the Confederation to resolve the differences between Connecticut and Massachusetts Bay over the impost levied on all goods exported down the Connecticut River past Saybrook Fort also proved futile. In 1647 the Bay challenged the duty on behalf of Springfield, but the impost was upheld by the other commissioners. The General Court of the Bay then retaliated in 1649 by levying a tax on all goods of the other colonies which passed through Boston, whether as imports or exports. The protest by the commissioners was as ineffective as if it had come from the General Court of Connecticut alone. The Confederation, while neither sanctioned nor prohibited by the Fundamental Orders, did not work contrary to its principles, but served as an institution parallel to the church synods. It was respected by the Connecticut Congregationalists, but its actual value to them is questionable.

The Fundamental Orders had been created by the first generation of settlers in the Connecticut River Valley to protect and preserve their Congregational churches. Both the constitution and the Congregational churches had satisfied the demands of the founding fathers, but by 1655, Thomas Hooker, Ephraim Huit (the teacher of the Windsor Church), Henry Smith (the first pastor of the Wethersfield Church), George Wyllys, John Haynes, and many additional founders of Connecticut had died. Others, like Edward Hopkins and Roger Ludlow, had returned to England to fight the battles for Puritanism directly under Oliver Cromwell.[17] Their positions were being taken by the second generation, advised by a ministry trained at Harvard instead of at Oxford or Cambridge. Many of this new generation in Connecticut had not experienced the personal rule of Charles I or the persecutions of Archbishop Laud. They had never struggled for their religious convictions in England and been forced to make the difficult decision to uproot themselves and their families and embark on the pilgrimage across the ocean to a wilderness in order to worship according to what they believed to be the truth. They had been too young to understand the tribulations of their fathers.

With the coming of age of the generation raised in Connecticut in the 1640's and 1650's, a crisis arose in the churches of the river towns, weakening the institutions established by the first generation. The first generation of ministers, led by Thomas Hooker, John Cotton, and John Davenport, had stood adamantly opposed to any child's receiving the sacrament of baptism unless he had at least one regenerate parent. But the question recurred with increasing frequency whether the baptized but unregenerate sons and daughters of the first generation had the right to have their children baptized. Many of the children of the founders of the Connecticut churches had been baptized in their infancy, but upon reaching adulthood could not make a confession of faith and provide sufficient evidence of a religious experience to warrant their admission to a church. They might behave like the saints and lead virtuous lives, but according to the original precepts of Congregationalism, because they were not members of a church, they could not have their children baptized.

Viewed with the advantage of historical hindsight, the adoption of the Halfway Covenant seems to be an inevitable and practical solution to the problem of keeping the younger generation under the wing of the churches. It was an expedient method of retaining their allegiance to the Congregational principles and preventing the membership of the churches from declining drastically as the original covenanters passed away. But the acceptance of the principle of the Halfway Covenant, in permitting the unregenerate faction in the church to transmit the right of baptism to their children, represented a compromise with the original creeds of Congregationalism. It denied the tenet that membership should be reserved exclusively for the saints.

The churches postponed their decisions on the issue until many of the first generation had died. The Cambridge Synod of 1646–1648 was called in part to settle the problem, but the Platform provided only an ambiguous answer. By 1650, however, both Samuel Stone, of Hartford, and John Warham, of Windsor, had accepted it in principle. In May 1656 the General Court appointed Governor Webster, Deputy Governor Welles, John Cullick, and John Talcott, of Hartford, to discuss the issue with the elders of the other Connecticut churches. But still the matter remained unsettled. Another meeting was arranged in 1657 at Boston for the sole purpose of resolving the controversy. It ruled in favor of the Halfway Covenant with the stipulation that the parents accept the obligations of church membership by acknowledging their faith in the gospel and their willingness to submit to the discipline of the church.[18] In January 1657/58 Warham introduced the policy into the Windsor Church. A synod called at Boston in 1662, which the churches of Connecticut did not attend, confirmed the practice, and in 1669 the General Assembly of Connecticut voted toleration for both types of membership.

The division of the membership of the churches into two classes, the full communion members and the members admitted according to the Halfway Covenant, represented a redefinition of Congregationalism. The Cambridge Platform in 1648 had defined each church as "the instititution [*sic*] of Christ a part of the Militant-visible-church, consisting of a company of Saints by calling, united into one body, by a holy covenant, for the publick worship of God, & the mutuall edification one of another, in the Fellowship of the Lord Iesus." [19] By 1660, therefore, the churches for whose sake the Connecticut towns had been founded and the Fundamental Orders adopted were modified, and their membership had been weakened by the infiltration of the noncommuning members. The Commonwealth of Connecticut and the Congregational churches were no longer synonymous.

Simultaneously, between 1653 and 1659 schisms split the Churches of Hartford and Wethersfield, leaving them irreconcilably divided. The Halfway Covenant was the leading point of contention, but other issues were involved. During Thomas Hooker's ministry the Hartford Church had been a model of peace and brotherly love. Ten years later it was in turmoil. Cotton Mather commented that the origin of the dispute was "almost as obscure as the Rise of *Connecticut*-River." [20] In Hartford the trouble apparently originated as a quarrel over the qualifications for baptism and church membership and over the rights of the brethren. On one side stood the teacher, Samuel Stone; on the other, the ruling elder, William Goodwin, supported by Governor Webster, William Whiting, and Captain Cullick.[21] After Thomas Hooker's death in 1647, Stone had led the Hartford Church, but without inspiring the same devotion. He was more formal in his relations with the congregation and less able to convey to them the intensity of belief that he himself felt. His sermons were duller and less heart-rending and therefore less convincing. The dispute was compounded by the personal animosity which existed between Stone and Goodwin and their conflicting opinions on whether the Hartford Church should lean toward Presbyterian or Congregational polity. They argued further about the successor for Hooker. Candidates Jonathan Mitchell, Michael Wigglesworth, John Davis, and John Cotton, Jr., were invited to Hartford in 1649, 1653, 1654, and 1655, but Stone ignored his congregation and refused to allow them to vote on a new pastor. Stormy church meetings ensued, and the quarrel continued.

Before 1659 this turmoil in the Hartford Church led to meetings with the elders of the other Connecticut churches in 1654, 1655, and 1656 and assemblies of the elders of Connecticut and Massachusetts Bay in June 1657 and again in September 1659. It caused the continual involvement of the General Court in the ecclesiastical affairs of the Commonwealth. On May 15, 1656, the Court appointed a committee to discuss the problem with the elders of the Connecticut churches. A special session was summoned on Feb-

ruary 26, 1656/57, to sanction the council which was to be held
at Boston and to submit to it the "Seventeen Questions." The
Court proclaimed a day of humiliation; it asked for peace and proposed another council for March 1657/58. The General Court
heard Stone's case in May 1658 and gave additional advice in August. By March 1658/59 it had determined to solicit outside advice
again and to allow a council to dispute the question. In June 1659
it ordered the two parties to appear in court in the fall to settle
the matter.[22] But for all its efforts the civil body was unable to
effect a reconciliation in the church.

Similar problems plagued the Wethersfield Church. From its
first settlement Wethersfield had faced dissension within its membership. The first members had departed from the Bay without
George Phillips, their pastor. Soon three of the members of the
new Connecticut church aligned themselves against the other four.
The Reverend John Davenport, of New Haven, attempted to end
the discord, but failed. Peace returned temporarily in 1643 and
1644 only after the departure of William Swain's faction. Strife
erupted again in 1656, when the minister, John Russell, excommunicated Lieutenant John Hollister without explanation and a
trial before the brethren. The members of the church and thirty-
eight of the leading citizens of the town supported the Lieutenant.
Several members of the church protested to the General Court in
August 1658. The Court found for the minister and pleaded with
the church to settle its differences. It was consulted again in March
1658/59 about the excommunication and answered that Russell
should present Lieutenant Hollister with the charges. In October
1659 it ordered another meeting to discuss the problem, but without result.[23]

The General Court utterly failed to restore peace in these two
churches; instead, harmony returned to the towns in 1659, when
William Goodwin and thirty-six or thirty-seven of the members
of the Hartford Church and John Russell with twenty members
of the Wethersfield Church, accompanied by two or three brethren
of the Windsor Church, moved up the Connecticut River to Had-
ley. Captain Cullick departed for Boston.[24] In February 1659/60
the Reverend John Cotton, Jr., accepted the invitation of the remainder of the Wethersfield Church to become their pastor, and

in 1660 the Reverend John Whiting was ordained pastor of the Hartford Church to serve with Stone. The interference of the General Court in the church controversies probably aggravated them; it certainly did not quell them.

Connecticut had changed since the days of its founding. New names appeared on the lists of magistrates and deputies; even responsible men like John Winthrop, Jr., had not ratified the Fundamental Orders. The Commonwealth became a less cohesive unit with the admission of the remote towns. Its homogeneity was shattered by the admission of newcomers and its tranquillity by the witchcraft mania and the threatened invasion by the Quakers. More crimes were committed, and greater authority was accruing in the hands of the magistracy.

At the same time Connecticut was growing sporadically under the eye of the ever watchful General Court. By the end of the period of the Fundamental Orders its population had risen to approximately four thousand, and several of its citizens had accumulated and retained large estates. Its economy remained agricultural and largely self-sustaining throughout this period. Only salt, sugar, and spices were imported on a large scale. In their home plots and in the fields the Congregationalists grew corn, wheat (known then as "English grain"), and peas and in the meadows and common pastures kept cows, pigs, oxen, and horses. When the hogs broke into the fields, pastures, or forests and rooted them up, the General Court or the town meetings had to pass laws requiring that all have rings in their snouts.[25]

When labor became scarce, the General Court acted in June 1641 to regulate the hours and wages of its working population. It froze the wages of carpenters, plowwrights, wheelwrights, masons, joiners, smiths, and coopers at 20 pence a day from March 10 to October 11 and 18 pence a day for the remainder of the year. In the summer the working day was eleven hours long and in the winter nine hours. In June 1649 the Court again asserted its authority over the population by instructing the magistrates to impress the fittest men of the Commonwealth to construct the public road at Saybrook. But when labor again became plentiful in March 1649/50 the Court repealed the fixed wages and restored bargaining.[26]

Massachusetts Bay grew wealthy as a shipping colony, but Connecticut's efforts to become either a trading center or a producer of a large staple for export failed. Its major cities were located too far inland. In February 1640/41 Connecticut began to feel the economic pinch that had been forecast by Jonathan Webster as early as August 1639 because of the decrease in the number of new settlers moving to the Commonwealth annually with the advent of the Civil War in England. The General Court acted to stimulate the production of wheat for export by giving each team 100 acres of plowing land and 20 acres of meadow in return for improving 20 tillable acres the first year, 80 the second, and the "whole hundred" the third year. The second phase of its economic program was to promote the manufacture of pipe staves. The Court prohibited the felling of trees and the selling of the finished staves without a license from the Particular Court. Furthermore, the Court ordered every family to plant one spoonful of hemp seed. In December 1642 Governor Wyllys, Messrs. Haynes, Hopkins, Whiting, Captain Mason, and Messrs. Chester, Hill, and Trott were chosen to investigate the possibility of building a ship to carry raw cotton and pipe staves to England.[27]

As a result of this program, Connecticut exported pipe staves, beaver, corn, livestock, biscuit and bread, and a little flour and linen to Boston, New Amsterdam, Long Island, Delaware, and some of the Caribbean colonies. But by 1644 Connecticut was exporting so much corn that it glutted the markets in Massachusetts Bay and Plymouth. Because of the complaints, the General Court was forced to rule that for the next two years no corn could be sold outside Connecticut except by William Whiting and Edward Hopkins. Later, in May 1650, Connecticut had become sufficiently self-supporting that the Court ordered that for one year after the next September 29 no foreigners could retail any goods within the Commonwealth on threat of confiscation of half their value. This step was specifically directed against the merchants of the Bay. But food again became scarce in the winter of 1652–1653. The Court ordered that none be exported from Connecticut before March without the consent of Deputy Governor Haynes, Mr. Welles, or Mr. Webster. The penalty imposed was the forfeiture of twice the value of the goods. It was rescinded just as soon as food became available again.[28]

A ferry soon crossed the Connecticut River at Windsor as the monopoly of the Bissell family. In January 1641/42 the Court authorized Windsor to provide a ferry and charge 3 pence for a single passenger, 2 pence each for several passengers, and 12 pence for a horse. It granted the monopoly to John Bissell for seven years in January 1648/49, allowing him to charge 8 pence for each horse or mare, 2 pence for each of several passengers, and 3 pence for a single passenger. It was renewed in May 1656 and again in May 1657. This monopoly descended to John Bissell, Jr., for a ten-year period in March 1657/58. By then Connecticut also had ferries at New London and Saybrook.[29] Under the Fundamental Orders, Connecticut managed its changing economic affairs unregulated by either England or Massachusetts Bay.

By 1660 the relationship with England had changed from what it had been in 1639. Charles I had sat on the throne when the majority of the Connecticut Congregationalists emigrated from England. From the cessation of the Great Migration in 1640 until the Restoration in 1660, England was preoccupied. The King was fighting for his very life and the survival of the Crown in the Bishops' Wars and the Civil War, which brought the final capture and beheading of the King and Archbishop. During the Commonwealth and Protectorate, England was absorbed in abolishing the political abuses employed to the disadvantage of the Puritans by Charles I, in eliminating the High Commission and Star Chamber, in reforming the Church of England, in waging war with the Dutch, and finally in the struggle for supremacy between the Independents and the Presbyterians. In 1642 Thomas Hooker, John Cotton, and John Davenport could decline an invitation to the Westminster Assembly, considering a discussion of church government an inadequate excuse for traveling a thousand leagues. The Assembly's decision would have little effect on the Connecticut churches.[30]

Only in June 1654 did Connecticut receive an order from the Lord Protector; it pertained to a matter close to the hearts of the men of Connecticut in its authorization of the expedition against the Dutch. Otherwise, England was so insensitive to the needs of Connecticut that in 1656 a movement was afoot to move the entire population of New England to Jamaica. The movement died a natural death shortly thereafter, and Parliament during the Protectorate delivered no further ultimatums to Connecticut. While England was in turmoil, Connecticut could act as a sovereign nation in both its internal and its external affairs, confident that it was safe from interference from abroad.

Until the Restoration the Congregationalists of Connecticut were content with their commonwealth status, just as they were content with their independent churches. Virtually unchallenged between 1639 and 1660, they were able to maintain both their temporal and their spiritual isolation from England. Throughout the period some settlers crossed the Atlantic repeatedly. Others preserved their ties with their mother country by correspondence, although the mail was delivered at a snail's pace. One letter written in Connecticut on December 7, 1648, did not arrive in England until the middle of June 1649.[31] On several occasions public days of humiliation were called in Connecticut to express the distress over events in England, as in January 1643/44 when the General Court ordered a day of humiliation to be held once a month because of its concern over the state of England. Upon occasion English creditors were allowed a certain number of months to assert their claims on an estate in Connecticut. In one instance in 1648 the General Court, in the same breath that it referred to Connecticut as a commonwealth, threatened to ship to England any Dutchman found guilty of selling shot and powder to the Indians and leave him at the mercy of Parliament. But even Thomas Hooker felt so strongly about the evils of living in England that in his will he wrote, "I do not forbid my sonne John from seeking and taking a wife in England, yet I doe forbid him from marrying and tarrying there." [32]

Yet the sentimental ties to England were strong. When in 1657/58 the time came to rename Pequot, John Winthrop, Jr.'s, settlement, the preamble to the order of the General Court read in part:

> This Court, considering that there hath yet noe place in any of the Colonies bene named in memory of yᵉ Citty of London, there being a new

plantation within this Jurisdiction of Conecticut setled vpon ye faire Riuer of Monhegin, in ye Pequot Countrey, it being an excellent harbour and a fit and convenient place for future trade, it being alsoe the only place wch ye English of these parts haue possessed by conquest, and y^t by a very iust war vpon y^t great and warlike people, ye Pequots, that therefore they might therby leaue to posterity the memory of y^t renowned citty of London, from whence we had our transportation, haue thought fit, in honour to that famous Citty, to cal ye said Plantation, New London.[33]

But the Commonwealth did not admit political subservience any more than the churches acknowledged dependence on the Anglican, Presbyterian, or Independent churches of England.

On May 8, 1660, however, Charles II was proclaimed King of England, supported by a coalition of Cavaliers, Presbyterians, and Anglicans. Oliver Cromwell had died in September 1658, and by July 1659 his son Richard had proved himself utterly incapable of governing England. News of the Restoration reached Boston on July 27 and traveled swiftly to Connecticut. The Restoration aroused concern in Connecticut that an anti-Congregational rule might be imposed on it by Charles II, who had little sympathy with its churches and political autonomy. There was also the danger that a claim to their territory might be asserted under the conflicting grant made in 1635 to James, Marquis of Hamilton, by the Council for New England. Though no attempt to pursue the rights conveyed in this patent had yet been made, the patent stood on the records, awarding the lands from the Narragansett to the Connecticut River and sixty miles inland to hostile forces. The need to protect their internal security compelled the Connecticut fathers to seek a patent from the King, even though it constituted a rejection of the concept of authority promulgated in the preamble of the Fundamental Orders. It now became expedient to abandon the theory of a divine sovereign and seek the protection of a temporal monarch as well.

Such action was preferable to subjection to a Sir Ferdinando Gorges or another William Laud or risk encroachments by Massachusetts Bay or the Dutch. In an undated letter to the Earl of Manchester, the General Court admitted that "we want a Pattent to secure o^r standing and to confirme o^r privilidges, and to strengthen vs against such as may oppose o^r p^{r}sent intrests in civil polecy." [34] In its dilemma the General Court opportunistically decided to avow its allegiance to the King, as a preliminary step in the regularization of its constitutional status.

On March 14, 1660/61, the Court elaborated on its position by declaring:

> In reference to former intentions and motions wch could not be brought to a ful conclusion for ye manner and meanes to accomplish the same, til this meeting of ye Generall Court, It is concluded and declared by this Court, That (as it was formerly agreed by those Magestrates and Deputies that then could be assembled together,) it is our duty and very necessary to make a speedy address to his Sacred Maiesty, our Soveraigne Lord Charles the Second, King of England, Scotland, France and Ireland, to acknowledge our loyalty & allegiance to his highnes, hereby declareing and professing ourselues, all the Inhabitants of this Colony, to be his Highnes loyall and faythfull subjects. And doe further conclude it necessary that we should humbly petition his Maiesty for grace and fauour, and for ye continuance and confirmation of such privilidges and liberties as are necessary for the comfortable and peaceable settlement of this Colony. [35]

Previously, with only rare exceptions, Connecticut had been designated the "Commonwealth" of Connecticut, emphasizing its independence from English civil authority. But by the spring of 1661 Connecticut wanted to consider itself a colony. It intended to swear allegiance to Charles II before the arrival of the royal command in order to assure the continuation and confirmation of the privileges and liberties it had enjoyed under the Fundamental Orders.

As the commissioners of the United Colonies later stated, in the seventeenth century jurisdictional rights depended on an indisputable patent.[36] And Connecticut had none. To eliminate the uncertainties inherent in the Warwick Patent the Commonwealth needed a royal charter. In December 1644 an agreement had been reached between George Fenwick, acting as the agent of the Patentees even though he had not their express instructions for this particular case, and Edward Hopkins, John Haynes, John Mason, John Steele, and James Boosy, representing the General Court. The Court confirmed the agreement in February 1644/45, and it was amended later several times. The bill of sale conveyed Saybrook Fort with its appurtenances and weapons, all the land along the Connecticut River, and the Patentees' common seal to the Commonwealth. Fenwick also included in the transfer any rights to the land between the Narragansett and Connecticut rivers that *might* come within the Patentees' jurisdiction. By 1662 this purchase had cost Connecticut about £1,600 in taxes on certain products that were exported past the river's mouth and on milk cows and mares raised in Connecticut and on the hogs slaughtered. The transaction, however, never provided the Commonwealth of Connecticut with a legally justifiable title to its lands and a valid authorization for the establishment of a corporate government.[37]

The reasons for Connecticut's lack of a case are found in the Patent itself. Much of the history of the Warwick Patent is nebulous. The Patent's very existence has been disputed. There is no surviving record of the original transfer of the land by the Council for New England to its president, the Earl of Warwick. The subsequent conveyance of the title of this tract by the Earl of Warwick to the Puritan lords is dated three months prior to their petition to the Council for the grant. The Patent is dated March 1631/32, but a rough draft of the Lords' petition was supposedly presented to the Council on June 26, 1632, at Warwick House in Holborne, England. The minutes of this meeting record the fact that the draft of the proposed patent was read and the order given that the territory extending thirty English miles west along the coast from the Narragansett River and fifty miles north be conferred upon Lord Robert Rich and his associates, provided it did not conflict with any other patent. Lord Gorges, Sir Ferdinando Gorges, Sir Henry Spellman, Sir James Bagg, and Captain J. Mason were asked to meet and agree on the contents before the next meeting of the Council.[38] But this is the final action on the Patent in the minutes. Warwick soon lost the presidency of the Council to the hostile Sir Ferdinando Gorges.[39]

The Massachusetts historian Thomas Hutchinson felt that the Connecticut settlers had never obtained a sealed copy of the Patent from Fenwick and consequently condemned them as intruders. Charles M. Andrews doubted that the Patent ever existed, for in 1648 Connecticut could not produce a copy of it to prove its rights to the commissioners from the Bay. Andrews was skeptical about any rights conferred by the Patent even had it been properly executed; it represented the transfer of the title to the land, rather than the authority to establish a corporate government.[40]

On the other hand, throughout the ages the Warwick Patent has been known as the "Old Patent of Connecticut." Thomas Lechford in 1641 wrote that there "are five or six townes, and Churches upon the River *Connecticot,* where are worthy master *Hooker,* master *Warham,* master *Hewet,* and divers others, and master *Fenwike* with the Lady *Boteler,* at the rivers mouth in a faire house, and well fortified, and one master *Higgison,* a young man, their Chaplain. These plantations have a Patent." [41] Actually, Lechford should have written that only Saybrook had a patent; at this time the Connecticut towns had the Fundamental Orders, but not a charter. Not until 1644 did Connecticut purchase the Patent. Benjamin Trumbull was convinced that at least a copy of the Warwick Patent had been exhibited when the New England colonies united in the New England Confederation and that Connecticut's legal rights were then generally recognized in the New World. He felt that the Patent was as valid as the Charter of the Bay, basing his premise on the offer of Governor Edward Hopkins in 1648 to swear that the copy of the Patent in his possession was an authentic duplicate of the original in England.[42]

The consensus today is that the Warwick Patent did exist. The original probably perished in a fire at Saybrook Fort, and the duplicate was either lost at sea by Lord Keeper Finch or returned to Connecticut in 1663 by John Winthrop, Jr., together with a copy a Mr. Dalley, Edward Hopkins' executor, gave him from Hopkins' possessions. The copy Winthrop discovered bore the endorsement, "The copye of the Patent for Connecticutt being the copy of that copy wch was shewed to the people here by m^r George Fenwick found amongst m^r Hopkins paps." It bore no seal of authenticity, however. Where Hopkins obtained the copy is unknown; possibly it was in Connecticut at the time of the Fenwick sale in 1644 and then Hopkins took it to England upon his return.[43]

After Rhode Island's successful endeavor to obtain a charter in 1644 Connecticut decided to apply to Parliament in 1645 for a confirmation of its title. On May 13, 1645, the General Court

Charles II, King of Great Britain and Ireland, 1660–1685, portrayed by an unidentified member of the School of Lely. *Courtesy of Colonial Williamsburg, Williamsburg, Virginia.*

desiered that the Gou^r [Haynes], Mr. Deputy [Hopkins], Mr. Fenwicke, Mr. Whiting and Mr. Welles should agitate the busines concerneing the enlardgement of the libertyes of the Patent for this Jurisdiction, and if they see a concurrence of op^rtunityes, both in regard of England [blank in original] they haue liberty to p^rceed therein, att such resonable chardge as they shall judge meete, and the Court will take some speedy course for the dischardge and satisfieing the same, as yt shalbe concluded and certified to the Court by the said Comittee or the greater p^rte of them.[44]

On July 9, 1645, it ordered a letter written to George Fenwick, asking him "to goe for Ingland to endeauor the enlardgement of Pattent, and to further other aduantages for the Country." [45] Fenwick did not undertake the journey himself, but sent a Mr. Gregson, who perished at sea on New Haven's "Phantom Ship" along with the manuscript of Thomas Hooker's *A Survey of the Summe of Church-Discipline*. As Benjamin Trumbull explained, in "consequence of these circumstances, and the state of affairs in England afterwards, the business rested until after the restoration." [46] And by then Fenwick was in his grave. The Warwick Patent remained Connecticut's best legal claim to the land and basis for its government until 1662, and its validity was extremely dubious.

Once England was again at peace, the magistrates and deputies who lived near enough to assemble on short notice met informally and emerged in agreement on the wisdom of approaching the King. The General Court on March 14, 1660/61, voted to address Charles II, acknowledging their loyalty and allegiance and at the same time to submit a petition for a charter to confirm its liberties and privileges. It intended to meet the expenses incurred with the £500 owed to Connecticut by Fenwick's heirs. This refund was the amount agreed on in the settlement of the estate because Fenwick had never been able to provide the Commonwealth with adequate jurisdictional rights to the territory it had purchased with the Fort Rate.[47]

On May 16 the Court voted to appoint a committee composed of Governor Winthrop, Deputy Governor John Mason, Magistrates Samuel Wyllys and Matthew Allyn, the Reverends Warham, Stone, Samuel Hooker, and John Whiting, and Secretary Daniel Clark to approve the address which had been drawn up by

Governor Winthrop and to prepare the petition to the King. It appointed the Governor its agent in obtaining the Charter and dispatched letters to Lord Brooke (the son of the Patentee) and to Lord Saye and Sele, the only survivor of the Warwick Patentees, who had since risen to become Lord Privy Seal and a member of the Privy Council and the Council for the Colonies. Lord Saye and Sele's health was failing, but he used what strength his gout left him in advancing Connecticut's cause until his death on April 14, 1662. In the Court's name a letter was also addressed to the Earl of Manchester, a son-in-law of the Earl of Warwick, who as a reward for his active role in the Restoration had been made Lord of the Bed Chamber, a member of the Privy Council, Knight of the Garter, Lord Lieutenant of Huntingdonshire, and, most important, Lord Chamberlain of his Majesty's Household. The Earl of Manchester in turn summoned the aid of Lord Chancellor Clarendon. Unfortunately for Connecticut, George Fenwick had died in England in 1657.[48]

The petition [49] to the King in the name of the "general court of the colony of Connecticut in New-England" was dated June 7, 1661. It emphasized Connecticut's great difficulties in settling the wilderness and the tremendous expenses incurred in purchasing the Warwick Patent. The Court requested a confirmation of the rights granted in the Patent.

It was accompanied by the address to the King, in which the General Court perhaps deviated from the truth slightly in defending Connecticut's period of isolation from England,

> when those sad and vnhappy times of troubles and wars begun in England, which we could only bewaile wth sighes and mournfull teares: And haue euer since hid our selues behind the Mountains, in this desolate desert, as a people forsaken, choosing rather to sit solitary and wait only vpon the Divine Providence for protection than to apply ourselves to any of those many changes of powers, o^r hearts as wel as o^r stations stil remaining free from illegal ingagements and intire to yor Maties intrests, euen now at ye returne of o^r Lord ye King to his Crowne and dignities.[50]

Unbidden they proclaimed their loyalty and allegiance. They begged that they be reinstated in the Crown's protection and favor. It is ironical that the Puritans should appear as Royalists, but removed from Charles I and Archbishop Laud, the Civil Wars and the Protectorate, by the Atlantic Ocean and the passage of many years, they could defend their independence in this manner and "implore your Maties fauour and gratious protection, y^t you would be pleased to accept this Collony, your owne Colony, a little branch of yor mighty Empire." [51]

At first glance it appears strange that Charles II should have granted so liberal a charter to a Puritan colony. But the General Court had been wise in its choice of agent. Without question, John Winthrop, Jr., was personally responsible for obtaining the Charter. Connecticut's first governor under the Massachusetts Bay Commission and its last under the Fundamental Orders was born in February 1605/06. He was the eldest son of Governor John Winthrop of Massachusetts, had been trained in medicine at Trinity College, Dublin, and afterward was admitted to the Inner Temple. Winthrop had traveled extensively abroad and continued to correspond with Robert Boyle, Sir Chistopher Wren, Sir Isaac Newton, and John Milton about his interests in optics, astronomy, and chemistry. He was a fellow of the society which in 1663 became the Royal Society.

He married his first cousin, Martha Fones, but she died in 1636. His second wife was Elizabeth Reade, a stepdaughter of the Reverend Hugh Peter. In his younger days this Winthrop had acted as agent for the Warwick Patentees at Saybrook and had been a founder of Ipswich in the Bay and an assistant in the Massachusetts Bay Company. His interest in mineralogy and his realization of the need to bolster Connecticut's economy led him to attempts at establishing ironworks at Saugus, Massachusetts Bay, graphite mines at Sturbridge, and salt mines at New Haven. He founded New London in 1646, hoping to find iron there. His water-purified gristmill there was Connecticut's first incorporated industry.

For several years both Connecticut and New Haven coaxed John Winthrop, the younger, to establish his permanent residence within their jurisdiction. In 1651 the General Court of Connecticut granted him the rights to any lead, copper, tin, antimony, vitriol, salt, black lead (graphite), and alum mines that he might discover, together with the land, timber, and waters within a three-mile radius. The offer was limited only by the provision that the mine not be within the boundaries of a town already established.[52]

In 1650 he had become a freeman of Connecticut and shortly afterward a magistrate. Without campaigning, he was elected governor in 1657. In fact, in May 1657 the Court had to appoint Captain Cullick to inform him that he had been elected to the office and to request that he come to Hartford to assume his duties. By August he had not appeared, and the Court once again had to beg him to come to live in Hartford with his family, offering him the use, at public expense, of the house and lands formerly belonging to John Haynes. In October the Court appointed the treasurer to supply men and horses to send for the recalcitrant governor. Not until March 11, 1657/58, do the records show him exercising the authority of his office. Thereafter he served Connecticut as its beloved governor until his death.[53]

Governor Winthrop sailed for Europe on July 23, 1661, aboard the Dutch ship *de Trouw*, arriving first in Holland on September 6, but embarking immediately for London. With him he carried detailed instructions from the General Court to address Lord Saye and Sele, the Earl of Manchester, Lord Brooke, Nathaniel Fiennes (Lord Saye and Sele's son), Samuel Peck (a doctor of physic), and a Mr. Floid of the Corporation. The Court directed him to do everything in his power to obtain a copy of the Warwick Patent; if impossible, it urged him to attempt to get the purchase price refunded. If, on the other hand, the Patent could be found and its conditions were comparable to the Bay's privileges, he was to seek a confirmation of it. Or, if he found that a new charter could be procured, he should ask for the rights and immunities previously granted to the Bay and the territory extending to Plymouth on the east, Massachusetts on the north, and the Delaware River on the south. It listed the men who should be named freemen of the corporation and requested that Connecticut be freed from import and export duties for twenty-one years. The Court also urged that a settlement be made concerning the ship that Prince Rupert and Captain Fernes had highjacked and that England send aid against the Dutch.[54] Besides these comprehensive instructions, Governor Winthrop carried the address and the petition, the letters to Lord Saye and Sele and the Earl of Manchester, £80 from the General Court to partially cover his expenses, and a letter of credit for the amount of £500 signed by John Talcott, treasurer of Connecticut, to cover his legal costs, perquisites, and gratuities.

Before his audience with the King, the Governor redrafted the petition.[55] He also made contact with his friend, Samuel Hartlib, who presented Connecticut's cause to the influential Dr. Benjamin Worsley, and sought the aid of William Jessop, the former secretary of the Patentees. Early in February 1661/62 Governor Winthrop presented the petition in its revised form to Sir Edward Nicholas, one of the secretaries of state, who in turn referred it to the Attorney-General, Sir Geoffrey Palmer. The Attorney-General then reported it favorably. The secretary, after receiving instructions from the King in Council, caused a warrant to be issued ordering that a bill for the Charter of Incorporation of Connecticut be prepared. The Attorney-General thereupon drew up the Charter, giving legal form to the requests expressed in the governor's petition. Connecticut's Charter was recorded at Westminster on April 23 and completed its journey through the seals on May 10, emerging as a writ of the Privy Seal. On the same day it was enrolled in the Six Clerks' Office in Chancery Lane, and the Great Seal was affixed to it.[56]

The success of the Winthrop mission was largely due to the personality of John Winthrop, Jr., coupled with the determination of Charles II to weaken Massachusetts Bay and New Haven in retaliation for their harboring the regicides. Connecticut also had powerful friends in the Lord Saye and Sele and the Earl of Manchester. The traditional explanation of the governor's success, as related by Cotton Mather, was "that while he was engaged in this Negotiation, being admitted unto a private Conference with the King, he presented His Majesty with a Ring, which King *Charles* I. had upon some Occasion given to his Grandfather; and the King not only accepted his Present, but also declared, that he accounted it one of his *Richest Jewels*." [57] Whether this tale is based on myth or fact is unimportant. That the King granted so liberal a charter to Connecticut is nothing less than phenomenal.

Word of the passage of the Charter was sent jubilantly in a letter from the governor to John Talcott on May 12. The governor was obviously delighted with it in spite of the expense because "it is so full & large in the grants & priveledges given." [58] He sent the original and sealed duplicate to New England in the care of Simon Bradstreet and the Reverend John Norton, who had been serving in England as agents for Massachusetts Bay. On September 3, 1662, they arrived in Boston, where the Charter was eagerly examined by the commissioners of the United Colonies between September 4 and 16 and then forwarded to Connecticut with its commissioners, Samuel Wyllys and John Talcott. Without their governor, who remained in England, the freemen assembled at the Court of Election heard the Charter read publicly on October 9, 1662, and voted their approval.[59]

Adoption of the Charter in 1662 did not signify an annulment or rejection of the Fundamental Orders; instead the Charter confirmed the government sanctioned by the Fundamental Orders and the lands granted in the Warwick Patent and provided Connecticut with an indisputable right to both. The Charter did not represent a revolutionary overthrow of the Commonwealth's constitution, but because the majority of the provisions of the Charter had been drafted in Connecticut,[60] the precepts espoused by the first constitution remained unchanged and endured throughout the colonial period.

The Charter confirmed the existing body politic. The nineteen recipients of the Patent served as freemen of the "Company and Society of our Collony of Conecticut in America." As the officers of the new corporation, the governor, deputy governor, the twelve assistants (magistrates), and the deputies appeared as before. They sat as the General Court, now transposed into the General Assembly of the Corporation. Councilors did not replace the magistrates. The assistants and deputies continued to be elected by the freemen and admitted inhabitants, respectively. John Winthrop retained his position as governor, and John Mason was reinstated as deputy governor. The twelve magistrates continued in office for the following year under the title of "assistants," and the deputies continued to represent the towns, although now a maximum of two for each town was applied. The General Assembly, like the General Court, was required to meet at least once in May and once in October.

The Charter confirmed much of Connecticut's autonomy. It

conferred on Connecticut greater powers of self-government than the King had permitted any colony except Rhode Island. Neither King nor Parliament possessed the right to verify appointments or interfere with elections, nor could the English courts act as courts of review. The supreme power in Connecticut continued to be the General Assembly. Its acts were not subject to the royal negative or even inspection. They were restricted only by the general provision that they not be contrary to the laws of England. At the October 9, 1662, session, the General Court ordered "and hereby declare[d] all yᵉ Lawes and orders of this Colony to stand in full force and vertue, vnles any be cross to yᵉ Tenour of oʳ Charter." Englishmen in Connecticut now possessed the same rights as Englishmen living in their native country. The Charter sanctioned their right to appoint juries, elect freemen and colonial officers, pass laws, levy fines, raise an army and a police force, plead and be impleaded in court, and own and transfer real and personal property.

Under the Charter, Connecticut retained the same seal it had used since the purchase of the Warwick Patent in 1644, but now the Great Seal authorized it. Anyone desiring to be admitted as a freeman of the colony had to fulfill similar requirements as others had had to meet to become freemen of the Commonwealth, but he also had to subscribe to the Oath of Supremacy. Church and state remained intimately related, as they had been under the Fundamental Orders; the General Assembly, in admitting South-old on Long Island to the colony, added with a familiar ring, "And we doe advice and order Capᵗ Yong to see that yᵉ Minister be duely paid his meet and competent maintenance." [61]

The Charter of 1662 approved many of the practices which had existed under the former constitution, but inevitably it wrought change. The Charter conferred on Connecticut all the land included formerly in the Warwick Patent. This meant that its western boundary extended to the Pacific Ocean and its southern line to Long Island Sound. Whether intentionally or accidentally is not known, but New Haven now fell within the jurisdiction of Connecticut. Charles II, perhaps because of his ignorance of the geography of New England, merely restated the boundaries set in the Patent. But more likely because New Haven had harbored the regicides, Edward Whalley, William Goffe, and John Dixwell, while Winthrop obligingly let his messengers search Connecticut, and had been the last New England colony to proclaim him king, Charles II legally ended New Haven's independent existence. Too, he may have been advised that an enlarged Connecticut would serve as a better foil to a powerful and often haughty Massachusetts Bay. Governor Winthrop was charged with encouraging the King to enlarge Connecticut's territory at the expense of New Haven, but he later denied it.[62] New Haven fought "the great sin of Connecticut" with fastings, prayers, heated letters of protest, and petitions to the King until 1665 and only then agreed to the union in preference to becoming attached to the royal colony of New York. Part of Long Island also fell within the new corporate limits of Connecticut. Opportunistically, Southold and Oyster Bay on Long Island withdrew from the New Haven jurisdiction to unite with the stronger colony. They were accepted as part of the Colony of Connecticut by the General Assembly at its meeting on October 9, 1662, along with the towns of Guilford, Westchester, Stamford, and Greenwich on the shore of Long Island Sound.[63] Connecticut also claimed jurisdiction over Mystic and Pawcatuck, but the boundary was not finally determined until many years later.

Under the Charter, land in Connecticut was held "as of our Manor of East Greenewich, in Free and Comon Soccage, and not in Capite nor by Knights Service," that is, not subject to feudal dues, nor even a quitrent.[64] This was little different from the system of land tenure under the Fundamental Orders, but now one-fifth of any gold or silver discovered was reserved for the King. The Charter officially pronounced Hartford the capital of Connecticut. Previously the majority of the sessions of the General and Particular Courts had met there, but the Fundamental Orders had not expressly named Hartford the capital. Under the new patent the governor became a more powerful officer; the right of the freemen and magistrates to convene the General Court was abrogated by the requirement that the governor or deputy governor be present at each of the meetings of the General Assembly.

The most significant change effected by the Charter was in the concept of authority. With the Charter, Charles II became the acknowledged sovereign of Connecticut. As the Congregational churches were gradually becoming aware of the necessity of admitting members through the Halfway Covenant, so the General Court had awakened to the fact that the constitutional status of Connecticut was precarious. Connecticut had been defenseless under English law. In self-protection the Court had to seek a royal patent. The Charter was in effect a new covenant. In the Fundamental Orders the covenant had been twofold: between God and the inhabitants and residents of Connecticut, and between the settlers of Connecticut themselves. In the Charter the King was admitted to the covenant in the place of God. Henceforth the officers of the Colony of Connecticut were required to subscribe to the Oath of Allegiance administered by the governor, deputy governor, or an assistant by authority of the King.[65]

The first mention in the records of loyalty due the King had appeared at the Particular Court on May 13, 1662, when the "Court considering the charg layd in against Mrs Skillinger respecting Treason agaynst his Matie and finding noe testimony to proue this charge doe acquit ye said Skilling^r and adiudge Wm Morton to pay to her the Sum of 40^s to beare her expences." [66] On May 15 the General Court could be found enforcing "the Proclamation sent forth from his Matie o^r Soveraigne or the Parliam^t of England, respecting the transporteing of Tobacco to forreigne nations." Custom officials had appeared in the Connecticut towns by July 22, 1662, after the passage of the Charter, but before it had been accepted by the freemen of Connecticut.[67]

The Fundamental Orders failed in their concept of authority when apparent peace returned to England with the Restoration. To assure their very survival the second generation in Connecticut realized the necessity of having their constitutional position regularized and their legal status as a corporate colony inhabited by loyal subjects of the King established. They required royal protection to prevent interference in their churches and state by Englishmen now free to look abroad once more. The acceptance of the Charter and rejection of the original covenant of the Fundamental Orders, like the adoption of the Halfway Covenant, was a sacrificial measure to preserve the Congregational state.

Prior to the Charter, Connecticut had enjoyed the autonomous

position of a commonwealth. It was the first settlement in America
to draw up a written instrument of government recognizing this
independence and providing a specific form for the body politic.
The government established by the Fundamental Orders more
than three centuries ago was neither a popular government nor a
modern democracy; a minority of its people, dedicated to creating
a Congregational commonwealth according to the Bible, governed
Connecticut from its founding until the Restoration. The creation
of a Congregational sanctuary in the wilderness had been the force
driving these Puritans from England to Massachusetts Bay and
from there to the Connecticut River in the 1630's. To build this
Congregational state they had tackled virgin country where provisions were desperately few and sickness and toil abounded. They
purchased the land from the Indians and then fought the Indians.
They cleared forests, planted fields, and built their homes and
their meetinghouses. And they drew up and adopted the Fundamental Orders to make certain that a reliable civil government
would support their churches.

Isolated from England by the Atlantic Ocean and England's
internal conflicts, the men in Connecticut did not create a paradise.
Human nature would not permit a society to exist without jealousies, feuds, and crime. But Connecticut's Congregationalists did
succeed in founding a Bible state enforced by its own constitution
and code of law, officers, and courts which satisfied their need for
freedom to worship God according to their beliefs, purified of
human innovations, impositions, and interference.

The actual system of government decreed in the Fundamental Orders was not basically altered by the Charter. Local autonomy for all intents and purposes was retained; the King did not
replace the governor, and Parliament did not supplant the General Court. The officers of the colony, the General Assembly, the
freemen, and the deputies remained essentially as they had been
under the Fundamental Orders. The laws enacted by the General
Court and codified into the Capital Laws of 1642 and the Ludlow
Code of 1650 remained unchanged. Nor was the judicial system
amended by the Charter, although it was soon revised, and the
Anglican hierarchy was not substituted for Congregational polity.
In turn, the Charter was not overthrown during the American

Revolution; only the loyalty due the Crown was omitted. Not until 1818 did Connecticut adopt a new constitution to replace the Charter.

In establishing a practical civil government for the Congregational churches, the Fundamental Orders succeeded for twenty-three years. But with the Restoration the men of Connecticut were forced to relinquish their isolation and return to the world as Englishmen. By October 1662 the General Court was ready to accept royal countenance and the protected position of a charter colony. Connecticut's joy in the transfer from Commonwealth to Colony, from the Fundamental Orders to the Charter of 1662, radiated from the order of October 9, 1662:

> This Court appoints that Wednesday come fortnight be set apart, throwout this Colony, for a solemne day of Thanksgiueing for ye mercies y^t God hath extended to this Colony ye yeare past, and p^{r}ticulerly for ye good success God hath giuen to ye indeauours of o^r Hon^d Gouerno^r in obteineing o^r Charter of his Maiestie o^r Soveraigne; as also for his gratious answer of o^r pray^r in ye late draught, in sending raine; and for abatement of ye sicknes; and for ye hopes we haue of settlement in v^e waies of peace and righteousnes.[68]

The men of Connecticut were seventeenth-century Englishmen in spite of their migrations from England to Massachusetts Bay and then to Connecticut. Their optimism was the result of the reaffirmation of their position as loyal subjects of the King, while their local institutions remained unchanged and unchallenged. They were in fact almost as independent in state and church under the new Charter as they had been under the Fundamental Orders of Connecticut from 1639 until 1662. But their civil and ecclesiastical privileges and liberties were more adequately protected from the new threat of outside interference by a temporal as well as a spiritual sovereign than by God alone.

The Warwick Patent,

or

THE OLD PATENT OF CONNECTICUT

To all people, unto whom this present writing shall come, Robert, Earl of Warwick, sendeth greeting, in our Lord God everlasting.

Know ye, that the said Robert, Earl of Warwick, for divers good causes and considerations him thereunto moving, hath given, granted, bargained, sold, enfeoffed, aliened, and confirmed, and by these presents doth give, grant, bargain, sell, enfeoff, aliene, and confirm, unto the right honorable William, Viscount Say and Seal, the right honorable Robert, Lord Brook, the right honorable Lord Rich, and the honorable Charles Fiennes, Esq. Sir Nathaniel Rich, Knt. Sir Richard Saltonstall, Knt. Richard Knightly, Esq. John Pym, Esq. John Hampden, John Humphrey, Esq. and Herbert Pelham, Esq. their heirs and assigns, and their associates forever, all that part of New-England, in America, which lies and extends itself from a river there called Narraganset river, the space of forty leagues upon a straight line near the sea shore towards the southwest, west and by south, or west, as the coast lieth towards Virginia, accounting three English miles to the league; and also all and singular the lands and hereditaments whatsoever, lying and being within the lands aforesaid, north and south in latitude and breadth, and in length and longitude of and within, all the breadth aforesaid, throughout the main lands there, from the western ocean to the south sea, and all lands and grounds, place and places, soil, wood, and woods, grounds, havens, ports, creeks and rivers, waters, fishings, and hereditaments whatsoever, lying within the said space, and every part and parcel thereof. And also all islands lying in America aforesaid, in the said seas, or either of them, on the western or eastern coasts, or parts of the said tracts of lands, by these presents mentioned to be given, granted, bargained, sold, enfeoffed, aliened, and confirmed, and also all mines and minerals, as well, royal mines of gold and silver, as other mines and minerals whatsoever, in the said land and premises, or any part thereof, and also the several rivers within the said limits, by what name or names soever called or known, and all jurisdictions, rights, and royalties, liberties, freedoms, immunities, powers, privileges, franchises, preeminencies, and commodities whatsoever, which the said Robert, Earl of Warwick, now hath or had, or might use, exercise, or enjoy, in or within any part or parcel thereof, excepting and reserving to his majesty, his heirs, and successors the fifth part of all gold and silver ore, that shall be found within the said premises, or any part or parcel thereof: To HAVE and to HOLD the said part of New-England in America, which lies and extends and is abutted as aforesaid. And the said several rivers and every part and parcel thereof, and all the said islands, rivers, ports, havens, waters, fishings, mines, minerals, jurisdictions, powers, franchises, royalties, liberties, privileges, commodities, hereditaments and premises, whatsoever with the appurtenances, unto the said William, Viscount Say and Seal, Robert, Lord Brook, Robert, Lord Rich, Charles Fiennes, Sir Nathaniel Rich, Sir Richard Saltonstall, Richard Knightly, John Pym, John Hampden, John Humphrey and Herbert Pelham, their heirs and assigns and their associates, to the only proper and absolute use and behoof of them the said William, Viscount Say and Seal, Robert, Lord Brook, Robert, Lord Rich, Charles Fiennes, Sir Nathaniel Rich, Sir Richard Saltonstall, Richard Knightly, John Pym, John Hampden, John Humphrey, and Herbert Pelham, their heirs and assigns, and their associates for ever more.

In witness whereof the said Robert, Earl of Warwick, hath hereunto set his hand and seal, the nineteenth day of March, in the seventh year of the reign of our sovereign Lord Charles, by the Grace of God, King of England, Scotland, France and Ireland, defender of the faith, &c. Annoq. Domini, 1631.

> *Signed, sealed, and delivered, in the presence of*
> WALTER WILLIAMS.
> THOMAS HOWSON.
> ROBERT WARWICK. *A Seal.*

The Massachusetts Bay Commission

A Comission graunted to seuall P[r]sons to governe the People att Coñecticott for the Space of a Yeare nowe nexte comeing, an Exemplificac̃on whereof ensueth:

Whereas, vpon some reason & grounds, there are to remove from this o[r] comonwealth & body of the Mattachusetts in America dyv['s] of o[r] loveing ffriends, neighb[r]s, ffreemen & members of Newe Towne, Dorchest[r], Waterton, & other places, whoe are resolved to transplant themselues & their estates vnto the Ryver of Coñecticott, there to reside & inhabite, & to that end dyv[rs] are there already, & dyv[rs] others shortly to goe, wee, in this present Court assembled, on the behalfe of o[r] said memb[rs], & John Winthrop, Junr, Esq, Goun[r], appoyncted by certaine noble personages & men of quallitie interested in the said ryv[r], wch are yet in England, on their behalfe, have had a serious consideraç̃on there[on], & thinke it meete that where there are a people to sitt down & cohabite, there will followe, vpon occaç̃on, some cause of difference, as also dyvers misdeamean[rs], wch will require a speedy redresse; & in regard of the distance of place, this state and goum[t] cannot take notice of the same as to apply timely remedy, or to dispence equall iustice to them & their affaires, as may be desired; & in regard the said noble psonages and men of quallitie have something ingaged themselues & their estates in the planting of the said ryver, & by vertue of a pattent, doe require jurisdicc̃on of the said place & people, & neither the mindes of the said psonages (they being writ vnto) are as yet knowen, nor any manner of goum[t] is yet agreed on, & there being a necessitie, as aforesaid, that some present goum[t] may be obserued, wee therefore thinke mee[te], & soe order, that Roger Ludlowe, Esq, Willm Pinchon, Esq, John Steele, Willm Swaine, Henry Smyth, Willm Phe[lps], Willm Westwood, & Andrewe Ward, or the greater p̄te of them shall haue full power & aucthoritie to hear & determine in a iudiciall way, by witnesses vpon oathe examine, w^t[^{h}in] the said plantacõn, all those differences wch may arise betweene p̄tie & p̄tie, as also, vpon misdemean^r, to inflicte corporall punishm^t or imprisonm^t, to ffinc & levy the same if occacõn soe require, to make & decree such orders, for the present, that may be for the peaceable & quiett ordering the affaires of the said plantacõn, both in tradeing, planting, building, lotts, millitarie dissipline, defensiue warr, (if neede soe require,) as shall best conduce to the publique good of the same, & that the said Roger Ludlowe, Willm Pinchon, John Steele, Willm Swaine, Henry Smyth, Willm Phelpes, Willm Westwood, Andrewe Warner, or the great^r p̄te of them, shall haue power, vnder the great^r p̄te of their ha[nds], att a day or dayes by them appoyncted, vpon convenient not[ice], to convent the said inhabitants of the said townes to any convenient place that they shall thinke meete, in a legall & open manner, by way of Court, to p̄ceede in execute[ing] the power & aucthoritie aforesaide, & in case of p̄sent necessitie, two of them ioyneing togeather, to inflict corpall punishm^t vpon any offender if they see good & warrantable ground soe to doe; provided, alwayes, that this comĩssion shall not extende any longer time then one whole yeare from the date thereof, & in the meane time it shalbe lawfull for this Court to recall the said p̄sents if they see cause, and if soe be there may be a mutuall and setled goum^t condiscended vnto by & with the good likeing & consent of the saide noble p̄sonages, or their agent, the inhabitants, & this comõnwealthe; provided, also, that this may not be any preiudice to the interst of those noble p̄sonages in the s^d ryver & confines thereof within their seuall lymitts.

The Fundamental Orders
of Connecticut

FORASMUCH as it hath pleased the Allmighty God by the wise disposition of his diuyne pʳuidence so to Order and dispose of things that we the Inhabitants and Residents of Windsor, Harteford and Wethersfield are now cohabiting and dwelling in and vppon the River of Conectecotte and the Lands thereunto adioyneing; And well knowing where a people are gathered togather the word of God requires that to mayntayne the peace and vnion of such a people there should be an orderly and decent Gouerment established according to God, to order and dispose of the affayres of the people at all seasons as occation shall require; doe therefore assotiate and conioyne our selues to be as one Publike State or Coṁonwelth; and doe, for our selues and our Successors and such as shall be adioyned to vs att any tyme hereafter, enter into Combination and Confederation togather, to mayntayne and pʳsearue the liberty and purity of the gospell of our Lord Jesus wᶜʰ we now pʳfesse, as also the disciplyne of the Churches, wᶜʰ according to the truth of the said gospell is now practised amongst vs; As also in oʳ Ciuell Affaires to be guided and gouerned according to such Lawes, Rules, Orders and decrees as shall be made, ordered & decreed, as followeth:——

1. It is Ordered, sentenced and decreed, that there shall be yerely two generall Assemblies or Courts, the on the second thursday in Aprill, the other the second thursday in September, following; the first shall be called the Courte of Election, wherein shall

be yerely Chosen frō tyme to tyme soe many Magestrats and other publike Officers as shall be found requisitte: Whereof one to be chosen Gouernour for the yeare ensueing and vntill another be chosen, and noe other Magestrate to be chosen for more then one yeare; p^{r}uided allwayes there be sixe chosen besids the Gouernour; wch being chosen and sworne according to an Oath recorded for that purpose shall haue power to administer iustice according to the Lawes here established, and for want thereof according to the rule of the word of God; wch choise shall be made by all that are admitted freemen and haue taken the Oath of Fidellity, and doe cohabitte wthin this Jurisdiction, . . . or the mayor p^{r}te of such as shall be then p^{r}sent.

2. It is Ordered, sentensed and decreed, that the Election of the aforesaid Magestrats shall be on this manner: euery p^{r}son p^{r}sent and quallified for choyse shall bring in (to the p^{r}sons deputed to receaue thē) one single pap^r wth the name of him written in yt whom he desires to haue Gouernour, and he that hath the greatest nūber of papers shall be Gouernor for that yeare. And the rest of the Magestrats or publike Officers to be chosen in this manner: The Secretary for the tyme being shall first read the names of all that are to be put to choise and then shall seuerally nominate them distinctly, and euery one that would haue the p^{r}son nominated to be chosen shall bring in one single paper written vppon, and he that would not haue him chosen shall bring in a blanke: and euery one that hath more written papers then blanks shall be a Magestrat for that yeare; wch papers shall be receaued and told by one or more that shall be then chosen by the court and sworne to be faythfull therein; but in case there should not be sixe chosen as aforesaid, besids the Gouernor, out of those wch are nominated, then he or they wch haue the most written pap^{r}s shall be a Magestrate or Magestrats for the ensueing yeare, to make vp the foresaid nūber.

3. It is Ordered, sentenced and decreed, that the Secretary shall not nominate any p^{r}son, nor shall any p^{r}son be chosen newly into the Magestracy wch was not p^{r}pownded in some Generall Courte before, to be nominated the next Election; and to that end yt shall be lawfull for ech of the Townes aforesaid by their deputyes to nominate any two whō they conceaue fitte to be put to

Election; and the Courte may ad so many more as they iudge requisitt.

4. It is Ordered, sentenced and decreed that noe p^rson be chosen Gouernor aboue once in two yeares, and that the Gouernor be alwayes a mēber of some approved congregation, and formerly of the Magestracy wthin this Jurisdiction; and all the Magestrats Freemen of this Comonwelth: and that no Magestrate or other publike officer shall execute any p^rte of his or their Office before they are seuerally sworne, wch shall be done in the face of the Courte if they be p^rsent, and in case of absence by some deputed for that purpose.

5. It is Ordered, sentenced and decreed, that to the aforesaid Courte of Election the seu^rall Townes shall send their deputyes, and when the Elections are ended they may p^rceed in any publike searuice as at other Courts. Also the other Generall Courte in September shall be for makeing of lawes, and any other publike occation, wch conserns the good of the Comonwelth.

6. It is Ordered, sentenced and decreed, that the Gou^rnor shall, ether by himselfe or by the secretary, send out sumons to the Constables of eu^r Towne for the cauleing of these two standing Courts, on month at lest before their seu^rall tymes: And also if the Gou^rnor and the gretest p^rte of the Magestrats see cause vppon any spetiall occation to call a generall Courte, they may giue order to the secretary soe to doe wthin fowerteene dayes warneing: and if vrgent necessity so require, vppon a shorter notice, giueing sufficient grownds for yt to the deputyes when they meete, or els be questioned for the same; And if the Gou^rnor and Mayor p^rte of Magestrats shall ether neglect or refuse to call the two Generall standing Courts or ether of thē, as also at other tymes when the occations of the Comonwelth require, the Freemen thereof, or the Mayor p^rte of them, shall petition to them soe to doe: if then yt be ether denyed or neglected the said Freemen or the Mayor p^rte of them shall haue power to giue order to the Constables of the seuerall Townes to doe the same, and so may meete togather, and chuse to themselues a Moderator, and may p^rceed to do any Acte of power, wch any other Generall Courte may.

7. It is Ordered, sentenced and decreed that after there are warrants giuen out for any of the said Generall Courts, the Consta-

ble or Constables of ech Towne shall forthw^th give notice distinctly to the inhabitants of the same, in some Publike Assembly or by goeing or sending frō howse to howse, that at a place and tyme by him or them lymited and sett, they meet and assemble thē selues togather to elect and chuse certen deputyes to be att the Generall Courte then following to agitate the afayres of the comonwelth; wch said Deputyes shall be chosen by all that are admitted Inhabitants in the seu^rall Townes and haue taken the oath of fidellity; p^ruided that non be chosen a Deputy for any Generall Courte wch is not a Freeman of this Comonwelth.

The foresaid deputyes shall be chosen in manner following: euery p^rson that is p^rsent and quallified as before exp^rssed, shall bring the names of such, written in seu^rall papers as they desire to haue chosen for that Imployment, and these 3 or 4, more or lesse, being the nūber agreed on to be chosen for that tyme, that haue greatest nūber of papers written for thē shall be deputyes for that Courte; whose names shall be endorsed on the backe side of the warrant and returned into the Courte, wth the Constable or Constables hand vnto the same.

8. It is Ordered, sentenced and decreed, that Wyndsor, Hartford and Wethersfield shall haue power, ech Towne, to send fower of their freemen as their deputyes to euery Generall Courte; and whatsoeuer other Townes shall be hereafter added to this Jurisdiction, they shall send so many deputyes as the Courte shall judge meete, a resonable p^rportion to the nūber of Freemen that are in the said Townes being to be attended therein; wch deputyes shall have the power of the whole Towne to giue their voats and alowance to all such lawes and orders as may be for the publike good, and unto wch the said Townes are to be bownd.

9. It is ordered and decreed, that the deputyes thus chosen shall haue power and liberty to appoynt a tyme and a place of meeting togather before any Generall Courte to aduise and consult of all such things as may concerne the good of the publike, as also to examine their owne Elections, whether according to the order, and if they or the gretest p^rte of them find any election to be illegall they may seclud such for p^rsent frō their meeting, and returne the same and their resons to the Courte; and if yt proue true, the Courte may fyne the p^rty or p^rtyes so intruding and the

Towne, if they see cause, and giue out a warrant to goe to a newe election in a legall way, ether in p^rte or in whole. Also the said deputyes shall haue power to fyne any that shall be disorderly at their meetings, or for not coming in due tyme or place according to appoyntment; and they may returne the said fynes into the Courte if yt be refused to be paid, and the Tresurer to take notice of yt, and to estreete or levy the same as he doth other fynes.

10. It is Ordered, sentenced and decreed, that euery Generall Courte, except such as through neglecte of the Gou^rnor and the greatest p^rte of Magestrats the Freemen themselues doe call, shall consist of the Gouernor, or some one chosen to moderate the Court, and 4 other Magestrats at lest, wth the mayor p^rte of the deputyes of the seuerall Townes legally chosen; and in case the Freemen or mayor p^rte of the̅, through neglect or refusall of the Gouernor and mayor p^rte of the magestrats, shall call a Courte, y^t shall consist of the mayor p^rte of Freemen that are p^rsent or their deputyes, wth a Moderator chosen by the̅: In wch said Generall Courts shall consist the supreme power of the Comonwelth, and they only shall haue power to make lawes or repeale the̅, to graunt leuyes, to admitt of Freemen, dispose of lands vndisposed of, to seuerall Townes or p^rsons, and also shall haue power to call ether Courte or Magestrate or any other p^rson whatsoeuer into question for any misdemeanour, and may for just causes displace or deale otherwise according to the nature of the offence; and also may deale in any other matter that concerns the good of this comon welth, excepte election of Magestrats, wch shall be done by the whole boddy of Freemen.

In wch Courte the Gouernour or Moderator shall haue power to order the Courte to giue liberty of spech, and silence vnceasonable and disorderly speakeings, to put all things to voate, and in case the voate be equall to haue the casting voice. But non of these Courts shall be adiorned or dissolued w^thout the consent of the maior p^rte of the Court.

11. It is ordered, sentenced and decreed, that when any Generall Courte vppon the occations of the Comonwelth haue agreed vppon any sume or somes of mony to be leuyed vppon the seuerall Townes w^thin this Jurisdiction, that a Comittee be chosen to sett out and appoynt w^t shall be the p^rportion of euery Towne to pay

of the said leuy, pᵛided the Coᵐittees be made vp of an equall nūber out of each Towne.

14ᵗʰ January, 1638, the 11 Orders abouesaid are voted.*

* The text of the Fundamental Orders as reproduced above appears in *The Public Records of the Colony of Connecticut*, ed. J. Hammond Trumbull (Hartford, 1850), I, 20–25. It differs substantially from the transliteration made by Albert Carlos Bates found in George M. Dutcher, *The Fundamental Orders of Connecticut*, Publications of the Tercentenary Commission of the State of Connecticut, XX (New Haven, 1934), pp. 3–9. The ellipsis marks the omission of a later addition to the first fundamental.

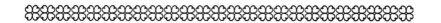

Notes

Chapter I *Prelude to Connecticut*

1. England did not begin using the Gregorian Calendar until 1752. During the seventeenth century time was reckoned according to the Julian Calendar, with the new year commencing on Lady Day, or the Feast of the Annunciation, which occurred on March 25. In this study the dates occurring between January 1 and March 24 will appear with the Julian Calendar year followed by the Gregorian Calendar year, such as 1638/39.

2. This figure is the one estimated by Charles M. Andrews, *The Fathers of New England* (New Haven, 1919), p. 34. It agrees approximately with Thomas Hutchinson, *The History of the Colony of Massachusets-Bay* (London, 1760), I, 93, who figured that 21,200 people immigrated to New England in the Great Migration. Cotton Mather, *Magnalia Christi Americana* (London, 1702), I, 23, underestimated the magnitude of the migration when he figured that only 4,000 persons were involved.

3. George L. Walker, *Thomas Hooker* (New York, 1891), p. 60.

4. Allen French, *Charles I and the Puritan Upheaval* (Boston, 1955), p. 266; William Haller, *The Rise of Puritanism* (New York, 1957 [1938]), pp. 80–81, 230.

5. On March 1, 1936/37, Robert Ryece, the "Suffolk Antiquary," wrote to John Winthrop: "This Summer the Bishop of Norwiche, by his deputyes, made as stricte a visitation in that Diocesse, as euer was seene before; all the weekely lectures putte downe, with sermons in the afternone on the Lord's daye, many mynisters sylenced, suspended, & putt from there places for not conformytie & readinge the Kings boocke [of Sports] for liberty & recreation on the Lords daye." *The Winthrop Papers*, in *Collections of the Massachusetts Historical Society*, Fourth Series (Boston, 1863), VI, 411.

6. Thomas Hooker, *The Danger of Desertion: or a Farwell Sermon* (London, 1641), p. 15.

7. John Cotton, "Letter to a puritan minister in England, December 3, 1634," *Chronicles of the First Planters of the Colony of Massachusetts Bay, from 1623–1636,* ed. Alexander Young (Boston, 1846), p. 439.

8. Samuel Eliot Morison, *The Founding of Harvard College* (Cambridge, Mass., 1935), p. 151.

9. Samuel Eliot Morison, *The Puritan Pronaos* (New York, 1936), p. 4.

10. Arthur P. Newton, *The Colonising Activities of the English Puritans* (New Haven, 1914), p. 3.

11. *Calendar of State Papers,* ed. John Bruce *et al.,* Domestic Series (London, 1859), III, cxli, No. 1, p. 521.

12. Nellis M. Crouse, "Causes of the Great Migration, 1630–1640," *New England Quarterly,* V, No. 1 (January 1932), 27–28.

13. William Hubbard, *A General History of New England* (Cambridge, Mass., 1815 [1680]), p. 87.

14. Morison, *The Founding of Harvard College,* p. 149.

15. James T. Adams, "Lion Gardiner," *Founders and Leaders of Connecticut,* ed. Charles E. Perry (Boston, 1934), p. 41.

16. "Captain Roger Clap's Memoirs," *Chronicles of the First Planters of the Colony of Massachusetts Bay,* p. 346.

17. "Deputy Governor Dudley's Letter," *ibid.,* p. 314.

18. Francis Higginson, *New-Englands Plantation* (Salem, Mass., 1908 [London, 1630]), p. 108.

19. *Records of the Governor and Company of the Massachusetts Bay in New England,* ed. Nathaniel B. Shurtleff (Boston, 1853), I, 3–19—hereafter cited as *Mass. Records.*

20. Benjamin Trumbull, *A Complete History of Connecticut* (Hartford, 1818 [1797]), I, 26; Sherman W. Adams and Henry R. Stiles, *The History of Ancient Wethersfield, Connecticut* (New York, 1904), I, 24.

21. On May 2, 1638, Newtown was renamed "Cambridge" by order of the General Court of Massachusetts Bay.

22. *Calendar of State Papers,* Domestic Series (London, 1862), V, ccx, No. 41, p. 255.

23. John Winthrop, *Winthrop's Journal, "History of New England," 1630–1649,* ed. James Kendall Hosmer (New York, 1908), I, 90—hereafter cited as Winthrop, *Journal.*

24. Mather, *Magnalia,* III, 57.

25. *Calendar of State Papers,* Domestic Series, III, cxlii, No. 112, p. 554.

26. *Ibid.,* cxliv, No. 36, p. 567.

27. *Ibid.,* IV, cli, No. 12, p. 87.

28. *Ibid.*, cli, No. 45, p. 92.

29. Mather, *Magnalia*, III, 62.

30. *Ibid.*, pp. 58–68; *Dictionary of American Biography*, ed. Dumas Malone (New York, 1932), IX, 199–200.

31. Mather, *Magnalia*, III, 20.

32. Winthrop, *Journal*, I, 111.

33. The humble Peticõn of John Winthrop Esq.ʳ in the name and by Order of your Maᵗⁱᵉˢ most Loyall, obedient and most dutifull Subjects: the Colony of Conectecut in New England, Connecticut State Library, Hartford, Conn. (photostat).

34. Winthrop, *Journal*, I, 124.

35. John Fiske, *The Beginnings of New England* (Boston, 1889), p. 126, estimated that between May 1635 and May 1636 more than 3,000 immigrants arrived in New England.

36. Edward Johnson, *Johnson's Wonder-Working Providence, 1628–1651*, ed. J. Franklin Jameson (New York, 1910 [London, 1654]), p. 74.

37. Winthrop, *Journal*, I, 74. "People" should be defined as "freemen."

38. *Mass. Records*, I, 167.

39. Hubbard, *op. cit.*, p. 173.

40. John Winthrop, "John Winthrop to Sir Simonds D'Ewes," *Publications of the Colonial Society of Massachusetts* (Boston, 1905), VII, 73.

41. *Calendar of State Papers*, ed. William Noël Sainsbury *et al.*, Colonial Series (London, 1860), I, ix, No. 72, p. 259.

42. Albert E. Van Dusen, *Connecticut* (New York, 1961), p. 63.

43. *Mass. Records*, I, 160–161.

44. French, *op. cit.*, p. 389; B. Trumbull, *op. cit.*, I, 96–97.

45. B. Trumbull, *op. cit.*, I, 40.

46. See *Historical Collections; Consisting of State Papers, and other Authentic Documents*, ed. Ebenezer Hazard (Philadelphia, 1792), I, 121–131.

47. See Appendix I.

48. "The old patent of Connecticut, 1631," in B. Trumbull, *op. cit.*, I, 495–496.

49. *Ibid.*, p. 61; Hutchinson, *op. cit.*, I, Appendix II, 490–495.

50. *The Public Records of the Colony of Connecticut*, ed. J. Hammond Trumbull (Hartford, 1850), I, 513 and note—hereafter cited as *Conn. Records*.

51. Winthrop, *Journal*, I, 124, 126, 128.

52. *Ibid.*, pp. 132–133. This information was not recorded in the September 3, 1634, session of the General Court (*Mass. Records*, I, 123–132), but comes entirely from Winthrop's *Journal*.

53. Winthrop, *Journal*, I, 134.

54. *Mass. Records*, I, 146.

55. Charles M. Andrews, *The River Towns of Connecticut*, in *Johns Hopkins University Studies in Historical and Political Science*, Seventh Series, VII, VIII, IX (July, August, September 1889), p. 17.

56. *Mass. Records*, I, 148.

57. *The Winthrop Papers*, in *Collections of the Massachusetts Historical Society, Fourth Series*, VI, 163.

58. Charles M. Andrews, *The Colonial Period of American History* (New Haven, 1936 [1934]), II, 73.

59. *Mass. Records*, I, 159–160; *The Winthrop Papers*, in *Collections of the Massachusetts Historical Society*, Fourth Series, VI, 381–382.

60. Winthrop, *Journal*, I, 163.

61. *The Register Book of the Lands and Houses in the "New Towne"* (Cambridge, Mass., 1896), pp. 15–16.

62. *Conn. Records*, I, 451.

63. See Appendix II.

64. Winthrop, *Journal*, I, 174.

65. Hutchinson, *op. cit.*, I, 99–100.

66. Andrews, *Colonial Period of American History*, II, 79, note 1.

67. *Mass. Records*, I, 171.

68. See Chapter III, note 3, for an explanation of the spelling of "Corte."

69. *Ibid.*

70. *Ibid.*

71. *Ibid.*, p. 321.

72. Winthrop, *Journal*, I, 180–181.

73. "The Matthew Grant Record," *Some Early Records and Documents of and Relating to the Town of Windsor Connecticut, 1639–1703* (Hartford, 1930), pp. 9–10.

74. B. Trumbull, *op. cit.*, I, 68. The estimates in Franklin B. Dexter, "Estimates of the Population in the American Colonies," *Proceedings of the American Antiquarian Society*, New Series, V (Worcester, 1889), 31, and Evarts B. Greene and Virginia D. Harrington, *American Population before the Federal Census of 1790* (New York, 1932), p. 47, were that there were approximately 3,000 people in the Connecticut Commonwealth by 1643 and 3,186 there by 1654.

75. Mather, *Magnalia*, I, 24.

Chapter II *The Way of the Churches of Connecticut*

1. John Cotton, in *The Way of Congregational Churches Cleared* (London, 1648), Part I, p. 11, objected to the title "Independent" applied to the New England churches because they were in fact dependent on the civil magistrates, on Christ and His Word, and on the synods. He also discouraged the appellation because the national church of Scotland, the Presbyterian Church, was sometimes called "The Independent Church" and in 1648 the Congregationalists were anxious to avoid any confusion and to assert their divergence from Presbyterian polity. "Independent" was also used in reference to the Antipaedo-baptists, Antinomians, Familists, and Seekers, with none of whom the Congregationalists wished to be associated.

2. *Conn. Records*, I, 373, 251, 39–40.

3. Cotton Mather, *Magnalia Christi Americana* (London, 1702), II, 23.

4. *Conn. Records*, I, 283–284.

5. *Ibid.*, pp. 303, 308, 324.

6. *A Platform of Church Discipline, Gathered Out of the Word of God: and Agreed upon by the Elders: and Messengers of the Churches, Assembled in the Synod at Cambridge in New England* (Cambridge, Mass., 1649), p. 1—hereafter cited as *Cambridge Platform*.

7. Thomas Hooker, *A Survey of the Summe of Church-Discipline* (London, 1648), Part I, p. 27—hereafter cited as Hooker, *Survey*.

8. Most notable among the other explanations were Thomas Allin and Thomas Shepard's *A Defence of the Answer made unto the Nine Questions or Positions sent from New England* (London, 1648) and John Cotton's *The True Constitution of A particular visible Church, proved by Scripture* (London, 1642) and *The Way of the Churches of Christ in New-England* (London, 1645).

9. See Thomas Hooker's preface to William Ames's *A Fresh Suit against Human Ceremonies in God's Worship* (Rotterdam, 1633).

10. Champlin Burrage, *The Early English Dissenters* (Cambridge, England, 1912), I, 291; Perry Miller, *Orthodoxy in Massachusetts, 1630–1650* (Cambridge, Mass., 1933), p. 82.

11. William Bradford, *Bradford's History "Of Plimouth Plantation"* (Boston, 1898), pp. 315–316.

12. Mather, *Magnalia*, III, 61.

13. *Ibid.*, I, 21.

14. William E. Barton, *Congregational Creeds and Covenants* (Chicago, 1917), p. 9.

15. *Cambridge Platform*, p. 2.

16. *Ibid.*

17. Samuel Stone, *A Congregational Church Is a Catholike Visible Church* (London, 1652), n.p.

18. Hooker, *Survey*, Part I, pp. 65, b 1.

19. Thomas Lechford, *Plain Dealing* (London, 1642), p. 2.

20. *Conn. Records*, I, 311–312.

21. Thomas Hooker, *The Poor Doubting Christian Drawn to Christ* (Boston, 1743 [London, 1629]), pp. 67–69, 95: Thomas Hooker, *The Soules Effectual Calling to Christ* (London, 1637), pp. 33–35.

22. Hooker, *Survey*, Part I, p. 46.

23. *Ibid.*, p. 48.

24. Barton, *op. cit.*, pp. 81–82.

25. *Cambridge Platform*, p. 6.

26. Williston Walker, *The Creeds and Platforms of Congregationalism* (New York, 1893), pp. 153–154.

27. *Cambridge Platform*, p. 13. Thomas Hooker in *A Survey of the Summe of Church-Discipline* (Part I, p. 206) and John Cotton in *The Keyes Of the Kingdom of Heaven* ([London, 1644], p. 36) reiterate this philosophy.

28. Hooker, *Survey*, Part I, p. 4.

29. Henry Wolcott, "Notes on Sermons," trans. Douglas H. Shepard (Typed copy, 1959), pp. 91–92. These cipher notes on sermons delivered by Hooker and several of his contemporary Connecticut ministers were discovered in 1850 in a notebook kept by Henry Wolcott, of Windsor. J. Hammond Trumbull and Douglas H. Shepard have subsequently deciphered this invaluable record of the first Connecticut sermons. The typescript is now located in the Connecticut Historical Society, Hartford, Connecticut.

30. *Cambridge Platform*, p. 13.

31. Hooker, *Survey*, Part I, pp. 284–285, 13; Stone, *A Congregational Church Is a Catholike Visible Church*, p. G 2.

32. *Cambridge Platform*, p. 3.

33. *Ibid.*; Hooker, *Survey*, Part I, p. 29; Perry Miller, *Errand into the Wilderness* (Cambridge, Mass., 1956), p. 32.

34. Hooker, *Survey*, Part III, pp. 4–5; *Cambridge Platform*, p. 17.

35. Hooker, *Survey*, Part III, p. 6; Cotton, *Keyes Of the Kingdom of Heaven*, pp. 43–44; Lechford, *op. cit.*, p. 12; Winthrop, *Journal*, II, 26.

36. Samuel Stone, *A Short Catechism Drawn out of the Word of God* (Hartford, 1899 [Boston, 1684]), pp. 11–12.

37. Hooker, *Survey*, Part II, p. 2.

38. *Cambridge Platform*, p. 10.

39. Hooker, *Survey*, Part I, p. 187.

40. Benjamin Trumbull, *A Complete History of Connecticut* (Hartford, 1818 [1797]), I, 280, 287.

41. Hooker, *Survey*, Part II, p. 68; Part I, p. 122.

42. Cotton, *Keyes Of the Kingdom of Heaven*, pp. 20–22.

43. Miller, *Errand into the Wilderness*, p. 28; Mather, *Magnalia*, III, 66–67.

44. *Conn. Records*, I, 531, 265, 19, 139, 175.

45. *Cambridge Platform*, p. 8.

46. Hooker, *The Poor Doubting Christian Drawn to Christ*, pp. 46, 140–143.

47. Mather, *Magnalia*, III, 121.

48. *Cambridge Platform*, p. 8.

49. Mather, *Magnalia*, III, 117.

50. *Ibid.*, p. 118.

51. Babette May Levy, *Preaching in the First Half Century of New England History* (Hartford, 1945), p. 3.

52. *Conn. Records*, I, 502, 459; Albert B. Hart, "Thomas Hooker," *Founders and Leaders of Connecticut*, ed. Charles E. Perry (Boston, 1934), p. 52.

53. Hooker, *Survey*, Part II, pp. 16–18.

54. *Founders and Leaders of Connecticut*, pp. 55–59.

55. Hooker, *Survey*, Part II, p. 30.

56. Henry M. Dexter, *The Congregationalism of the Last Three Hundred Years* (New York, 1880), pp. 108–109.

57. B. Trumbull, *op. cit.*, I, 285.

58. Wolcott, *op. cit.*, p. 233.

59. Edward Johnson, *Johnson's Wonder-Working Providence, 1628–1951*, ed. J. Franklin Jameson (New York, 1910 [London, 1654]), p. 239.

60. Hooker, *Survey*, Part I, p. 230; Part IV, pp. 18, 52–53.

61. *Ibid.*, Part I, p. 4.

Chapter III *The Fundamental Orders*

1. "Copy of a Letter from Mr. Cotton to Lord Say and Seal in the Year 1636," *The Puritans*, ed. Perry Miller and Thomas H. Johnson (New York, 1938), p. 209.

2. Benjamin Trumbull, *A Complete History of Connecticut*, (Hartford, 1818 [1797]), I, 78, note, and 95.

3. To make a distinction between the courts, the court that sat from May 1, 1637, until January 1638/39 will be referred to as the "General Corte," and its successor that met under the Fundamental Orders as the "Gen-

eral Court." The spelling is arbitrary, but may help to distinguish between them.

4. On February 21, 1636/37.

5. *Conn. Records*, I, 13.

6. *Ibid.*, p. 12.

7. Thomas Hooker, "Rev. Thomas Hooker's Letter, in Reply to Governor Winthrop," *Collections of the Connecticut Historical Society* (Hartford, 1860), I, 12.

8. See Albert E. Van Dusen, *Connecticut* (New York, 1961), pp. 34–40, for an excellent, brief narration of the Pequot War.

9. Elias B. Sanford, *A History of Connecticut* (Hartford, 1889), p. 28, note 8.

10. *Conn. Records*, I, 14, 19.

11. *Ibid.*, pp. 15, 11.

12. *Ibid.*, p. 39.

13. Henry Wolcott, "Notes on Sermons," trans. Douglas H. Shepard (Typed copy, 1959), p. 9.

14. Perry Miller, *Errand into the Wilderness* (Cambridge, Mass., 1956), p. 44.

15. *The Winthrop Papers*, in *Collections of the Massachusetts Historical Society*, Fifth Series (Boston, 1871), I, 260–261.

16. George L. Walker, *History of the First Church in Hartford* (Hartford, 1884), p. 103.

17. Charles M. Andrews, *The Colonial Period of American History* (New Haven, 1936 [1934]), II, 102; Sherman W. Adams and Henry R. Stiles, *The History of Ancient Wethersfield, Connecticut* (New York, 1904), I, 77.

18. *Conn. Records*, I, 17, 34; *Mass. Records*, I, 147, 174–175.

19. Roy V. Coleman, *A Note Concerning the Formulation of The Fundamental Orders* (Westport, Conn., 1934), pp. 6–13; John M. Taylor, *Roger Ludlow* (New York, 1900), pp. 28–31, 92; *Dictionary of American Biography*, ed. Dumas Malone (New York, 1933), XI, 493–494.

20. Samuel Eliot Morison, *The Founding of Harvard College* (Cambridge, Mass., 1935), p. 388; Taylor, *Roger Ludlow*, p. 96; Coleman, *op. cit.*, p. 10; B. Trumbull, *op. cit.*, I, 218.

21. *Conn. Records*, I, 34–35. Roger Ludlow was not present at the General Court on September 10, 1639, but had returned to Connecticut before the session of the Particular Court held on October 3. The proceedings of the General Court for October 10, 1639, begin, "Mr. Deputy [Ludlow] informed the Court that he hath vnderstood since his returne, offence hath

beene taken att some of his p^rceedings in his late journey to Pequannocke, and the parts thereabouts."

22. Herbert Parker, *Courts and Lawyers of New England* (New York, 1931), III, 611; B. Trumbull, *op. cit.*, I, 100; John Fiske, *The Beginnings of New England* (Boston, 1889), p. 127; Rockwell H. Potter, *Hartford's First Church* (Hartford, 1932), p. 7; Breckinridge Long, *Genesis of the Constitution of the United States of America* (New York, 1926), p. 29; *The Judicial and Civil History of Connecticut*, ed. Dwight Loomis and J. Gilbert Calhoun (Boston, 1895), p. 9; Connecticut Historical Society and the Towns of Windsor, Hartford, and Wethersfield, *Celebration of the Two Hundred and Fiftieth Anniversary of the Adoption of the First Constitution of the State of Connecticut* (Hartford, 1889), p. 26.

23. *Conn. Records*, I, 26.

24. *Ibid.*, opposite p. 64.

25. Edwin Stanley Welles, *The Origin of the Fundamental Orders, 1639* (Hartford, 1936), p. 20; George M. Dutcher, "Introduction," *The Fundamental Orders of Connecticut*, Publications of the Tercentenary Commission of the State of Connecticut, XX (New Haven, 1934), 2; Adams and Stiles, *op. cit.*, I, 76–77; *Conn. Records*, I, 28, 34.

26. Roger Welles, "Constitutional History of Connecticut," *Connecticut Magazine*, V, No. 2 (February 1899), 87.

27. Located in the Probate Room, Connecticut State Library, Hartford, Connecticut.

28. *Conn. Records*, I, 150.

29. Charles Borgeaud, *Adoption and Amendment of Constitutions in Europe and America*, trans. Charles D. Hazen (New York, 1895), p. xv.

30. Perry Miller, *The New England Mind, From Colony to Province* (Cambridge, Mass., 1953), p. 21.

31. Miller, *Errand into the Wilderness*, p. 38; Wallace Notestein, *The English People on the Eve of Colonization, 1603–1630* (New York, 1954), p. 159.

32. *Records of the Colony and Plantation of New Haven*, ed. Charles J. Hoadly (Hartford, 1857), p. 15; *Records of the Colony of Rhode Island and Providence Plantations, in New England*, ed. John R. Bartlett (Providence, 1856), I, 14, 52, 87.

33. *Conn. Records*, I, 21.

34. *Ibid.*, pp. 13, 19; Perry G. Miller, "Thomas Hooker and the Democracy of Early Connecticut," *New England Quarterly*, IV, No. 4 (October 1931), 700–701.

35. Henry Wolcott, William Phelps, Matthew Grant, Henry Smith,

Andrew Warner, John Winthrop, Jr., John Branker, William Goodwin, John
Talcott, Thomas Hooker, Samuel Stone, John Steele, Andrew Ward, John
Spenser, Captain John Mason, William Westwood, Matthew Allyn, Richard
Lord, William Butler, George Stockin, William Blumfeild, William Swain,
Thomas Welles, and Thomas Hale were some of the Connecticut settlers who
had been made freemen of the Colony of Massachusetts Bay before their re-
moval to Connecticut. See *Mass. Records*, I, 366–375.

36. *Conn. Records*, I, 290.

37. "Papers Relating to the Controversy in the Church in Hartford,
1656–1659," *Collections of the Connecticut Historical Society* (Hartford,
1870), II, 95–96.

38. *Conn. Records*, I, 138.

39. *Ibid.*, pp. 290, 331.

40. Charles M. Andrews, *The River Towns of Connecticut*, in *Johns
Hopkins University Studies in Historical and Political Science*, Seventh Series,
VII, VIII, IX (July, August, September 1889), p. 87.

41. Albert E. McKinley, *The Suffrage Franchise in the Thirteen English Colonies in America*, in *Publications of the University of Pennsylvania*,
Series in History, No. 2 (Philadelphia, 1905), p. 390.

42. *Conn. Records*, I, 346; Samuel Hart, "The Fundamental Orders
and the Charter," *Papers of the New Haven Colony Historical Society* (New
Haven, 1914), VIII, 251.

43. *Conn. Records*, I, 96, 293, 351.

44. *Hartford Town Votes*, I, in *Collections of the Connecticut Historical Society* (Hartford, 1897), VI, 132.

45. *Conn. Records*, I, 36.

46. Winthrop, *Journal*, I, 78.

47. Cotton Mather, *Magnalia Christi Americana* (London, 1702), II,
33.

48. *Ibid.*, p. 17.

49. *Conn. Records*, I, 161–162.

50. *Ibid.*, pp. 252, 256.

51. *Ibid.*, p. 348.

52. *Ibid.*, pp. 555–556.

53. *Ibid.*, pp. 559, 30, 307.

54. *Ibid.*, p. 51.

55. Charles M. Andrews, "The Beginnings of the Connecticut Towns,"
Annals of the American Academy of Political and Social Science, I (October
1890), 186–187.

56. At the previous Court of Election, on May 16, 1661, thirty-seven
men had been elected to the General Court, that is, the governor, deputy

governor, ten magistrates, the treasurer, the secretary, and twenty-three deputies. This is in comparison with the nineteen men, including both magistrates and deputies, elected at the first Court of Election in 1639. *Conn.
Records,* I, 27, 364–365, 378–379.

57. *Conn. Records,* I, 119.

58. *Ibid.,* pp. 27, 41.

59. *Ibid.,* p. 140.

60. *Ibid.,* p. 25.

61. Hooker, "Rev. Thomas Hooker's letter, in Reply to Governor
Winthrop," *Collections of the Connecticut Historical Society,* I, 12.

62. *Mass. Records,* I, 116–117; *Conn. Records,* I, 17, 27.

63. *Conn. Records,* I, 279, 34–36.

64. *Ibid.,* p. 186.

65. Hooker, *op. cit.,* I, 14; Charles M. Andrews, "Colonial Connecticut," *Founders and Leaders of Connecticut,* ed. Charles E. Perry (Boston,
1934), pp. 9, 17.

66. *Conn. Records,* I, 96, 119, 138, 150, 290, 293, 331.

67. *Ibid.,* pp. 140, 256, 346–347.

68. Wolcott, *op. cit.,* p. 68.

Chapter IV *Law and the Courts*

1. Leonard Bacon, *Thirteen Historical Discourses, on the Completion
of Two Hundred Years, From the Beginning of the First Church in New
Haven* (New Haven, 1839), p. 34.

2. *Conn. Records,* I, 77–78.

3. Alexis de Tocqueville, *Democracy in America,* trans. Henry Reeve
(London, 1835), I, 35.

4. *Conn. Records,* I, 21.

5. *Ibid.,* pp. 77–78; J. Hammond Trumbull, *The True-Blue Laws of
Connecticut and New Haven and the False Blue-Laws Invented by the Rev.
Samuel Peters* (Hartford, 1876), p. 59, note.

6. *Conn. Records,* I, 78, 80, 514.

7. See John Cotton, "Moses his Judicialls," *Collections of the Massachusetts Historical Society,* First Series (Boston, 1798), V, 173–192.

8. J. H. Trumbull, *op. cit.,* pp. 10–11.

9. *Conn. Records,* I, 103.

10. *Records of the Particular Court of Connecticut, 1639–1663,* in
Collections of the Connecticut Historical Society (Hartford, 1928), XXII,
13, 3—hereafter cited as *Particular Court Records; Conn. Records,* I, 159.

11. *Particular Court Records,* pp. 106–107, 114.

12. *Ibid.*, pp. 143–145, 194.

13. *Ibid.*, pp. 56, 93.

14. John M. Taylor, *The Witchcraft Delusion in Colonial Connecticut, 1647–1697* (New York, 1908), pp. 119–121; *Particular Court Records,* pp. 131, 188, 238, 240, 251; *Conn. Records,* I, 220, 572–573.

15. *Conn. Records,* I, 36, 39.

16. *Ibid.*, pp. 138, 154.

17. *Ibid.*, p. 216.

18. John M. Taylor, *Roger Ludlow* (New York, 1900), pp. 97–105; Charles W. Burpee, *History of Hartford County, Connecticut, 1633–1928* (Hartford, 1928), I, 63; William A. Beers, "Roger Ludlowe: The Father of Connecticut Jurisprudence," *Magazine of American History,* VIII, Part I, No. 4 (New York, April 1882), 269.

19. George Lee Haskins and Samuel E. Ewing, III, "The Spread of Massachusetts Law in the Seventeenth Century," *University of Pennsylvania Law Review,* CVI (1957–1958), 415, notes 18–20.

20. *The Winthrop Papers,* in *Collections of the Massachusetts Historical Society,* Fourth Series (Boston, 1863), VI, 386.

21. This is Book Number B. or the Second Book of the Records of the Colony of Connecticut, pp. 6–65. The pages of the Ludlow Code are upside down in relation to the rest of the entries, and the numbers begin at the end of the volume and continue in sequence toward the front of the book.

22. Benjamin Trumbull, *A Complete History of Connecticut* (Hartford, 1818 [1797]), I, 178.

23. *Conn. Records,* I, 509.

24. *Ibid.*

25. "Capitall Lawes," *Conn. Records,* I, 514–515.

26. *Ibid.*, pp. 510, 539–541, 545–546, 551–556, 559.

27. "Lands; Free Lands," *ibid.*, pp. 536–537.

28. "Escheats," *ibid.*, p. 525.

29. *Ibid.*, pp. 3, 500, 88.

30. George Lee Haskins, "The Beginnings of Partible Inheritance in the American Colonies," *Yale Law Journal,* LI (June 1942), 1301–1303.

31. A typical apportionment of an estate may be seen in the case of the estate of Jonathan Brundish, of Wethersfield, probated by the Particular Court on April 2, 1640. *Conn. Records,* I, 40, 45–46.

32. "Rates," *ibid.*, pp. 547–551; "Ministers Meintenance," *ibid.*, p. 545.

33. "Levyes," *ibid.*, p. 537.

34. "Ecleseasticall," *ibid.*, pp. 523–525.

35. *Ibid.,* pp. 524, 514; *Particular Court Records,* pp. 134–135, 138.

36. *Conn. Records,* I, 514, 194, 168–169.

37. *Hartford Town Votes,* I, in *Collections of the Connecticut Historical Society* (Hartford, 1897), VI, 74; *Conn. Records,* I, 106, 111, 56.

38. *Conn. Records,* I, 520–521, 554–555.

39. "Indians," *ibid.,* pp. 529–533.

40. *Particular Court Records,* pp. 79, 128–129.

41. "Masters; Servants; Sojourners," *Conn. Records,* I, 538–539; "Idlenes," *ibid.,* p. 528; *Particular Court Records,* p. 103.

42. John Robinson, *The Works of John Robinson,* ed. Robert Ashton (Boston, 1851), II, 464–466; William Bradford, *Bradford's History "Of Plimouth Plantation"* (Boston, 1898), p. 393.

43. *Conn. Records,* I, 47–48; "Marriage," *ibid.,* I, 540; *Particular Court Records,* pp. 124–125.

44. *Conn. Records,* I, 275, 301, 362, 376, 379, 351–352.

45. "Gaming," *ibid.,* p. 527; "Inkeepers," *ibid.,* pp. 533–535; "Wyne and Strong Water," *ibid.,* p. 560.

46. *Ibid.,* pp. 533, 155, 255.

47. "Lying," *ibid.,* pp. 537–538; "Profane Swearing," *ibid.,* p. 547; "Tobacko," *ibid.,* p. 558; *Particular Court Records,* p. 126.

48. *Particular Court Records,* pp. 236, 252–253; *Conn. Records,* I, 167.

49. *Particular Court Records,* p. 182.

50. *Conn. Records,* I, 100, 224; *Particular Court Records,* pp. 79–80, 187, 218–219, 119.

51. *Conn. Records,* I, 527, 542–545, 560–561.

52. William M. Maltbie, "Judicial Administration in Connecticut Colony before the Charter of 1662," *Connecticut Bar Journal,* XXIII, No. 2 (June 1949), 228–236; *Conn. Records,* I, 196, 512.

53. *Particular Court Records,* pp. 161, 222, 226, 232; *Conn. Records,* I, 360–361.

54. *Particular Court Records,* pp. 97, 202–203.

55. *Ibid.,* p. 88; *Conn. Records,* I, 211.

56. *Conn. Records,* I, 226, 231, 360–361.

57. *Ibid.,* pp. 51–52.

58. *Ibid.,* p. 376.

59. *Ibid.,* pp. 377–378.

60. *Ibid.,* pp. 86, 119, 150.

61. *Particular Court Records,* p. vii.

62. *Conn. Records,* I, 71, 81, 139, 231.

63. The session of April 18, 1654, was probably the one exception.

64. *Particular Court Records,* p. 197; *Conn. Records,* I, 4, 205, 117–118, 535–536; Maltbie. *op. cit.,* p. 236.

65. *Particular Court Records,* pp. 191, 199–200, 233–234.

66. *Ibid.,* pp. 6–8.

67. "Juryes and Jurors," *Conn. Records,* I, 535–536.

68. "Death Vntimely," *ibid.,* p. 523; "Grand Jury," *ibid.,* pp. 536, 91.

69. *Particular Court Records,* pp. 118–119.

70. *Ibid.,* pp. 86–88.

71. Roger Ludlow, John Winthrop, Jr., and George Fenwick were the exceptions.

72. Thomas Hooker, *The Poor Doubting Christian Drawn to Christ* (Boston, 1743 [London, 1629]), pp. 71–72.

73. *Conn. Records,* I, 87, 89, 202; *Particular Court Records,* pp. 99, 162–163; *The Judicial and Civil History of Connecticut,* ed. Dwight Loomis and J. Gilbert Calhoun (Boston, 1895), p. 182; Charles M. Andrews, *The River Towns of Connecticut,* in *Johns Hopkins University Studies in Historical and Political Science,* Seventh Series, VII, VIII, IX (July, August, September 1889), p. 103; Maltbie, *op. cit.,* pp. 232–233.

74. *Conn. Records,* I, 117–118.

75. *Ibid.,* pp. 53, 86, 125–126, 186, 191.

76. *Ibid.,* pp. 226–227, 233, 257–258, 336–337.

77. *Ibid.,* p. 37.

78. *Particular Court Records,* pp. 112, 133.

79. *Conn. Records,* I, 29, 33, 50, 115, 127, 140.

80. *Particular Court Records,* p. 127; *Conn. Records,* I, 203.

81. *Particular Court Records,* p. 140.

82. *Conn. Records,* I, 513, 110, 115; *Particular Court Records,* pp. 236–237.

83. *Conn. Records,* I, 242.

84. *Ibid.,* pp. 129, 142, 194, 203, 124.

85. *Particular Court Records,* pp. 81–82; *Conn. Records,* I, 209, 222, 226, 232.

86. *Conn. Records,* I, 47, 204, 124.

87. *Ibid.,* pp. 510–512, 151–153, 518–520, 472.

88. *Particular Court Records,* p. 219; *Conn. Records,* I, 225–226, 96.

89. "Constables," *Conn. Records,* I, 521–522; *ibid.,* pp. 26, 560–561, 555.

90. *Ibid.,* p. 130; *Particular Court Records,* p. 156.

91. Thomas Hooker, *The Danger of Desertion: or a Farwell Sermon* (London, 1641), pp. 4, 9.

92. George Lee Haskins, *Law and Authority in Early Massachusetts* (New York, 1960), p. 4.

Chapter V *From Commonwealth to Colony*

1. Windsor's Law Book has been preserved and is now in the possession of the Connecticut Historical Society, Hartford, Connecticut.

2. *Hartford Town Votes*, I, in *Collections of the Connecticut Historical Society* (Hartford, 1897), VI, 2–3.

3. *Conn. Records*, I, 234, 279, 290, 377, 298.

4. *Ibid.*, pp. 309, 351.

5. *Ibid.*, p. 36.

6. *Hartford Town Votes*, I, 49–51.

7. *Conn. Records*, I, 37. The registration had been ordered on October 10, 1639. See also *Original Distribution of the Lands in Hartford Among the Settlers, 1639*, in *Collections of the Connecticut Historical Society* (Hartford, 1912), XIV.

8. *Conn. Records*, I, 24.

9. *Ibid.*, pp. 112 and note, 133–134, 200, 224, 365, 377.

10. Winthrop, *Journal*, I, 231–232.

11. *Conn. Records*, I, 74–75.

12. The fourth member, Plymouth, signed the Articles of Confederation in September 1643, after the General Court of Plymouth had granted permission to Edward Winslow and William Collyer to subscribe to them. *Acts of the Commissioners of the United Colonies of New England*, I, in *Records of the Colony of New Plymouth in New England* (Boston, 1859), X, 8.

13. *Ibid.*, pp. 3–4.

14. Elias B. Sanford, *A History of Connecticut* (Hartford, 1889), pp. 45–47.

15. *Acts of the Commissioners of the United Colonies of New England*, I, in *Records of the Colony of New Plymouth in New England*, X, 190; *The Winthrop Papers*, in *Collections of the Massachusetts Historical Society*, Fourth Series (Boston, 1865), VII, 193–194; *Conn. Records*, I, 254, 275 and note.

16. *Conn. Records*, I, 259–260.

17. Edward Hopkins became Warden of the Fleet, Keeper of the Palace of Westminster, Commissioner of the Admiralty and the Navy Office, and a Member of Parliament. He died in London in 1657. Roger Ludlow served as a Master of Chancery in Ireland. He died after the Restoration.

18. Williston Walker, *A History of the Congregational Churches in the United States* (Boston, 1894), pp. 175–176.

19. *Cambridge Platform*, p. 3.

20. Cotton Mather, *Magnalia Christi Americana* (London, 1702), III, 117.

21. See "Papers Relating to the Controversy in the Church in Hartford," *Collections of the Connecticut Historical Society* (Hartford, 1870), II. These papers were discovered by the Hon. John G. Palfrey among the Lansdowne Manuscripts in the British Museum.

22. *Conn. Records*, I, 281, 288–289, 312, 314, 317, 320–321, 333–334, 339.

23. Sherman W. Adams and Henry R. Stiles, *The History of Ancient Wethersfield, Connecticut* (New York, 1904), I, 160–162; *Conn. Records*, I, 319–320, 330, 342.

24. Adams and Stiles, *op. cit.*, I, 163.

25. *Conn. Records*, I, 214.

26. *Ibid.*, pp. 65, 188, 205.

27. *Ibid.*, pp. 32, 58–61, 80.

28. *Ibid.*, pp. 116–117, 207, 236–237.

29. *Ibid.*, pp. 71, 174–175, 281, 298, 310–311.

30. Thomas Hutchinson, *The History of the Colony of Massachusets-Bay* (London, 1760), I, 115–117.

31. *The Wyllys Papers*, in *Collections of the Connecticut Historical Society* (Hartford, 1924), XXI, 115.

32. *Conn. Records*, I, 99, 90, 163, 499.

33. *Ibid.*, p. 313.

34. *Ibid.*, p. 584.

35. *Ibid.*, pp. 361–362.

36. *Ibid.*, p. 571.

37. *Ibid.*, pp. 266–270, 584.

38. "Records of the Council for New England," *Proceedings of the American Antiquarian Society* (Cambridge, Mass., April 1867), pp. 107–108.

39. Charles M. Andrews, *The Colonial Period of American History* (New Haven, 1936 [1934]), II, 128, note 3.

40. Hutchinson, *op. cit.*, I, 47 and note; Andrews, *Colonial Period of American History*, II, 129, note 3.

41. Thomas Lechford, *Plain Dealing* (London, 1642), p. 42.

42. Benjamin Trumbull, *A Complete History of Connecticut* (Hartford, 1818 [1797]), I, 174, 183.

43. Albert C. Bates, *The Charter of Connecticut* (Hartford, 1932), p. 17. This copy is now located in the Connecticut Archives.

44. *Conn. Records*, I, 126.

45. *Ibid.*, p. 128.

46. B. Trumbull, *op. cit.*, I, 155.

47. This point has been debated, but the records clearly state, "It is ordered, that the Fiue hundred pounds that Capt John Cullick is to pay to ye Countrey, shalbe kept and improued in pursueance of our Address to his Highnes our Soveraigne Lord Charles etc.," and that "whateuer charges or expenses the attendance on those affaires of this Colony shall require in England, shalbe defraied out of that 500l. that is by ord^r of Court appointed and set apart for y^t service." The Fenwick account was not settled in time to pay for the Winthrop mission; therefore, in October 1662 the Patent Rate had to be levied on the towns to meet the expenses incurred in obtaining the Charter. *Conn. Records*, I, 362, 369, 385–386, 389, 573–574.

48. *Ibid.*, pp. 361–362, 367–368, 583–585; Andrews, *Colonial Period of American History*, II, 133.

49. Located in B. Trumbull, *op. cit.*, I, 511–512.

50. *Conn. Records*, I, 582–583.

51. *Ibid.*, p. 583.

52. *Ibid.*, p. 223.

53. *Ibid.*, pp. 298, 301, 306, 308.

54. *Ibid.*, pp. 579–581.

55. Charles M. Andrews found this revision among the Rawlinson Manuscripts in the Bodleian Library. See Andrews, *op. cit.*, II, 132, note 3.

56. *Calendar of State Papers*, Colonial Series, V, No. 229, pp. 74–75; No. 246, p. 79; No. 284, pp. 86–88; Andrews, *op. cit.*, II, 131–135; Richard S. Dunn, *Puritans and Yankees* (Princeton, 1962), p. 129.

57. Mather, *op. cit.*, II, 31. The ring had been given to Adam Winthrop by Charles I while he was still Prince of Wales.

58. John Winthrop, Jr., Letter to Samuel Wyllys regarding Connecticut Charter, London, May 12(?), 1662. Connecticut State Library, Hartford, Connecticut. Governor Winthrop did not return to Connecticut until the summer of 1663, when the financial obligations of Connecticut to the London merchants, Cowes, Silvester, and Maskeline, had been discharged. The debt to the merchants was repaid in the form of two thousand bushels of wheat, valued at 3s. 6d. a bushel, and twelve hundred bushels of peas, valued at 2s. 6d. a bushel. The merchants had to send a ship from England to New London to collect their wheat and peas.

59. After the acceptance of the Charter by the General Court, the Charter and one duplicate were assigned to the custody of Lieutenant John Allyn, who became secretary of Connecticut in 1663. One copy remained in his possession until the incident of Governor General Sir Edmund Andros

and the Charter Oak in 1687. Why there has been a dispute over the number of copies of the Charter that Connecticut received is a mystery. The *Public Records of the Colony of Connecticut*, I, 407, clearly refer to the "Charter" and the "Duplicate." They are now in the possession of the Connecticut Historical Society and the Connecticut State Library.

60. *The Judicial and Civil History of Connecticut*, ed. Dwight Loomis and J. Gilbert Calhoun (Boston, 1895), p. 19; J. Hammond Trumbull, *Historical Notes on the Constitutions of Connecticut, 1639–1818* (Hartford, 1901), p. 13.

61. *Conn. Records*, I, 386–387, 389.

62. *Calendar of State Papers*, Colonial Series, V, No. 422, p. 125.

63. *Conn. Records*, I, 386–390.

64. *Charter of the Colony of Connecticut, 1662* (Hartford, 1900), p. 19.

65. *Ibid.*, pp. 11, 13.

66. *Particular Court Records*, p. 248.

67. *Conn. Records*, I, 379–380, 383.

68. *Ibid.*, p. 390.

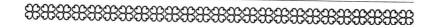

Bibliography

I. MANUSCRIPTS

Book Number A. or the First Book of the Records of the Colony of Connecticutt. Probate Room, Connecticut State Library, Hartford, Connecticut.

Book Number B. or the Second Book of the Records of the Colony of Connecticut. Probate Room, Connecticut State Library, Hartford, Connecticut.

The humble Peticõn of John Winthrop Esq.ʳ in the name and by Order of your Maᵗⁱᵉˢ most Loyall, obedient and most dutifull Subjects: the Colony of Conectecutt in New England. Connecticut State Library, Hartford, Connecticut (Photostatic copy of the original in the British Archives).

TALLCOTT, JOHN, Treasurer of the Colony of Connecticut. Letter of Credit to John Winthrop, Jr., June 16, 1661. Robert Winthrop Collection, Connecticut State Library, Hartford, Connecticut.

The Town's Law Book of Windsor, Connecticut, 1650–1708. Connecticut Historical Society, Hartford, Connecticut.

WINTHROP, JOHN, JR. Letter to Samuel Wyllys regarding Connecticut Charter. London, May 12(?), 1662. Connecticut State Library, Hartford, Connecticut (Photostatic copy of the original in the Boston Atheneum, Boston).

WOLCOTT, HENRY. Notes on Sermons 1638–1641 by the Reverends Warham, Hooker, Stone, Davenport, Huit, Branker, Witchfield, Moxon. Translated from shorthand by Douglas H. Shepard, 1959. Connecticut Historical Society, Hartford, Connecticut (Typescript).

II. PUBLISHED DOCUMENTS AND MANUSCRIPTS

Acts of the Commissioners of the United Colonies of New England, 2 vols., in *Records of the Colony of New Plymouth in New England,* IX–X. Boston, 1859.

BRADFORD, WILLIAM. *Bradford's History "Of Plimouth Plantation."* Boston, 1898.

Calendar of State Papers, ed. John Bruce *et al.* Domestic Series, 23 vols. London, 1858–1897.

Calendar of State Papers, ed. William Noël Sainsbury *et al.* Colonial Series, 38 vols. London, 1860–1942.

Charter of the Colony of Connecticut, 1662. Hartford, 1900.

Chronicles of the First Planters of the Colony of Massachusetts Bay, from 1623–1636, ed. Alexander Young. Boston, 1846.

COTTON, JOHN. *The Keyes Of the Kingdom of Heaven, and Power thereof, according to the Word of God.* London, 1644.

———. *The Way of Congregational Churches Cleared: in two Treatisies.* London, 1648.

Hartford Town Votes, I, in *Collections of the Connecticut Historical Society,* VI. Hartford, 1897.

HIGGINSON, FRANCIS. *New-Englands Plantation.* Salem, Mass., 1908 (London, 1630).

Historical Collections; Consisting of State Papers, and Other Authentic Documents; Intended as Materials for an History of the United States of America, ed. Ebenezer Hazard. 2 vols. Philadelphia, 1792, 1794.

HOOKER, THOMAS. *The Danger of Desertion: or a Farwell Sermon.* London, 1641.

———. *The Poor Doubting Christian Drawn to Christ.* Boston, 1743 (London, 1629).

———. "The Preface," in William Ames. *A Fresh Suit against Human Ceremonies in God's Worship.* Rotterdam, 1633.

———. "Rev. Thomas Hooker's Letter, in Reply to Governor Winthrop," *Collections of the Connecticut Historical Society,* I. Hartford, 1860.

———. *The Soules Effectual Calling to Christ.* London, 1637.

———. *A Survey of the Summe of Church-Discipline.* London, 1648.

HUBBARD, WILLIAM. *A General History of New England, From the Discovery to MDCLXXX.* Cambridge, Mass., 1815 (1680).

JOHNSON, EDWARD. *Johnson's Wonder-Working Providence, 1628–1651,* ed. J. Franklin Jameson. Original Narratives of Early American History. New York, 1910 (London, 1654).

LECHFORD, THOMAS. *Plain Dealing: or, Newes from New-England.* London, 1642.

MATHER, COTTON. *Magnalia Christi Americana: or, the Ecclesiastical History of New-England, from Its First Planting in the Year 1620. unto the Year of our Lord, 1698.* 7 vols. London, 1702.

MILLER, PERRY, and JOHNSON, THOMAS H., eds. *The Puritans.* New York, 1938.

Original Distribution of the Lands in Hartford Among the Settlers, 1639, in

Collections of the Connecticut Historical Society, XIV. Hartford, 1912.

"Papers Relating to the Controversy in the Church in Hartford. 1656–1659," *Collections of the Connecticut Historical Society*, II. Hartford, 1870.

A Platform of Church Discipline, Gathered Out of the Word of God: and Agreed upon by the Elders: and Messengers of the Churches, Assembled in the Synod at Cambridge in New England. Cambridge, Mass., 1649.

The Public Records of the Colony of Connecticut, ed. J. Hammond Trumbull. 15 vols. Hartford, 1850–1890.

Records of the Colony and Plantation of New Haven, from 1638 to 1649, ed. Charles J. Hoadly. Hartford, 1857.

Records of the Colony of Rhode Island and Providence Plantations in New England, ed. John R. Bartlett. 10 vols. Providence, 1856–1865.

"Records of the Council for New England," *Proceedings of the American Antiquarian Society.* Cambridge, Mass., April 1867.

Records of the Governor and Company of the Massachusetts Bay in New England, ed. Nathaniel B. Shurtleff. 5 vols. Boston, 1853–1854.

Records of the Particular Court of Connecticut, 1639–1663, in *Collections of the Connecticut Historical Society*, XXII. Hartford, 1928.

The Register Book of the Lands and Houses in the "New Towne," and the Town of Cambridge, with the Records of the Proprietors of the Common Lands, being the Records Generally Called "The Proprietors' Records." Cambridge, Mass., 1896.

ROBINSON, JOHN. *The Works of John Robinson, Pastor of the Pilgrim Fathers*, ed. Robert Ashton. 3 vols. Boston, 1851.

Some Early Records and Documents of and Relating to the Town of Windsor Connecticut, 1639–1703. Hartford, 1930.

STONE, SAMUEL. *A Congregational Church Is a Catholike Visible Church. OR An Examination of M. Hudson his Vindication concerning the Integrity of the Catholike Visible Church. Wherein also satisfaction is given to what M. Cawdrey writes touching that subject, in his Review of M. Hooker's Survey of Church Discipline.* London, 1652.

———. *A Short Catechism Drawn out of the Word of God.* Hartford, 1899 (Boston, 1684).

WINTHROP, JOHN. "John Winthrop to Sir Simonds D'Ewes," *Publications of the Colonial Society of Massachusetts*, VII (Boston, 1905), 73.

———. *Winthrop's Journal, "History of New England," 1630–1649*, ed. James Kendall Hosmer. 2 vols. New York, 1908.

The Winthrop Papers, in *Collections of the Massachusetts Historical Society*, Fourth Series, VI–VII. Boston, 1863, 1865.

The Winthrop Papers, in *Collections of the Massachusetts Historical Society*, Fifth Series, I. Boston, 1871.

The Wyllys Papers, in *Collections of the Connecticut Historical Society*, XXI. Hartford, 1924.

III. SECONDARY SOURCES: BOOKS

ADAMS, SHERMAN W., and STILES, HENRY R. *The History of Ancient Wethersfield, Connecticut.* 2 vols. New York, 1904.

ANDREWS, CHARLES M. *The Colonial Period of American History.* 4 vols. New Haven, 1936 (1934).

———. *The Fathers of New England.* Chronicles of America Series, VI. New Haven, 1919.

BACON, LEONARD. *Thirteen Historical Discourses, on the Completion of Two Hundred Years, From the Beginning of the First Church in New Haven.* New Haven, 1839.

BARTON, WILLIAM E. *Congregational Creeds and Covenants.* Chicago, 1917.

BATES, ALBERT CARLOS. *The Charter of Connecticut.* Hartford, 1932.

BORGEAUD, CHARLES. *Adoption and Amendment of Constitutions in Europe and America*, trans. Charles D. Hazen. New York, 1895.

BURPEE, CHARLES W. *History of Hartford County, Connecticut, 1633–1928.* 2 vols. Hartford, 1928.

BURRAGE, CHAMPLIN. *The Early English Dissenters, in the Light of Recent Research, 1550–1641.* 2 vols. Cambridge, England, 1912.

CAMPBELL, DOUGLAS. *The Puritan in Holland, England and America.* 2 vols. New York, 1892.

Connecticut Historical Society and the Towns of Windsor, Hartford, and Wethersfield. *Celebration of the Two Hundred and Fiftieth Anniversary of the Adoption of the First Constitution of the State of Connecticut.* Hartford, 1889.

DEXTER, HENRY MARTYN. *The Congregationalism of the Last Three Hundred Years, as seen in its Literature.* New York, 1880.

Dictionary of American Biography, ed. Dumas Malone. 22 vols. New York, 1928–1937.

DUNN, RICHARD S. *Puritans and Yankees, The Winthrop Dynasty of New England, 1630–1717.* Princeton, 1962.

FISKE, JOHN. *The Beginnings of New England, or the Puritan Theocracy in its Relation to Civil and Religious Liberty.* Boston, 1889.

FRENCH, ALLEN. *Charles I and the Puritan Upheaval, a Study of the Causes of the Great Migration.* Boston, 1955.

GREENE, EVARTS B., and HARRINGTON, VIRGINIA D. *American Population before the Federal Census of 1790.* New York, 1932.

HALLER, WILLIAM. *The Rise of Puritanism.* New York, 1957 (1938).

HASKINS, GEORGE LEE. *Law and Authority in Early Massachusetts.* New York, 1960.

HUTCHINSON, THOMAS. *The History of the Colony of Massachusets-Bay, from the First Settlement thereof in 1628, until its Incorporation with the Colony of Plimouth, Province of Main, &c. by the Charter of King William and Queen Mary, in 1691.* 2nd ed., 3 vols. London, 1760.

LEVY, BABETTE MAY. *Preaching in the First Half Century of New England History.* Studies in Church History, VI. Hartford, 1945.

LONG, BRECKINRIDGE. *Genesis of the Constitution of the United States of America.* New York, 1926.

LOOMIS, DWIGHT, and CALHOUN, J. GILBERT, eds. *The Judicial and Civil History of Connecticut.* Boston, 1895.

MCKINLEY, ALBERT E. *The Suffrage Franchise in the Thirteen English Colonies in America.* Publications of the University of Pennsylvania, Series in History, No. 2. Philadelphia, 1905.

MILLER, PERRY. *Errand into the Wilderness.* Cambridge, Mass., 1956.

———. *The New England Mind, From Colony to Province.* Cambridge, Mass., 1953.

———. *Orthodoxy in Massachusetts, 1630–1650.* Cambridge, Mass., 1933.

MORISON, SAMUEL ELIOT. *The Founding of Harvard College.* Cambridge, Mass., 1935.

———. *The Puritan Pronaos, Studies in the Intellectual Life of New England in the Seventeenth Century.* New York, 1936.

NEWTON, ARTHUR P. *The Colonising Activities of the English Puritans.* New Haven, 1914.

NOTESTEIN, WALLACE. *The English People on the Eve of Colonization, 1603–1630.* New American Nation Series. New York, 1954.

PARKER, HERBERT. *Courts and Lawyers of New England.* 4 vols. New York, 1931.

PERRY, CHARLES E., ed. *Founders and Leaders of Connecticut, 1633–1783.* Boston, 1934.

PETERS, SAMUEL A. *A General History of Connecticut, from its First Settlement Under George Fenwick, Esq. to its Latest Period of Amity with Great Britain.* London, 1781.

POTTER, ROCKWELL H. *Hartford's First Church.* Hartford, 1932.

SANFORD, ELIAS B. *A History of Connecticut.* Hartford, 1889.

STILES, HENRY R. *The History and Genealogies of Ancient Windsor, Connecticut, 1635–1891.* 2 vols. Hartford, 1891, 1892.

TAYLOR, JOHN M. *Roger Ludlow, the Colonial Lawmaker.* New York, 1900.

————. *The Witchcraft Delusion in Colonial Connecticut, 1647–1697.* The Grafton Historical Series. New York, 1908.

TOCQUEVILLE, ALEXIS DE. *Democracy in America,* trans. Henry Reeve. 2 vols. London, 1835.

TRUMBULL, BENJAMIN. *A Complete History of Connecticut, Civil and Ecclesiastical, From the Emigration of its First Planters, from England, in the year 1630, to the year 1764; and to the close of the Indian Wars,* 2 vols. Hartford, 1818 [1797].

TRUMBULL, J. HAMMOND. *The True-Blue Laws of Connecticut and New Haven and the False Blue-Laws Invented by the Rev. Samuel Peters.* Hartford, 1876.

VAN DUSEN, ALBERT E. *Connecticut.* New York, 1961.

WALKER, GEORGE LEON. *History of the First Church in Hartford, 1633–1883.* Hartford, 1884.

————. *Thomas Hooker, Preacher, Founder, Democrat.* New York, 1891.

WALKER, WILLISTON. *The Creeds and Platforms of Congregationalism.* New York, 1893.

————. *A History of the Congregational Churches in the United States.* The American Church History Series, III. Boston, 1894.

IV. SECONDARY SOURCES: ARTICLES, PAMPHLETS, ADDRESSES

ANDREWS, CHARLES M. "The Beginnings of the Connecticut Towns," *Annals of the American Academy of Political and Social Science,* I (October 1890), 165–191.

————. *The Connecticut Intestacy Law.* New Haven, 1933.

————. *The River Towns of Connecticut, A Study of Wethersfield, Hartford, and Windsor,* in *Johns Hopkins University Studies in Historical and Political Science,* Seventh Series, VII, VIII, IX (July, August, September 1889).

ARCHIBALD, WARREN SEYMOUR. *Thomas Hooker.* Tercentenary Pamphlet Series, IV. New Haven, 1933.

BEERS, WILLIAM A. "Roger Ludlowe: The Father of Connecticut Jurisprudence," *Magazine of American History,* VIII, Part I, No. 4 (April 1882), 264–271.

COLEMAN, ROY V. *A Note Concerning the Formulation of The Fundamental Orders Uniting the Three River Towns of Connecticut, 1639.* Westport, Conn., 1934.

————. *Roger Ludlow in Chancery.* Westport, Conn., 1934.

CROUSE, NELLIS M. "Causes of the Great Migration, 1630–1640," *New England Quarterly,* V, No. 1 (January 1932), 3–36.

DEXTER, FRANKLIN BOWDITCH. "Estimates of the Population in the American Colonies," *Proceedings of the American Antiquarian Society*, New Series, V. Worcester, Mass., 1889.

DUTCHER, GEORGE M., and BATES, ALBERT CARLOS. *The Fundamental Orders of Connecticut*. Publications of the Tercentenary Commission of the State of Connecticut, XX. New Haven, 1934.

HART, SAMUEL. "The Fundamental Orders and the Charter," *Papers of the New Haven Colony Historical Society*, VIII (New Haven, 1914), 238–254.

HASKINS, GEORGE LEE. "The Beginnings of Partible Inheritance in the American Colonies," *Yale Law Journal*, LI (June 1942), 1280–1315.

HASKINS, GEORGE LEE, and EWING, SAMUEL E., III. "The Spread of Massachusetts Law in the Seventeenth Century," *University of Pennsylvania Law Review*, CVI (1957–1958), 413–418.

MALTBIE, WILLIAM M. "Judicial Administration in Connecticut Colony before the Charter of 1662," *Connecticut Bar Journal*, XXIII, No. 1 (March 1949), 147–158; No. 2 (June 1949), 228–247.

MILLER, PERRY G. "Thomas Hooker and the Democracy of Early Connecticut," *New England Quarterly*, IV, No. 4 (October 1931), 663–712.

OSGOOD, HERBERT L. "The Political Ideas of the Puritans," *Political Science Quarterly*, VI, No. 1 (March 1891), 1–28; No. 2 (June 1891), 201–231.

TRUMBULL, J. HAMMOND. *The Composition of Indian Geographical Names, Illustrated from the Algonkin Languages*, reprinted from *Collections of the Connecticut Historical Society*, II. Hartford, 1870.

———. *Historical Notes on the Constitutions of Connecticut, 1639–1818*. Hartford, 1901.

WELLES, EDWIN STANLEY. *The Origin of the Fundamental Orders, 1639*. Hartford, 1936.

WELLES, ROGER. "Constitutional History of Connecticut," *Connecticut Magazine*, V, No. 2 (February 1899), 86–93; No. 3 (March 1899), 159–162.

Index

Confessions by torture, 108
Confiscation, 119
Conformist clergymen of Essex, 16
Congregational churches, 9, 38, 45, 47, 61, 71; and Fundamental Orders, 61; aristocracy within, 52; attendance, 51, 114; autonomy, 58; chosen people in, 37; code of, 60; defined, 40-41, 44, 189n1; discipline, 45, 53, 55; faith, 44, 47, 49; fiscal needs, 112; gathered, 45, 51-52, 58; heritage, 41-43; keys, 43, 45; members (brethren), 20, 48-51, 58, 113, 150-151; model for reform, 9; monarchy within, 47-48; particular visible, 44-46, 150; polity, 39-60, 97, 151; redefined, 149-151, 169; reforms of Church of England demanded, 36, 39, 41; schisms in, 143, 151-153; separation from Church of England, 42-44; tenets, 71; visible saints in, 51; unite in synods, 58-59, 144; withdrawal from, 47. *See* Boston Church; Brethren; Cambridge Platform; Covenants; Dorchester Church; Hartford Church; Middletown Church; Newtown Church; Saints; Watertown Church; Westminster Confession; Wethersfield Church; Windsor Church
Congregationalists, 36-38
Connecticut Archives, 200n43
Connecticut Historical Society, 100, 190n29, 199n1, 202n59
Connecticut River, xi, xii, 23, 26, 157, 159, 170
Connecticut State Library, 202n59
Connecticut Valley, 19, 22, 29-30, 32
Constables, 28, 63, 64, 89, 90, 140; duties of, 113, 135-136; oath of office, 94, 127; summon freemen, 83
Constitution, xi, 41, 60, 61, 77, 170; discussions regarding, 70-73; of 1818, 62, 171; of United States, 96. *See* Fundamental Orders
Constitutional crisis, English, 7
Contempt of court, 131

Contempt of ordinances, 102
Coo, Robert, 33
Cooper, John, 124
Coopers, 153
Corn, 22, 69, 79, 90, 116, 120, 126-127, 153, 154
Cornewell, Thomas, 131
Corte, General. *See* General Corte
Costs of court, 120, 122, 123-124, 128
Cotton, 154
Cotton, John, 6, 15, 42, 43, 59, 62, 78, 149; arrives in Massachusetts Bay, 18; explains Congregationalism, 189n1; *Keyes Of the Kingdom of Heaven*, 50; "Moses his Judicialls," 102; opposes removal to Connecticut, 26; opposes attending Westminster Assembly, 155; rivalry with Thomas Hooker, 20-21
Cotton, John, Jr., 151, 152
Council for New England, 12, 23, 157, 159
Councils, church, 58-59, 152. *See* Synods
Court, General. *See* General Court
Court, Particular. *See* Particular Court
Courtiers, 7
Court of Election, 85-92, 95-96, 129-130, 166; freemen attend, 82, 97-98, 139. *See* General Court
Courtship, 117
Courts of law, Connecticut, 121-131
Courts of law, English, Admiralty, 92; Baron, 123; Chancery, 92, 123; Common Pleas, 92; High Commission, 5, 16, 17, 41, 92, 155; Kings Bench, 22, 92, 123; Leet, 11, 123; Star Chamber, 5, 92, 123, 155. *See page 123 for miscellaneous courts*
Covenants, 9, 26, 45-47, 60, 62, 78-80, 95; church, xi, 49, 53, 58, 78, 79, 94, 150; civil, 94, 97; in Charter, 138, 169; in Fundamental Orders, 77, 98, 102, 144; of grace, 21; of Hartford Church, 46-47; of works, 21
Cowes, Silvester and Maskeline, 201n58
Cowherds, 140